Scottish SECONDARY MATHEMATICS

Tom Sanaghan

Jim Pennel

Carol Munro

Carole Ford

John Dalton

James Cairns

Heinemann

Inspiring generations

Heinemann Educational Publishers
Halley Court, Jordan Hill, Oxford OX2 8EJ
Part of Harcourt Education

Heinemann is the registered trademark of
Harcourt Education Limited

© Tom Sanaghan, Jim Pennel, Carol Munro, Carole Ford, John Dalton,
James Cairns, 2003

First published 2003

08 07 06 05 04 03
10 9 8 7 6 5 4 3 2 1

British Library Cataloguing in Publication Data is available
from the British Library on request.

ISBN 0 435 04012 X

Designed by Bridge Creative Services Ltd.
Illustrations by Bridge Creative Services Ltd, Inkwell Design, Phil Burrows
Cover design by Miller Craig & Cocking Ltd.
Printed in Spain by Mateu Cromo S.A.
Cover photo: © StockScotland

Acknowledgements
The authors and publishers would like to thank the following for permission to
use photographs:

P8: StockScotland; P9: Kobal/Lucas Films; P20: Corbis; P44: Corbis; P49: Corbis;
P86: Harcourt/Peter Evans; P95: Jim Newall; P131: Corbis; P137: Corbis; P143:
Corbis; P164: Cordon Art BV; P167: Cordon Art BV; P174: Empics; P176:
ActionPlus; P208: Cordon Art BV

'Little Red Riding Hood' from *Revolting Rhymes* by Roald Dahl, published by
Jonathan Cape, reprinted by permission of The Random House Group Ltd.

Tel: 01865 888058 www.heinemann.co.uk

Contents

How to use this book

Every chapter is divided into sections.
Each section begins with a list of key points:

1.1 Place value

> Our numbers were developed from the Arabic system giving the digits 0–9.

An exercise follows:

Exercise 1.1

1 Write the following numbers in figures:
   (**a**) twelve thousand, six hundred and forty

At the end of the chapter is a review exercise and a summary of all the key points.

Special instructions are shown by these symbols:

 You may use the matching numbered worksheet on the website to answer this question. These questions are for extra practice.

 Use a calculator to answer these questions.

1 Whole numbers

In this chapter you will use numbers in everyday situations and explore patterns of numbers.

From early cave dwellers to today, humans have invented different methods of recording numbers.

1.1 Place value

Our numbers were developed from the Arabic system giving the digits 0–9.
Like the Roman system, where you put the digits is important.

M	HTh	TTh	Th	H	T	U	the 5 stands for	
						5	5 units	
				2	5	6	5 tens	
			5	0	1	3	5 thousands	
	2	5	4	9	0	9	5 ten thousands	fifty thousand
5	3	1	1	0	0	6	5 millions	

In large numbers, grouping the digits in threes makes the number easier to read.

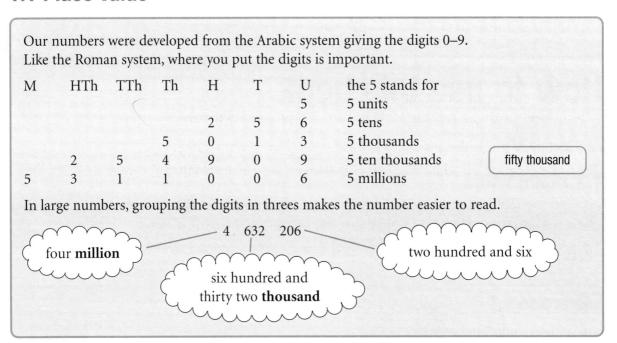

four **million**

six hundred and thirty two **thousand**

4 632 206

two hundred and six

Exercise 1.1

1 Write the following numbers in figures:
   (**a**) twelve thousand, six hundred and forty
   (**b**) fifty thousand, three hundred
   (**c**) two million, four hundred and thirteen thousand, six hundred and twenty seven
   (**d**) five million, six hundred and two thousand and fifty
   (**e**) fourteen million, two hundred and twenty thousand.

2 Write the following numbers in words:

  (**a**) 2406   (**b**) 15 212   (**c**) 5004   (**d**) 120 300

  (**e**) 7 364 000 (**f**) 1 300 010 (**g**) 4 230 146 (**h**) 3 034 659

> NEW BANK Date 26/01/03
> Pay Windsor Antiques
> Thirty six pounds   £36.00
> only
> A.N.Other
> 0005468   60-1234 607895

3 Play this game with a partner.

Player 1

- Write down six numbers. Don't let your partner see them.
  Add them up using a calculator.
- Write down the answer.
- Read the six numbers aloud to player 2.

Player 2

- Write down the six numbers.
- Add them up using a calculator.
- Compare your answers with player 1.

If player 2's answers agree with player 1's then player 2 scores 2 points.
If not, check your numbers with player 1 to find out why you were wrong.

Player 2 should now choose six numbers and repeat the above.
The first player to reach six points wins.

4 Write the number that is

  (**a**) 200 bigger than 10 640   (**b**) 8000 bigger than 91 400

  (**c**) 40 000 bigger than 1 415 200   (**d**) 2000 less than 63 520

  (**e**) 700 less than 17 800   (**f**) 300 000 less than 1 940 000.

5 The estimated crowd for a football match was 17 500.
The actual crowd was 2000 higher. How many people went to the match?

6 Grossman's Superstore estimated they would give away 380 000 catalogues in
December, but the actual number was 50 000 lower. How many did they give away?

7 In 2001 the Daily Chronicle was delivered to 264 000 people. In 2002 this number
had risen by 30 000. How many people had the newspaper delivered in 2002?

8 Read a to f from these scales.

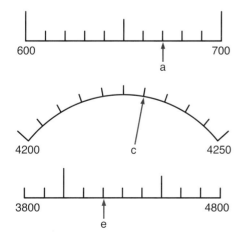

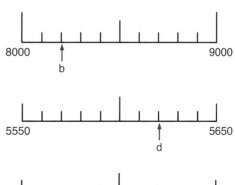

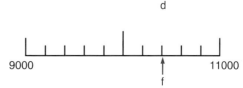

9 Put these numbers in order starting with the smallest:

(**a**) 10 900, 9800, 10 110, 9090, 9099, 10 090

(**b**) 313 509, 312 540, 312 509, 314 210, 312 000

10 The number of secondary school pupils in Scotland is shown in the table below:

Year	Number of pupils
1970	314 442
1975	397 997
1980	407 844
1985	360 642
1990	293 702
1995	316 883
2000	314 293

Put the numbers in order starting with the smallest.

1.2 Rounding numbers

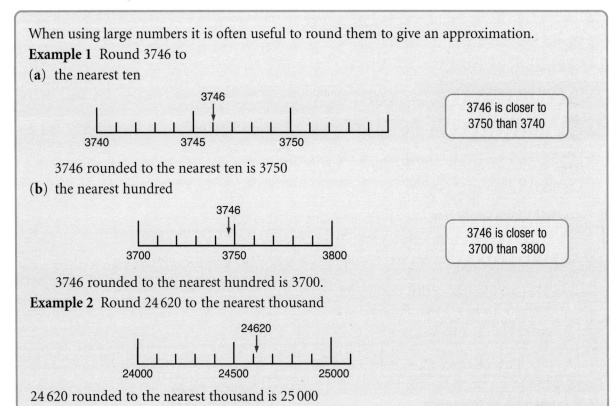

When using large numbers it is often useful to round them to give an approximation.

Example 1 Round 3746 to

(**a**) the nearest ten

3746 is closer to 3750 than 3740

3746 rounded to the nearest ten is 3750

(**b**) the nearest hundred

3746 is closer to 3700 than 3800

3746 rounded to the nearest hundred is 3700.

Example 2 Round 24 620 to the nearest thousand

24 620 rounded to the nearest thousand is 25 000

Exercise 1.2

1 Round the heights of these mountains to the nearest 10 metres:

(**a**) Ben Cruachan 1126 m   (**b**) Ben Alder 1148 m

(**c**) Ben Nevis 1344 m   (**d**) Sgurr nan Gillean 964 m

2 Round these numbers to (**a**) the nearest ten

(**b**) the nearest hundred:

(**i**) 7856 (**ii**) 67 (**iii**) 145 (**iv**) 289 (**v**) 699

(**vi**) 34 (**vii**) 5112 (**viii**) 3999 (**ix**) 15 670 (**x**) 18 727

3 The number of customers in a department store over one holiday weekend was:

Saturday	Sunday	Monday
1968	1532	2195

Round these figures to the nearest hundred.

4 Round the football stadium capacities shown below to the nearest

(**a**) hundred (**b**) thousand.

Pittodrie	22 199	Celtic Park	60 294
Fir Park	13 742	McDiarmid Park	10 673
Ibrox	50 411	Tynecastle	17 990

5

Authority	Population	Land Area (km²)
East Ayrshire	120 940	1262
Edinburgh	451 710	263
Glasgow	611 440	175
Highland	208 600	25 728
Aberdeenshire	227 440	6317
Dumfries & Galloway	146 800	6934
Shetland	22 740	1442
Renfrewshire	177 230	260
Midlothian	81 680	355

Using the information in the table above, round:

(**a**) the land areas to the nearest (**i**) ten (**ii**) hundred

(**b**) the populations to the nearest (**i**) hundred (**ii**) thousand (**iii**) ten thousand.

6 Max read in his newspaper that the number of shops in the
United Kingdom was 311 844. Round this to the nearest

(**a**) hundred (**b**) thousand.

7 In the year 2000 the United Kingdom sent 928 511 545 items of mail abroad.
Round this to the nearest

(**a**) thousand (**b**) million.

8 The gross income in the United Kingdom from
one of the *Star Wars* film series was £51 063 811.
Round this to the nearest hundred thousand.

1.3 Estimating – addition and subtraction

Rounding helps estimate answers to our calculations.

Example 1

$$87 - 28$$
estimate $90 - 30 = 60$
exact value $87 - 28 = 59$

Example 2

$$532 + 176$$
estimate $500 + 200 = 700$
exact value $532 + 176 = 708$

Exercise 1.3

1 By rounding each number to the nearest ten, give **approximate** answers to the following:

(**a**) $46 + 27$ (**b**) $837 + 129$ (**c**) $79 - 25$
(**d**) $87 + 64$ (**e**) $99 - 36$ (**f**) $733 - 265$

2 By rounding each number to the nearest hundred, give **approximate** answers to the following:

(**a**) $689 + 380$ (**b**) $743 - 560$ (**c**) $7569 + 365$
(**d**) $990 + 450$ (**e**) $1560 - 820$ (**f**) $940 - 176$

3 By rounding each number to the nearest thousand, give **approximate** answers to the following:

(**a**) $8560 + 1980$ (**b**) $7640 + 2222$ (**c**) $9891 + 7600$
(**d**) $1590 - 999$ (**e**) $5123 - 2950$ (**f**) $12\,433 - 1972$

4 The boiling point of calcium is 1484 °C. The boiling point of potassium is 759 °C. Find the approximate difference between these boiling points.

5 When Kilmarnock played St Johnstone at Rugby Park there were 9630 Kilmarnock supporters and 5460 St Johnstone supporters.
(**a**) Approximately how many supporters attended the match?
(**b**) If the capacity of the stadium is 18 128, approximately how many more people could have attended?

1.4 Mental strategies for adding

Example Calculate 63 + 28:

Method 1
- 60 + 20 = 80
- 3 + 8 = 11
- 80 + 11 = 91

Method 2
- 63 + 20 = 83
- 83 + 8 = 91

Method 3
- 63 + 30 = 93
- 30 is 2 too many so subtract 2
- 93 − 2 = 91

Exercise 1.4

1 Use method 1 to find:
   (**a**) 64 + 23   (**b**) 26 + 85   (**c**) 91 + 64   (**d**) 76 + 156   (**e**) 36 + 74

2 Use method 2 to find:
   (**a**) 72 + 28   (**b**) 36 + 65   (**c**) 34 + 85   (**d**) 48 + 73   (**e**) 95 + 27

3 Use method 3 to find:
   (**a**) 29 + 36   (**b**) 47 + 24   (**c**) 79 + 130   (**d**) 77 + 56   (**e**) 159 + 25

4 Find mentally:
   (**a**) 28 + 45   (**b**) 36 + 74   (**c**) 142 + 65   (**d**) 99 + 126
   (**e**) 138 + 22   (**f**) 400 + 320   (**g**) 175 + 130   (**h**) 198 + 86
   (**i**) 108 + 43   (**j**) 1040 + 70   (**k**) 499 + 15   (**l**) 999 + 999

5 Every week Mr and Mrs Price buy a TV guide for 35p and a copy of *Puzzle Break* for 58p. How much does this cost them every week?

6 On a Saturday 157 people visited an art gallery, while 85 people visited on Sunday. How many people visited that weekend?

7 Mrs Kamkoff was buying chocolate prizes for everyone in her classes at Efton Primary School. In her 3 classes there were 28 pupils, 25 pupils and 30 pupils. How many prizes did she need to buy?

8 Mr Jarvis had 4 rolls of material holding 23 metres, 14 metres, 36 metres and 18 metres. How much material does he have in total?

1.5 Mental strategies for subtracting

Example Calculate 64 − 29

Method 1

Method 2

Method 3

Exercise 1.5

1 Use method 1 to find:
  (**a**) 55 − 31   (**b**) 89 − 44   (**c**) 75 − 26   (**d**) 142 − 36   (**e**) 275 − 57

2 Use method 2 to find:
  (**a**) 96 − 87   (**b**) 56 − 28   (**c**) 72 − 19   (**d**) 80 − 26   (**e**) 134 − 75

3 Use method 3 to find:
  (**a**) 96 − 29   (**b**) 84 − 58   (**c**) 124 − 39   (**d**) 57 − 48   (**e**) 192 − 69

4 Find mentally:
  (**a**) 76 − 24   (**b**) 24 − 12   (**c**) 34 − 18   (**d**) 68 − 29
  (**e**) 54 − 38   (**f**) 112 − 20   (**g**) 150 − 62   (**h**) 268 − 199
  (**i**) 2000 − 5   (**j**) 1063 − 49   (**k**) 245 − 99   (**l**) 1254 − 999

5 A curtain with drop length of 192 centimetres was needed for a window.
  Lana's curtains are 148 centimetres. By how much are they short?

6 Tamsin has a 350 millilitre bottle of shampoo. She uses it to fill an 85 millilitre travel bottle.
  How much is now left in the original bottle?

7 Rowan and Bernie have to put adverts through 530 letterboxes.
  On the first evening they delivered 155. How many had they still to deliver?

1.6 Adding and subtracting

Example 1
1634 + 2040 + 509

$$
\begin{array}{r}
1634 \\
+\ 2040 \\
509 \\
\hline
4183 \\
11
\end{array}
$$

Example 2
4500 − 3867

$$
\begin{array}{r}
{\scriptstyle 3\ 1\ 9\ 1} \\
4800 \\
-\ 3867 \\
\hline
633
\end{array}
$$

> Remember to estimate your answer first

Exercise 1.6

1 Without using a calculator, find:

(**a**) 387 + 211   (**b**) 519 + 242   (**c**) 318 + 262
(**d**) 445 + 271   (**e**) 633 + 298   (**f**) 494 + 406 + 318
(**g**) 494 + 700 + 23   (**h**) 235 + 1026 + 108   (**i**) 2010 + 890
(**j**) 4560 + 1354   (**k**) 12 546 + 1380 + 4100   (**l**) 3999 + 1056 + 89

2 Without using a calculator, find:

(**a**) 276 − 42   (**b**) 340 − 106   (**c**) 876 − 139
(**d**) 766 − 147   (**e**) 712 − 168   (**f**) 562 − 188
(**g**) 1342 − 175   (**h**) 202 − 125   (**i**) 1050 − 287
(**j**) 3568 − 1084   (**k**) 4367 − 1902   (**l**) 4007 − 135

3 Jesse received her weekly pay of £540. On her way to the bank she spent £68 at the supermarket. How much did she have left?

4 In the final vote for the winner on 'Biggest Brother' Su-Lin received 7470 votes and Mike received 9692 votes.
(**a**) How many votes were there in total?
(**b**) By how much did Mike win?

5 Jenny calculated that her journey from Edinburgh to Bath would be 391 miles. When she reached Birmingham there were still 98 miles to Bath. How far had she travelled?

BATH
98 miles

6 At Beldrun High School there are 1132 pupils. There are 297 pupils in first year and 246 pupils in second year.
(**a**) What is the total number of pupils in first and second year?
(**b**) How many pupils are in the other years?

7 The diameter of Ganymede, the largest moon of Jupiter, is 5269 kilometres. The diameter of Europa, another moon, is 3130 kilometres. What is the difference in diameter between Ganymede and Europa?

8 Over three consecutive years the staff at Bainwells raised £1654, £1940 and £990 for charity. How much had they raised altogether?

9 The length of the main span of the Forth Road Bridge is 1006 m. The main span of the Golden Gate bridge in San Fransisco is 1280 m. Which is longer and by how much?

10 The Beldrun High School Christmas Show cost £2346 to produce. £3580 was made from ticket sales and £640 from refreshment sales. How much profit did the school make?

11 The Milton family won £100 000 in the lottery and used some of the money to redecorate their house. They bought a 3 piece suite for £1299, carpets for £2680 and a kitchen for £3400. How much money did they have left?

12 Think of a three digit number which is **not** palindromic. Reverse the number and **subtract** the smallest from the largest. Now reverse your answer and **add** it to your previous answer.

> Something which reads the same backwards as forwards is called **palindromic**, for example 686

   (**a**) What is your answer?
   (**b**) Choose another number and repeat the process. What do you notice?

1.7 Revision of simple multiplying and dividing

Exercise 1.7

1 Find mentally:

(**a**) 5 × 6	(**b**) 4 × 8	(**c**) 9 × 6	(**d**) 5 × 7
(**e**) 7 × 8	(**f**) 15 × 2	(**g**) 8 × 12	(**h**) 9 × 9
(**i**) 56 ÷ 2	(**j**) 32 ÷ 4	(**k**) 100 ÷ 5	(**l**) 63 ÷ 9
(**m**) 18 ÷ 3	(**n**) 42 ÷ 6	(**o**) 48 ÷ 8	(**p**) 40 ÷ 5
(**q**) 72 ÷ 9	(**r**) 64 ÷ 8	(**s**) 120 ÷ 12	(**t**) 99 ÷ 11

2 Chocolate frogs cost 11p, orange bottles cost 8p and sherbert fizzys cost 5p. Jenny buys 3 chocolate frogs, 6 orange bottles and 3 sherbet fizzys. How much did she spend altogether?

3 Fiona is making cakes for the school fair. The recipe uses 6 eggs. If she has 4 dozen eggs, how many cakes could she make?

4 In Cut Price CDs' closing down sale Joe buys 12 CDs at £7 each, 6 books at £5 each, 7 posters at £4 each and 8 DVDs at £11 each. How much did he spend altogether?

5 Bob is playing Scrabble. He uses the word QUICKLY:

(**a**) Use the scores on the letters to find his total word score.
(**b**) If he places the word on a triple word square he gets three times as many points. What would his score be then?

6 Amy needs 4 metres of ribbon to edge a cushion. She has 8 cushions and 36 metres of ribbon. Will she be able to edge them all?

1.8 Mental strategies for multiplying and dividing

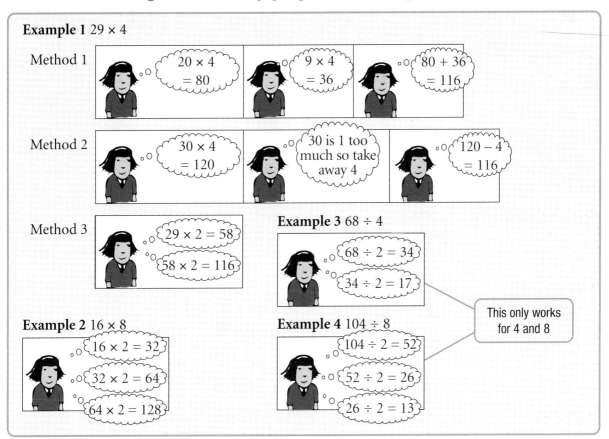

Exercise 1.8

1 Find mentally:
  (**a**) 75×4 (**b**) 34×4 (**c**) 17×8 (**d**) 42×6 (**e**) $292 \div 4$
  (**f**) $360 \div 8$ (**g**) 62×5 (**h**) 34×9 (**i**) 44×4 (**j**) $6432 \div 4$

2 Stratford's Bookshop ordered 57 copies of each of the first four Harry Potter books. How many books was this?

3 Mr Kingston can make 34 cones from one tub of ice cream. In one weekend he used seven tubs. How many cones did he make?

4 The doctor tells Mrs Mackie that she needs to take four tablets every day.
If she is given 64 tablets, how many days will they last?

5 If there are 8 furlongs in a mile how many furlongs will there be in 592 miles?

6 It was estimated that on average a person eats approximately 22 pounds of
chocolate a year. How much chocolate would the person eat in 7 years?

7 Tins of soup are sold in special 4 packs.
(**a**) How many tins would there be in 46 packs?
(**b**) How many packs could be made from 364 tins?

1.9 Multiplying and dividing

Example 1
A table is 168 cm wide. How wide will 7 tables be?

$$
\begin{array}{r}
168 \\
\times \quad 7 \\
\hline
1176
\end{array}
$$
   Total width is 1176 cm.

Example 2
Roy, Amy and Tariq win £384 in a raffle. If they share it equally among
themselves, how much will each get?

$$
\begin{array}{r}
128 \\
3\overline{)384}
\end{array}
$$
   Each receives £128.

Exercise 1.9

1 Calculate:
(**a**) 74 × 9   (**b**) 119 × 5   (**c**) 342 × 3   (**d**) 246 × 7
(**e**) 242 × 4   (**f**) 1277 × 6   (**g**) 2246 × 8   (**h**) 2568 × 9

2 Calculate:
(**a**) 138 ÷ 3   (**b**) $\dfrac{768}{8}$ (**c**) 572 ÷ 4   (**d**) 994 ÷ 7

(**e**) 108 ÷ 9   (**f**) 696 ÷ 6   (**g**) $\dfrac{1850}{5}$ (**h**) 2403 ÷ 9

3 Storewares is having a mid season sale.
What is the cost of a table and 4 chairs?

4 Sharon has 192 CDs. Each shelf on her stand holds 8 CDs. How many shelves can she fill?

5 The Astor Hotel is being recarpeted. There are 6 floors which each require 414 square metres, and the ground floor, which requires 87 square metres. How much carpet is needed?

6 A group of 136 pupils from Toddington Primary School are visiting the science museum. They are split into groups of 8 pupils. How many groups are there?

7 Mr Hussain inherits £7600. He decides to keep £3000 and share the rest equally among his 5 grandchildren. How much does each grandchild receive?

1.10 Multiplying by multiples of 10 and 100

To multiply a number by 10 you move every digit one place to the left.

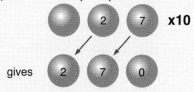

To multiply a number by 100 you move every digit two places to the left.

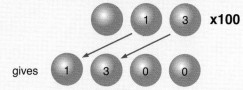

You can use this to multiply by multiples of 10 and 100.

Example 1

$$43 \times 20$$
$$43 \times 2 = 86 \longrightarrow 86 \times 10 = 860$$
so $$\mathbf{43 \times 20 = 860}$$

> To multiply by 20, multiply by 2 then by 10

Example 2

$$574 \times 300$$
$$574 \times 3 = 1722 \longrightarrow 1722 \times 100 = 172\,200$$
so $$\mathbf{574 \times 300 = 172\,200}$$

> To multiply by 300, multiply by 3 then by 100

Exercise 1.10

1 Multiply the following numbers by 10 and 100:

(**a**) 26   (**b**) 823   (**c**) 450   (**d**) 300   (**e**) 5620
(**f**) 2200   (**g**) 3867   (**h**) 3030   (**i**) 12 406   (**j**) 30 506

2 Calculate:

(**a**) 14 × 30 (**b**) 27 × 30 (**c**) 32 × 50 (**d**) 50 × 60 (**e**) 40 × 84
(**f**) 105 × 60 (**g**) 60 × 405 (**h**) 200 × 200 (**i**) 19 × 800 (**j**) 182 × 400
(**k**) 2060 × 30 (**l**) 360 × 400 (**m**) 1709 × 30 (**n**) 234 × 300 (**o**) 1050 × 600

3 Buzz collected the £14 Christmas party payment from each of the 70 staff at Walkers Bookshop. How much money did he collect altogether?

4 Mrs Sugar charges £50 for a decorated cake. In one year she sold 160 cakes. How much money did she make?

5 When Elvis was cashing up at the end of the day he counted the bank notes in the till. He had six £50 notes, seventeen £20 notes, forty-three £10 notes and twenty £5 notes. How much did he have in total?

6 Mr Bell bought fifteen 20-litre tins of cooking oil. If he uses 4 litres each day, how long will it last?

1.11 Dividing by multiples of 10 and 100

To divide a number by 10 you move every digit one place to the right.

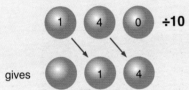

To divide a number by 100 you move every digit two places to the right.

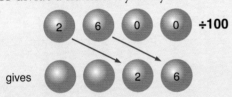

You can use this to divide by multiples of 10 and 100.

Example 1

$480 ÷ 20$
$480 ÷ 2 = 240 \longrightarrow 240 ÷ 10 = 24$
so **$480 ÷ 20 = 24$**

> To divide by 20, divide by 2 then by 10

Example 2

$1800 ÷ 300$
$1800 ÷ 3 = 600 \longrightarrow 600 ÷ 100 = 6$
so **$1800 ÷ 300 = 6$**

> To divide by 300, divide by 3 then by 100

Exercise 1.11

1 Divide the following numbers by 10 and 100:

(**a**) 300   (**b**) 200   (**c**) 8000   (**d**) 6000   (**e**) 3400

(**f**) 6200   (**g**) 17 800   (**h**) 200 000   (**i**) 15 500   (**j**) 289 500

2 Calculate:

(**a**) $880 \div 20$ (**b**) $\dfrac{960}{30}$ (**c**) $320 \div 40$ (**d**) $1190 \div 70$ (**e**) $650 \div 50$

(**f**) $\dfrac{6300}{70}$ (**g**) $3600 \div 80$ (**h**) $4920 \div 60$ (**i**) $\dfrac{6000}{300}$ (**j**) $\dfrac{4900}{700}$

(**k**) $\dfrac{4800}{400}$ (**l**) $\dfrac{5100}{300}$ (**m**) $19\,200 \div 600$ (**n**) $7200 \div 900$

3 Mrs Sheikh drove to London to visit her family. The journey was 480 miles long and she decided to stop every 80 miles for a break. How many times did she stop?

4 A box holds 500 sheets of paper. How many boxes are needed for:

(**a**) 3000 sheets   (**b**) 10 000 sheets   (**c**) 24 000 sheets?

5 Rynan's sells folders in packets of 40. How many packets can George make from:

(**a**) 400 folders   (**b**) 2000 folders   (**c**) 12 000 folders?

6 Vernon bought $730 of travellers cheques. He received nine $20 cheques and the rest were $50 cheques. How many $50 cheques did he receive?

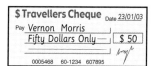

1.12 Estimating – multiplication and division

Examples

Estimate the following:

(**a**) 32×48

30×50 Estimate
$= 1500$

(**b**) 682×41

700×40 Estimate
$= 28\,000$

(**c**) $216 \div 12$

$200 \div 10$ Estimate
$= 20$

Exercise 1.12

1 Caterers who are supplying food for a three-day conference calculate they will need 684 sandwiches every day. Approximately how many sandwiches will they need altogether?

2 A counsellor can see 16 patients a day. If he works for 26 days each month, approximately how many patients would he be able to see in:

(**a**) 1 month   (**b**) 4 months?

3 A school is awarded £1850. They decide to split it evenly between 12 clubs. Approximately how much will each club receive?

4 Eighteen teams of school children are to take part in the opening ceremony of an athletics competition. If 776 children are chosen, approximately how big will each team be?

5 While on a driving holiday in the USA, Jill calculates that she will drive about 180 miles per day. The route she plans to take is 1350 miles long. Approximately how many days will this take her?

6 Nauru has an area of 21 square kilometres and a population of 22 696. Approximately how many people are there per square kilometre?

1.13 Multiplying by two digit numbers

Example   A datalogger records the air temperature 18 times an hour. How many measurements will it take in twenty four hours?

$$18 \times 24 \qquad 18 \times 20 = 360$$
$$18 \times 4 = 72$$
$$18 \times 24 = 432$$

Exercise 1.13

1 Meri's new car travels 15 kilometres per litre of petrol. The tank holds 49 litres of fuel. How far can her car travel on a full tank of petrol?

2 Macy spends £18 each week buying her lunch. How much will she spend after 52 weeks?

3 Vela has calculated she will need £15 per day spending money when she is on holiday. If she is going on holiday for two weeks, how much will she need to save?

4 Robbie saves £38 a month. How much will he have after 2 years?

5 The admission fee to Funland theme park is £25 for adults and £12 for children. How much will the total admission be for:
   (a) 10 adults and 16 children
   (b) 16 adults and 80 children
   (c) 22 adults and 34 children?

6 Good Books Ltd have decided to replace 12 of their company cars with new models.

(**a**) Each new car costs £8650. What was the total cost of the 12 new cars?

(**b**) Each old car was sold for £3400. How much did the company receive?

(**c**) How much did it cost the company to replace the 12 cars?

7 (**a**) What is the largest number you can make using the digits 2, 3, 5 and 6 and the multiplication symbol once each?

(**b**) What is the smallest number you can make?

Miscellaneous Exercise 1.14

1 Toni is baking almond biscuits.
He uses this recipe to make 10 biscuits:

150 g flour
75 g sugar
50 g ground almonds
125 g margarine
Salt
Makes 10 biscuits

If Toni wants to bake 30 biscuits, how much of each ingredient will he need?

2 Queen Victoria reigned from 1837 to 1901. How many years was this?

3 Loftlys furnishing fabrics have received a large order:

17 metres black velvet – £14 per metre
28 metres of cream damask – £11 per metre
28 metres of red brocade – £23 per metre
36 metres of blue silk – £9 per metre

What is the total cost of the order?

4 Sweetlys chocolates cost £3 per box. In one year the company sold £354 000 worth of chocolates. How many boxes did they sell?

5 Brian is head of sales for the Jeto car company. In 2002 they sold 79 943 cars. Approximately how many cars did they sell each week?

6 In 1998 in the UK there were 114 000 people employed in the army, 43 770 in the navy and 54 750 in the airforce. What was the total number of people employed?

7 (a) What was the total amount of strawberries produced by Spain and the USA?

(b) How much more does Spain produce than the UK?

(c) How much more does the USA produce than the UK?

Strawberry production 2001 (tonnes)	
USA	822 800
Spain	350 000
Italy	138 514
UK	38 500

8 Mr Wright is building a platform for the tigers at Newton zoo to sit on. It will need to withstand the weight of the 4 tigers. He estimates that the tigers weigh 275 kilogrammes each. What would their combined weight be?

9 Janice wants to buy wine for her party. She estimates that each of the 36 guests will drink 3 glasses of wine. If she can fill 5 glasses from 1 bottle, how many bottles will she need to buy?

10 Jane has £76 which she wants to spend on new clothes.

She sees a special offer on in her favourite clothes shop: 3 items for the price of 2 (cheapest item free).

The items she likes are:

Skirt	£36
Blouse	£17
Jumper	£25
Trousers	£32
Jacket	£40

Copy and complete the table to find how many different combinations of clothes she could buy and how much each would cost her.

Item 1	Item 2	Item 3	Cost
skirt	trousers	jumper	£68

Review exercise 1

1 Write the following numbers in words:

(a) 482 (b) 8020 (c) 120 310 (d) 271 015 (e) 2 672 000

2 Write the following numbers in figures:

(a) six thousand and eighty two

(b) twenty four thousand five hundred

(c) sixty four thousand five hundred and eighty seven

(d) one hundred and fifty thousand and twenty

(e) nine million, six hundred and seventy two thousand, three hundred

3 Put these numbers in order starting with the smallest:

16 865, 16 856, 16 809, 16 880, 16 980

4 Round to the nearest (**a**) ten (**b**) hundred:

(**i**) 345   (**ii**) 486   (**iii**) 798   (**iv**) 5365   (**v**) 12 284

5 Round these magazine circulation numbers to the nearest thousand:

Magazine	Circulation
TV Now	1 684 399
Look at TV	1 269 721
Lifestyles Weekly	982 851
Real Life	567 490

6 There were 6852 supporters at a football match. 2349 supported Middleton Athletic and the rest supported Newton Rangers.

(**a**) Estimate how many supported Newton Rangers.

(**b**) Calculate exactly how many supported Newton Rangers.

7 In one year a company spent £76 682 on research. The following year they spent £76 243.

(**a**) Estimate the difference between these amounts.

(**b**) Calculate exactly the difference between these amounts.

8 The asteroid Ceres has a diameter of 936 kilometres. The asteroid Euphrosyne has a diameter of 370 kilometres. Calculate the difference between their diameters.

9 During his climbing career Mr MacDonald climbed Mount McKinley (6194 metres high) and K2 (8607 metres high). What is the difference in height between these two mountains?

10 Olivier has just bought a house. He needs to buy the following:

Suite   £845
Fridge   £570
Bed   £399
Table and chairs   £459

Calculate the total price for these items.

11 Calculate:

(**a**) 4625 + 7298   (**b**) 4730 + 782   (**c**) 12 725 + 1390

(**d**) 17 640 + 21 950 + 897   (**e**) 986 − 227   (**f**) 16 522 − 4532

12 Calculate mentally:

(**a**) 39 + 47   (**b**) 63 + 27   (**c**) 247 + 35   (**d**) 542 + 90   (**e**) 136 + 43

(**f**) 84 − 27   (**g**) 65 − 46   (**h**) 143 − 95   (**i**) 192 − 59   (**j**) 84 − 66

(**k**) 24 × 8   (**l**) 17 × 6   (**m**) 107 × 7   (**n**) 299 × 5   (**o**) 122 × 5

(**p**) 188 ÷ 4   (**q**) 430 ÷ 5   (**r**) 126 ÷ 3   (**s**) 504 ÷ 8   (**t**) 240 ÷ 10

13 The six children of the White family inherit £3 147 000 to be shared equally among themselves. How much does each receive?

14 Multiply by 10 and 100:
    (a) 47   **(b)** 360   **(c)** 52 640   **(d)** 13 456   **(e)** 25 600

15 Divide by 10 and 100:
    (a) 2800   **(b)** 153 000   **(c)** 592 000   **(d)** 601 200

16 Calculate:
    (a) 27×40 **(b)** 161×30 **(c)** 4300×50 **(d)** 36×200
    (e) 78×300 **(f)** 21×400 **(g)** $1680 \div 20$ **(h)** $1470 \div 70$
    (i) $18 000 \div 60$ **(j)** $4200 \div 300$ **(k)** $7000 \div 500$ **(l)** $620 000 \div 400$

17 Nails are sold in boxes of two hundred. How many nails are in 34 boxes?

18 Brenda estimated that she needs 42 000 ice cubes for a party.
If ice cubes are sold in boxes of 500 how many boxes will be needed?

19 Sonia pays £146 council tax every month. How much will she have
paid after 12 months?

Summary

Writing numbers

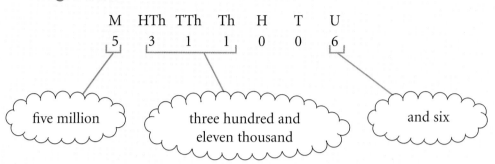

M	HTh	TTh	Th	H	T	U
5	3	1	1	0	0	6

five million

three hundred and eleven thousand

and six

Rounding numbers

4281 is 4280 to the nearest ten
        is 4300 to the nearest hundred

Estimating – addition and subtraction

$93 + 58$
Estimate is $90 + 60$
$= 150$

$186 - 29$
Estimate is $200 - 30$
$= 170$

Multiplying and dividing

23×10

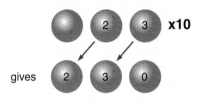

gives

213×200
$= 426 \times 100$

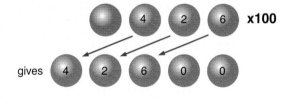

gives

$280 \div 10$

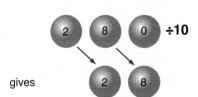

gives

$1600 \div 400$
$= 400 \div 100$

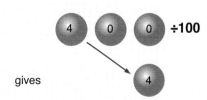

gives

Estimating – multiplication and division

46×29
Estimate is 50×30
$= 1500$

$315 \div 9$
Estimate is $300 \div 10$
$= 30$

2 Sequences, multiples and factors

2.1 Sequences

A sequence is a list of numbers that are in a particular order.
You have met some sequences already:

2, 4, 6, 8, 10, 12, 14, 16…
1, 3, 5, 7, 9, 11, 13, 15, 17…
3, 6, 9, 12, 15, 18, 21…
Do you recognise them?

Sometimes you will be able to find a pattern or rule for continuing the sequence.

Example

Sequence	Rule
3, 7, 11, 15, 19, 23…	add 4 to find the next number
2000, 1000, 500, 250, 125…	divide by 2 to find the next number

Exercise 2.1

1 Write (**a**) the next two numbers in each sequence and
   (**b**) a rule to find the next number:
     (**i**) 3, 7, 11, 15…   (**ii**) 3, 8, 13, 18, 23…
   (**iii**) 100, 96, 92…   (**iv**) 5, 10, 20, 40…
     (**v**) 2, 9, 16, 23…   (**vi**) 81, 27, 9…
   (**vii**) 250, 200, 150, 100…   (**viii**) 3, 4, 6, 9, 13, 18…
    (**ix**) 2400, 1200, 600, 300…   (**x**) 2, 8, 7, 28, 27, 108…

2 Each time a ball bounces its height decreases by 11 centimetres.
   If it bounces 120 centimetres on the first bounce, how high will it be on:
   (**a**) the third bounce   (**b**) the fourth bounce?

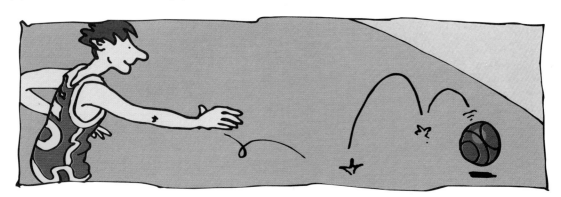

3 Every time Sam cuts the lawn he is given double the amount he received the previous time.
   He is given £1 the first time he cuts the lawn, £2 the second time, £4 the third time…
   How much will he get the tenth time he cuts the lawn?

4 Anna has written down the start of two squences:
120, 110, 100, 90...   and   1, 4, 7, 10, 13...
Which numbers will appear in both sequences?

5 Find the next three numbers in each of these special sequences:
(**a**) Triangular numbers   1, 3, 6, 10, 15...

(**b**) Rectangular numbers   2, 6, 12, 20, 30...

(**c**) Square numbers   1, 4, 9, 16, 25...

6 These sequences are called Fibonacci sequences.
(**a**) Find the next two numbers in each sequence.
   (**i**)   1, 1, 2, 3, 5, 8, 13...   (**ii**) 3, 4, 7, 11, 18...
   (**iii**) 20, 24, 44, 68...   (**iv**) 17, 19, 36, 55, 91...
(**b**) Make up a Fibonacci sequence of your own.

7 Complete the square:

5	7	12	19	31	50
18	15	33	48	81	129
23		45		112	
41			193		
64	59	123			
105	96				

8 Here is the start of Pascal's triangle:

```
                1
            1       1
        1       2       1
     1      3       3       1
  1      4      6       4       1
 ...    ...    ...     ...    ...    ...
 ...    ...    ...     ...    ...    ...    ...
```

Copy the triangle and complete the next two lines.

2.2 Multiples and factors

The multiples of 6 are   6, 12, 18, 24, 30, 36…
The multiples of 5 are   5, 10, 15, 20, 25…

The factors of 50 are   1, 2, 5, 10, 25, 50
The factors of 35 are   1, 5, 7, 35

Exercise 2.2

 1 The sieve of Erastothenes

You will need coloured pencils. You may use worksheet 2.1 or follow these instructions in your jotter.

Draw a square 10 cm by 10 cm and divide it into rows and columns of 1 cm width as shown:

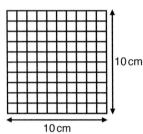

10 cm

10 cm

Starting at the top left hand corner, write in the numbers from 1 to 100.

1	2	3	4	5
11	12	13	14	
21	22			

Colour: (**a**) the number 1

(**b**) all the multiples of 2

(**c**) all the multiples of 3, then 4 … until you cannot colour in any more multiples.

The numbers which are left are called prime numbers.

A prime number has only two factors: 1 and itself.

2 (a) Which of these numbers are multiples of 4?

2, 16, 28, 14, 52, 36

(**b**) Which of these numbers are multiples of 9?

19, 81, 32, 36, 54

(**c**) Which of the numbers above are multiples of both 4 and 9?

3 Find:
   (**a**) a multiple of 7 which lies between 32 and 39
   (**b**) three multiples of 5 which are even
   (**c**) a multiple of 4 which is over 50
   (**d**) a number which is a multiple of 3 and 4
   (**e**) a number which is a multiple of 7 and 9
   (**f**) the smallest number which is a multiple of 6 and 8.

4 Find the lowest common multiple of:
   (**a**) 3 and 5   (**b**) 3 and 7   (**c**) 6 and 4   (**d**) 3, 5 and 7

5 Write down all the factors of:
   (**a**) 15   (**b**) 48   (**c**) 100   (**d**) 5   (**e**) 36

6 ⓐ120 ⑮15 ⑥60 ㊵40 ③3 ⑧8 ①1 ⑨9

   Which of these numbers are factors of:
   (**a**) 60   (**b**) 45?

7 Find a number which is a factor of 20 and 28.

8 (**a**) Find all the factors of:
       (**i**) 8   (**ii**) 6
   (**b**) Which factors do the answers have in common?
   (**c**) Find all the factors of:
       (**i**) 3   (**ii**) 15   (**iii**) 18
   (**d**) Which factors do the answers have in common?

9 Find the highest common factor of:
   (**a**) 6 and 8   (**b**) 20 and 28   (**c**) 15 and 45

2.3 Number puzzles

Exercise 2.3

1 Find three consecutive numbers which add up to 12 and multiply to give 60.

2 Tony thinks of a number. Its units digit is six less than its tens digit. The sum of the two digits is ten. Find Tony's number.

3 Numbers which are divisible by 5 end in a 0 or 5. Numbers which are divisible by 3 have a digit sum which is divisible by three. Which of these numbers can be divided by:
   (**a**) three   (**b**) five   (**c**) both?

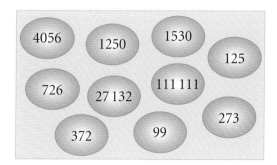

4 Each square contains the product of the numbers in the circles on either side.
Copy and complete each diagram.

(**a**)
```
 4 —28— ○
 □     56
 3 —□— 8
```

(**b**)
```
18 —□— 7
 □    161
12 —□— ○
```

(**c**)
```
 ○ —8000— 400
 □         □
 ○ —4800— 80
```

5 A magic square is a square in which the sum of the numbers on every row column and diagonal
have the same total.

Example

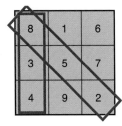

$8 + 3 + 4 = 15$
$8 + 5 + 2 = 15$

Copy and complete each magic square
(**a**) using the digits 2 to 10
(**b**) using the digits 6 to 14.

(**a**)

9		5
2		
7		

(**b**)

13		
	10	
11		7

6 This magic square has had a pair of numbers swapped.
Draw the corrected magic square.

6	13	8
11	7	9
10	5	12

Rows and columns add to 27

7 In this grid each block of 4 adds up to 12.

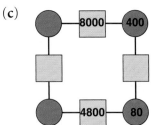

$1 + 4 + 4 + 3 = 12$

Copy and complete this
grid so that every block
of four adds up to 12.

6	1	4	0
3	2		
	5		
		7	

8 Complete these calculations:

(a)
```
  1 6
+ ▨ 2
-----
  9 8
```
(b)
```
  1 3 4
-   8 ▨
-------
  ▨ 9
```
(c)
```
    ▨ 9
×     5
-------
  1 4 ▨
```
(d)
```
  ▨ 6 5 7
+ 2 4 3 ▨
---------
  6 0 ▨ 5
```

9 Use the digits 1, 2, 3, 4, 5, 6, 7, 8, 9 and + or − signs to make a total of 100.
Example $12 + 3 − 4 + 5 + 67 + 8 + 9 = 100$

10 How many times does the digit 4 appear in all the numbers from 1 to 1000?

Review exercise 2

1 Write (a) the next two numbers in each sequence and
(b) a rule to find the next number.
(i) 15, 18, 21, 24...   (ii) 100, 94, 88, 82...
(iii) 640, 320, 160...   (iv) 3, 9, 27, 81...

2 (a) Which of these numbers are multiples of
(i) 4   (ii) 7?
(b) Which of these numbers are factors of
(i) 32   (ii) 80?
(c) Which of these numbers is a multiple of 5 and 6?

30	7	14	40	18
13	20	14	56	32
2	6	24	8	17

3 Find the lowest common multiple of:
(a) 3 and 5   (b) 6 and 10   (c) 4 and 8   (d) 4 and 6

4 Find the highest common factor of:
(a) 12 and 18   (b) 20 and 30   (c) 16 and 40   (d) 27 and 36

Summary

Sequence

A **sequence** is a list of numbers in a particular order.

Sequence	Rule
2, 6, 10, 14 ...	add 4 to find the next number.

Multiples and factors

Multiples of 7 are   7, 14, 21, 28 ...
Factors of 54 are   1, 2, 3, 6, 9, 18, 27, 54

3 Symmetry

In this chapter you will learn about lines of symmetry and reflection.

3.1 Lines of symmetry

The dotted line cuts this shape in half so that one half will fold exactly onto the other.
This is called a **line of symmetry**
            or **axis of symmetry**.

Some shapes have more than one line of symmetry.

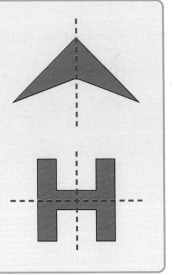

Exercise 3.1

1 List any shapes that you can see in the room which have a line or lines of symmetry.

2 Look at the following shapes:

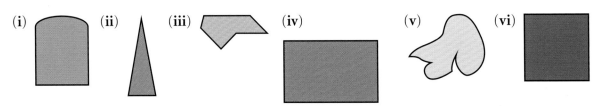

(i)   (ii)   (iii)   (iv)   (v)   (vi)

(**a**) Which shapes have only one line of symmetry?
(**b**) Which shapes have no lines of symmetry?
(**c**) How many lines of symmetry could you draw on shape (iv)?
(**d**) How many lines of symmetry could you draw on shape (vi)?

3 Which of the following pictures have an axis of symmetry?

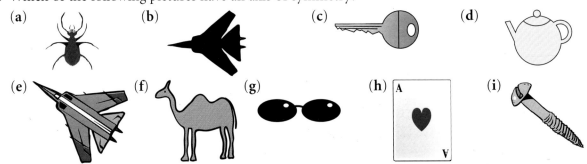

(**a**)   (**b**)   (**c**)   (**d**)

(**e**)   (**f**)   (**g**)   (**h**)   (**i**)

4 Copy these shapes into your jotter.
Draw all lines of symmetry for each.

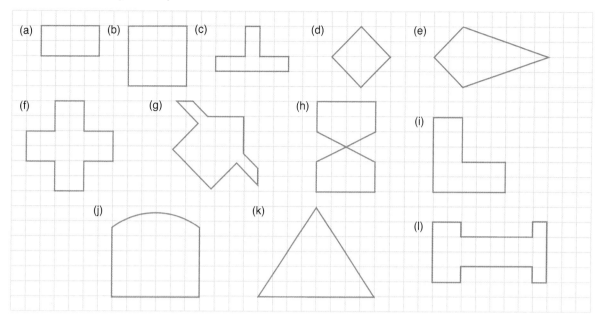

5 How many lines of symmetry can you draw on the shapes below?

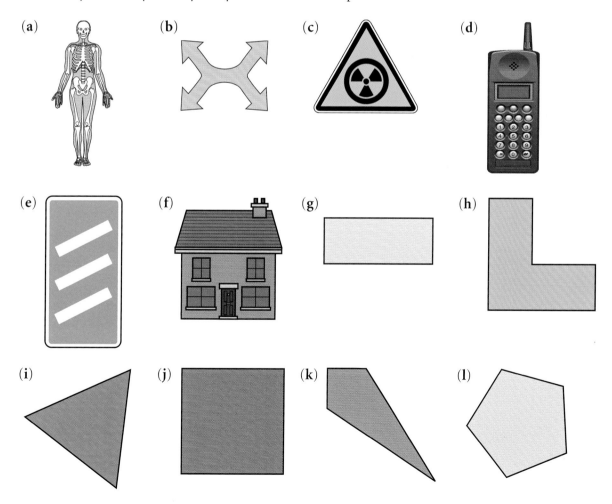

6 Here is the capital letter A.

Use a page in your jotter to write **all** the
capital letters of the alphabet.
Keep them all approximately the same size.
(**a**) Show all the lines of symmetry for each, if any.
(**b**) Which letter has too many lines for you to draw?

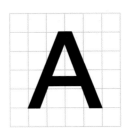

 7 You may use worksheet 3.1 for this question.

3.2 Reflection

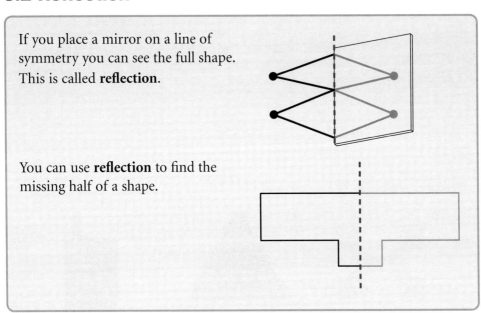

If you place a mirror on a line of
symmetry you can see the full shape.
This is called **reflection**.

You can use **reflection** to find the
missing half of a shape.

Exercise 3.2

1 Copy and complete the following shapes using reflection.

(**a**) (**b**) (**c**) (**d**)

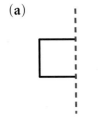   

(**e**) (**f**) (**g**)

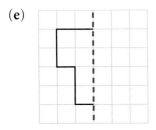 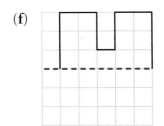 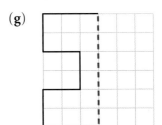

2 The symmetrical letters have been used to form a code.
Write down each coded message.

(a) HELLO, I LOVE MATHS

(b) MY NAME IS BOD

(c) PASSWORD IS BADDY

3 Use the code above to write in your jotters:

(a) HELP ME
(b) the name of your school
(c) your own full name.

4 Copy and complete the calculations using symmetry.

(a)    (b)

5 Copy and complete the following shapes using reflection.

(a)   (b)   (c)   (d)

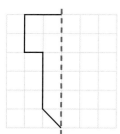   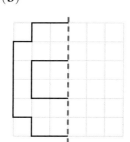   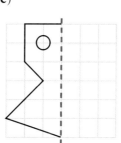   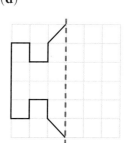

 6 You may use worksheet 2.2 for this question.

3.3 Images

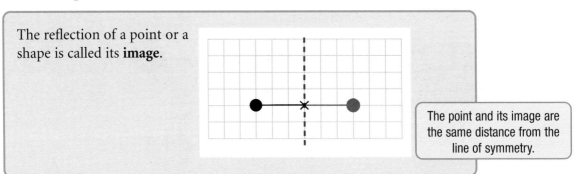

The reflection of a point or a shape is called its **image**.

The point and its image are the same distance from the line of symmetry.

Exercise 3.3

W You may use worksheet 3.3 for this exercise.

Copy and complete the diagrams, showing all images.

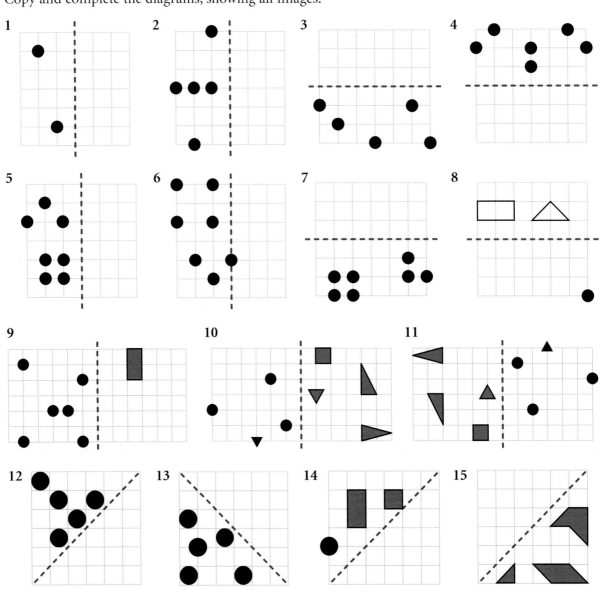

Review exercise 3

1 Which of these pictures have a line of symmetry?

(**a**)    (**b**)   (**c**)    (**d**)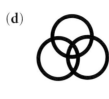

2 How many axes of symmetry could you draw on each diagram?

(**a**)   (**b**) 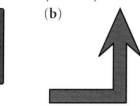   (**c**) 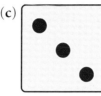   (**d**)   (**e**)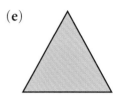

3 Copy each shape and draw any lines of symmetry.

(**a**) 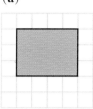   (**b**)   (**c**) 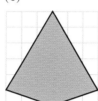   (**d**) 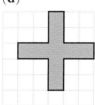   (**e**)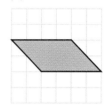

4 Copy and complete the shapes for each axis of symmetry.

(**a**) 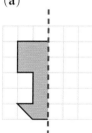   (**b**) 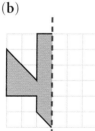   (**c**) 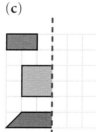   (**d**) 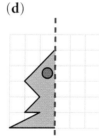   (**e**)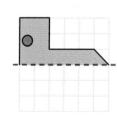

5 Copy the shapes and use reflection to show each image.

(**a**) 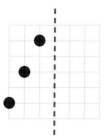   (**b**) 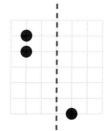   (**c**) 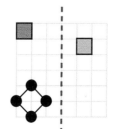   (**d**)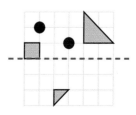

Summary

Symmetry

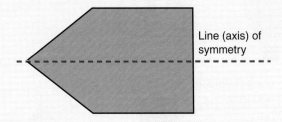 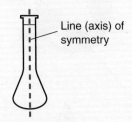

Some shapes have more than one line of symmetry.

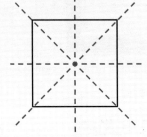

Reflection

Reflection may be used to complete the missing half of a symmetrical shape.

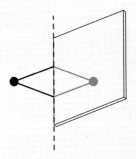

The reflection of a point or shape is called its **image**.

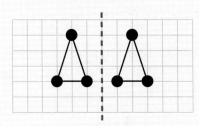

4 Fractions

In this chapter you will review your knowledge of fractions, learn more about equivalent fractions and calculate fractions of quantities.

4.1 Understanding fractions

Example

From the picture below find the fraction of the barber's pole which is
(**a**) red   (**b**) white.

There are 9 **identical** hoops on the pole so each hoop is $\frac{1}{9}$ of the pole.

(**a**) Four hoops are red so $\frac{4}{9}$ of the pole is red.

(**b**) Five hoops are white so $\frac{5}{9}$ of the pole is white.

Exercise 4.1

1 Use the picture to find the fraction of:
   (**a**) the billboard outside the sweet shop which is   (**i**) white   (**ii**) blue
   (**b**) people in the queue who   (**i**) have a hat   (**ii**) do not have a hat
   (**c**) people in the queue who are   (**i**) men   (**ii**) women
   (**d**) the animals which are   (**i**) cats   (**ii**) dogs
   (**e**) the awning which is   (**i**) green   (**ii**) blue
   (**f**) the jars in the window which are   (**i**) red   (**ii**) blue   (**iii**) green
   (**g**) the letters above the sweet shop which are   (**i**) vowels   (**ii**) consonants
   (**h**) the numbers on the route board which are   (**i**) even   (**ii**) odd.

2 This cake has been cut into 8 equal slices.
   (**a**) What fraction of the cake is:
       (**i**) 1 slice   (**ii**) 3 slices   (**iii**) 7 slices?
   (**b**) How many slices are in:
       (**i**) 2 cakes   (**ii**) half a cake   (**iii**) $1\frac{1}{8}$ cakes?

4.2 Equivalent fractions

Multiplying the numerator and denominator of a fraction by the same number makes an **equivalent fraction**.

The **numerator** is on the **top** and the **denominator** is on the **bottom**.

$$\frac{5}{8} \xrightarrow{\times 3} = \xrightarrow{\times 3} \frac{15}{24}$$

$$\frac{2}{3} \xrightarrow{\times 5} = \xrightarrow{\times 5} \frac{10}{15}$$

$\frac{5}{8}$ and $\frac{15}{24}$ are equivalent fractions. $\frac{2}{3}$ and $\frac{10}{15}$ are equivalent fractions.

Exercise 4.2

1 Copy and complete by filling in the missing numbers.

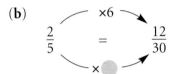

(a) $\frac{1}{3} = \frac{5}{15}$ ×5 / ×◯

(b) $\frac{2}{5} = \frac{12}{30}$ ×6 / ×◯

(c) $\frac{3}{4} = \frac{30}{40}$ ×◯ / ×10

(d) $\frac{1}{7} = \frac{4}{28}$ ×◯ / ×4

(e) $\frac{4}{11} = \frac{12}{33}$ ×◯ / ×◯

(f) $\frac{5}{12} = \frac{10}{24}$ ×◯ / ×◯

(g) $\frac{3}{8} = \frac{18}{48}$ ×◯ / ×◯

(h) $\frac{2}{9} = \frac{18}{81}$ ×◯ / ×◯

(i) $\frac{7}{10} = \frac{42}{60}$ ×◯ / ×◯

(j) $\frac{3}{7} = \frac{21}{49}$ ×◯ / ×◯

(k) $\frac{5}{6} = \frac{40}{48}$ ×◯ / ×◯

(l) $\frac{4}{5} = \frac{400}{500}$ ×◯ / ×◯

(m) $\frac{1}{4} = \frac{8}{32}$ ×◯ / ×◯

(n) $\frac{2}{3} = \frac{18}{27}$ ×◯ / ×◯

(o) $\frac{3}{5} = \frac{33}{55}$ ×◯ / ×◯

4.3 Further equivalence

Example Copy and complete: $\dfrac{3}{5} = \dfrac{6}{\square}$

$$\dfrac{3}{5} \begin{array}{c} \xrightarrow{\times 2} \\ = \\ \xrightarrow{\times 2} \end{array} \dfrac{6}{10}$$

3 has been multiplied by 2 to give 6

5 must also be multiplied by 2 to give 10

$$\dfrac{3}{5} = \dfrac{6}{10}$$

Exercise 4.3

1 Copy and complete:

(a) $\dfrac{3}{8} = \dfrac{\square}{16}$ (b) $\dfrac{1}{5} = \dfrac{\square}{15}$ (c) $\dfrac{7}{10} = \dfrac{\square}{30}$ (d) $\dfrac{2}{3} = \dfrac{8}{\square}$ (e) $\dfrac{9}{10} = \dfrac{63}{\square}$ (f) $\dfrac{3}{5} = \dfrac{\square}{35}$

(g) $\dfrac{1}{4} = \dfrac{5}{\square}$ (h) $\dfrac{2}{7} = \dfrac{6}{\square}$ (i) $\dfrac{5}{9} = \dfrac{40}{\square}$ (j) $\dfrac{6}{11} = \dfrac{\square}{44}$ (k) $\dfrac{7}{12} = \dfrac{14}{\square}$ (l) $\dfrac{10}{11} = \dfrac{100}{\square}$

2 Copy and complete:

(a) $\dfrac{1}{2} = \dfrac{\square}{4} = \dfrac{\square}{8}$ (b) $\dfrac{1}{3} = \dfrac{\square}{6} = \dfrac{\square}{9}$ (c) $\dfrac{2}{3} = \dfrac{4}{\square} = \dfrac{\square}{15}$

(d) $\dfrac{3}{4} = \dfrac{\square}{8} = \dfrac{12}{\square}$ (e) $\dfrac{1}{5} = \dfrac{4}{\square} = \dfrac{\square}{40}$ (f) $\dfrac{4}{5} = \dfrac{20}{\square} = \dfrac{40}{\square}$

(g) $\dfrac{5}{6} = \dfrac{\square}{18} = \dfrac{25}{\square}$ (h) $\dfrac{4}{7} = \dfrac{24}{\square} = \dfrac{36}{\square}$ (i) $\dfrac{3}{8} = \dfrac{\square}{24} = \dfrac{18}{\square}$

(j) $\dfrac{5}{9} = \dfrac{20}{\square} = \dfrac{80}{\square}$ (k) $\dfrac{7}{10} = \dfrac{14}{\square} = \dfrac{\square}{60}$ (l) $\dfrac{2}{11} = \dfrac{\square}{44} = \dfrac{16}{\square}$

4.4 Simplifying fractions

To simplify a fraction, divide the numerator and denominator by the same number.

$$\dfrac{28}{49} \begin{array}{c} \xrightarrow{\div 7} \\ = \\ \xrightarrow{\div 7} \end{array} \dfrac{4}{7}$$

Exercise 4.4

Simplify these fractions.

1 $\dfrac{2}{4}$ **2** $\dfrac{3}{6}$ **3** $\dfrac{5}{10}$ **4** $\dfrac{7}{14}$ **5** $\dfrac{5}{15}$ **6** $\dfrac{3}{9}$ **7** $\dfrac{2}{18}$ **8** $\dfrac{7}{21}$

9 $\dfrac{11}{33}$ **10** $\dfrac{3}{30}$ **11** $\dfrac{2}{10}$ **12** $\dfrac{3}{15}$ **13** $\dfrac{5}{25}$ **14** $\dfrac{7}{49}$ **15** $\dfrac{15}{20}$ **16** $\dfrac{6}{9}$

17 $\dfrac{9}{12}$ **18** $\dfrac{15}{25}$ **19** $\dfrac{21}{35}$ **20** $\dfrac{14}{49}$ **21** $\dfrac{3}{39}$ **22** $\dfrac{5}{75}$ **23** $\dfrac{2}{50}$ **24** $\dfrac{17}{34}$

4.5 Simplest form

To express a fraction in simplest form, keep dividing if necessary.

$$\frac{60}{84} \xrightarrow[\div 12]{\div 12} = \frac{5}{7} \qquad \text{or} \qquad \frac{60}{84} \xrightarrow[\div 3]{\div 3} = \frac{20}{28} \xrightarrow[\div 4]{\div 4} = \frac{5}{7}$$

Exercise 4.5

1 Copy and complete these simplifications by filling in the missing numbers.

(a)

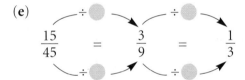

$$\frac{60}{80} \xrightarrow[\div \bullet]{\div 10} = \frac{6}{8} \xrightarrow[\div \bullet]{\div 2} = \frac{3}{4}$$

(b)

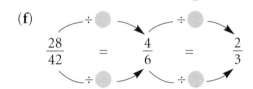

$$\frac{30}{45} \xrightarrow[\div \bullet]{\div 5} = \frac{6}{9} \xrightarrow[\div 3]{\div \bullet} = \frac{2}{3}$$

(c)

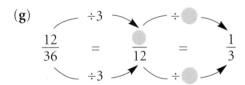

$$\frac{16}{40} \xrightarrow[\div 4]{\div 4} = \frac{4}{10} \xrightarrow[\div \bullet]{\div 2} = \frac{2}{5}$$

(d)

$$\frac{36}{48} \xrightarrow[\div \bullet]{\div 4} = \frac{9}{12} \xrightarrow[\div \bullet]{\div \bullet} = \frac{3}{4}$$

(e)

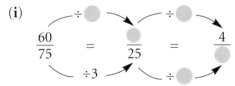

$$\frac{15}{45} \xrightarrow[\div \bullet]{\div \bullet} = \frac{3}{9} \xrightarrow[\div \bullet]{\div \bullet} = \frac{1}{3}$$

(f)

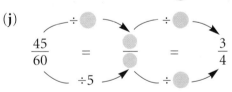

$$\frac{28}{42} \xrightarrow[\div \bullet]{\div \bullet} = \frac{4}{6} \xrightarrow[\div \bullet]{\div \bullet} = \frac{2}{3}$$

(g)

$$\frac{12}{36} \xrightarrow[\div 3]{\div 3} = \frac{\bullet}{12} \xrightarrow[\div \bullet]{\div \bullet} = \frac{1}{3}$$

(h)

$$\frac{12}{42} \xrightarrow[\div 2]{\div \bullet} = \frac{\bullet}{21} \xrightarrow[\div \bullet]{\div \bullet} = \frac{2}{\bullet}$$

(i)

$$\frac{60}{75} \xrightarrow[\div 3]{\div \bullet} = \frac{\bullet}{25} \xrightarrow[\div \bullet]{\div \bullet} = \frac{4}{\bullet}$$

(j)

$$\frac{45}{60} \xrightarrow[\div 5]{\div \bullet} = \frac{\bullet}{\bullet} \xrightarrow[\div \bullet]{\div \bullet} = \frac{3}{4}$$

(k)

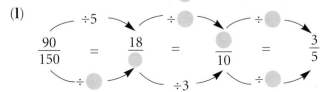

$$\frac{140}{700} \xrightarrow[\div \bullet]{\div 10} = \frac{14}{\bullet} \xrightarrow[\div \bullet]{\div 7} = \frac{\bullet}{10} \xrightarrow[\div \bullet]{\div 2} = \frac{1}{\bullet}$$

(l)

$$\frac{90}{150} \xrightarrow[\div \bullet]{\div 5} = \frac{18}{\bullet} \xrightarrow[\div 3]{\div \bullet} = \frac{\bullet}{10} \xrightarrow[\div \bullet]{\div \bullet} = \frac{3}{5}$$

2 Express these fractions in simplest form:

(a) $\frac{12}{72}$ (b) $\frac{40}{60}$ (c) $\frac{90}{120}$ (d) $\frac{14}{70}$ (e) $\frac{24}{48}$ (f) $\frac{72}{84}$

(g) $\frac{63}{72}$ (h) $\frac{48}{108}$ (i) $\frac{16}{112}$ (j) $\frac{490}{560}$ (k) $\frac{100}{160}$ (l) $\frac{24}{72}$

4.6 Calculating a fraction of a quantity

To calculate a fraction of a quantity, divide by the denominator.

To find $\frac{1}{2}$ divide by 2   To find $\frac{1}{3}$ divide by 3   To find $\frac{1}{4}$ divide by 4

To find $\frac{1}{10}$ divide by 10   To find $\frac{1}{5}$ divide by 5

Example Calculate $\frac{1}{5}$ of £25.

$\frac{1}{5}$ of £25 = £25 ÷ 5

= **£5**

Exercise 4.6

1 Calculate:

(a) $\frac{1}{2}$ of £30 (b) $\frac{1}{3}$ of 63 g (c) $\frac{1}{4}$ of 24 kg (d) $\frac{1}{7}$ of 35 m

(e) $\frac{1}{6}$ of 48 tonnes (f) $\frac{1}{5}$ of 45 cm (g) $\frac{1}{8}$ of 56 litres (h) $\frac{1}{9}$ of 72 pence

(i) $\frac{1}{10}$ of £80 (j) $\frac{1}{2}$ of 56 km (k) $\frac{1}{7}$ of 63 litres (l) $\frac{1}{3}$ of 102 g

(m) $\frac{1}{4}$ of 112 m (n) $\frac{1}{5}$ of £65 (o) $\frac{1}{6}$ of 72 cm (p) $\frac{1}{8}$ of 248 m

(q) $\frac{1}{9}$ of £207 (r) $\frac{1}{10}$ of 560 g (s) $\frac{1}{4}$ of £960 (t) $\frac{1}{6}$ of 306°

2 There are 960 pupils at Alnwath Academy. Calculate the number of pupils in each category.

(a) $\frac{1}{2}$ are boys (b) $\frac{1}{3}$ have fair hair

(c) $\frac{1}{4}$ wear glasses (d) $\frac{1}{5}$ are in first year

(e) $\frac{1}{8}$ have their own computer (f) $\frac{1}{10}$ travel to school by bicycle.

3 The Mathematics Department at Alnwath Academy spent £5600 last year on books and equipment. Calculate the amount spent on each item.

(a) $\frac{1}{4}$ on jotters (b) $\frac{1}{5}$ on calculators

(c) $\frac{1}{7}$ on photocopying (d) $\frac{1}{8}$ on stationery items

(e) $\frac{1}{10}$ on other equipment (f) The rest was spent on books: how much was this?

4.7 Fractions of a quantity

Example   There are 960 pupils at Alnwath Academy.

$\frac{3}{4}$ of the pupils walk to school.

How many pupils walk to school?

$\frac{1}{4}$ of 960 = 240

So $\frac{3}{4}$ of 960 = 3 × 240 = 720

720 pupils walk to school.

Exercise 4.7

1 Calculate:

(a) $\frac{5}{8}$ of 400   (b) $\frac{2}{5}$ of 25   (c) $\frac{2}{3}$ of 15   (d) $\frac{3}{5}$ of 45   (e) $\frac{2}{7}$ of 28   (f) $\frac{3}{8}$ of 64

2 Find:

(a) $\frac{2}{9}$ of 54 tonnes   (b) $\frac{9}{10}$ of 70 mm   (c) $\frac{4}{9}$ of £99   (d) $\frac{7}{8}$ of 96 cm

(e) $\frac{6}{7}$ of £147   (f) $\frac{8}{9}$ of 270 kg   (g) $\frac{5}{6}$ of £3 (in pence)   (h) $\frac{3}{7}$ of 1470 g

(i) $\frac{3}{10}$ of 20 km   (j) $\frac{3}{4}$ of 80 kg   (k) $\frac{4}{5}$ of 15 litre   (l) $\frac{4}{9}$ of 180 km

3 There are 960 pupils at Alnwath Academy. Find the number of pupils in each group if:

(a) $\frac{2}{3}$ have lunch in school   (b) $\frac{3}{4}$ wear school uniform

(c) $\frac{5}{6}$ say they enjoy school   (d) $\frac{2}{5}$ expect to go to university or college

(e) $\frac{3}{5}$ never play sport   (f) $\frac{5}{8}$ attend after-school clubs

(g) $\frac{7}{8}$ enjoy maths   (h) $\frac{9}{10}$ complete their homework.

4 A bag contains 480 coloured beads.

$\frac{3}{8}$ are red, $\frac{1}{6}$ are blue, $\frac{3}{10}$ are yellow and the rest are white.

(a) Calculate the number of:
   (i) red beads   (ii) blue beads   (iii) yellow beads
(b) How many of the beads are white?

5 One complete revolution is 360°.
Calculate the sizes of the angles which are:

(a) $\frac{2}{3}$ of a revolution   (b) $\frac{3}{4}$ of a revolution   (c) $\frac{2}{5}$ of a revolution

(d) $\frac{4}{5}$ of a revolution   (e) $\frac{5}{6}$ of a revolution   (f) $\frac{3}{8}$ of a revolution

(g) $\frac{2}{9}$ of a revolution   (h) $\frac{7}{9}$ of a revolution   (i) $\frac{3}{10}$ of a revolution

4.8 Mixed numbers

Example

How many $\frac{1}{4}$ litre cartons of milk can be filled from:

(**a**) a 1 litre bottle   (**b**) a $2\frac{1}{4}$ litre bottle?

(**a**) One litre has 4 quarters so a 1 litre bottle fills 4 cartons.
(**b**) Two litres have 8 quarters so a $2\frac{1}{4}$ litre bottle fills 9 cartons.

$1 = \frac{4}{4}$

Exercise 4.8

1 How many $\frac{1}{2}$ litre glasses of Iron Brew can be filled from bottles containing:

(**a**) 1 litre   (**b**) 2 litres   (**c**) 3 litres   (**d**) 5 litres   (**e**) $1\frac{1}{2}$ litres?

$1 = \frac{2}{2}$

2 How many $\frac{1}{3}$ litre glasses of milk can be filled from containers which hold:

(**a**) 1 litre   (**b**) 2 litres   (**c**) 3 litres   (**d**) 5 litres   (**e**) $1\frac{2}{3}$ litres?

$1 = \frac{3}{3}$

3 How many $\frac{1}{4}$ kg tubs can be filled from a carton containing:

(**a**) 1 kg   (**b**) 2 kg   (**c**) 4 kg   (**d**) $1\frac{1}{4}$ kg   (**e**) $3\frac{1}{2}$ kg?

4 How many $\frac{1}{5}$ kg packets can be filled from a box containing:

(**a**) 1 kg   (**b**) 3 kg   (**c**) $1\frac{2}{5}$ kg   (**d**) $2\frac{4}{5}$ kg   (**e**) $5\frac{3}{5}$ kg?

5 Find the number of:

(**a**) thirds of a pizza in 2 pizzas   (**b**) fifths of an apple in 3 apples

(**c**) eighths of a cake in 5 cakes   (**d**) quarters of a pie in $1\frac{1}{4}$ pies

(**e**) sevenths of a loaf in $3\frac{2}{7}$ loaves   (**f**) sixths of a tart in $2\frac{5}{6}$ tarts.

6 In Fazzini's café Alasdair sells ice cream in tubs like these.

(**a**) How many large tubs can he fill from a one litre container?
(**b**) How many medium tubs can he fill from a 3 litre container?
(**c**) How many small tubs can he fill from a 7 litre container?

7 A small coffee cup holds $\frac{1}{6}$ litre.

How many of these cups can be filled from:
(**a**) a 1 litre pot   (**b**) a $1\frac{1}{2}$ litre pot?

4.9 Multiplying a fraction by a whole number

Example Calculate the total weight of nine $\frac{1}{4}$ kg packets of butter.

Nine $\frac{1}{4}$ kg packets weigh $9 \times \frac{1}{4} = \frac{9}{4}$

Total weight $= 2\frac{1}{4}$ kg

$\frac{4}{4} = 1$

$\frac{8}{4} = 2$

So $\frac{9}{4} = 2\frac{1}{4}$

Exercise 4.9

1 Calculate:

(**a**) $6 \times \frac{1}{2}$ (**b**) $9 \times \frac{1}{3}$ (**c**) $3 \times \frac{1}{4}$ (**d**) $10 \times \frac{1}{5}$ (**e**) $5 \times \frac{1}{6}$ m (**f**) $7 \times \frac{1}{7}$ km

(**g**) $5 \times \frac{1}{8}$ litre (**h**) $9 \times \frac{1}{9}$ m (**i**) $4 \times \frac{1}{10}$ g (**j**) $10 \times \frac{1}{2}$ kg (**k**) $8 \times \frac{1}{5}$ m (**l**) $11 \times \frac{1}{4}$ litre

2 Calculate the weight of:

(**a**) ten $\frac{1}{2}$ kg bags of rice (**b**) twelve $\frac{1}{4}$ kg bags of flour

(**c**) seven $\frac{1}{3}$ kg bags of sugar (**d**) twelve $\frac{1}{5}$ kg packets of curry powder

(**e**) twenty $\frac{1}{9}$ kg packets of nutmeg (**f**) seventeen $\frac{1}{10}$ kg packets of parmesan

3 Calculate the volume of:

(**a**) fourteen $\frac{1}{3}$ litre bottles of lemonade (**b**) eighteen $\frac{1}{5}$ litre cups of water

(**c**) twenty five $\frac{1}{8}$ litre glasses of cola (**d**) thirty $\frac{1}{9}$ litre glasses of wine

4.10 More mixed numbers

Example A bottle of shampoo holds $\frac{2}{5}$ litre.

Calculate the total volume of 6 bottles of shampoo.

Total volume $= 6 \times \frac{2}{5}$

$= \frac{12}{5}$

$= 2\frac{2}{5}$ litres

$\frac{5}{5} = 1$

$\frac{10}{5} = 2$

So $\frac{12}{5} = 2\frac{2}{5}$

Exercise 4.10

1 Calculate:

(**a**) $3 \times \frac{2}{3}$ (**b**) $8 \times \frac{3}{4}$ (**c**) $5 \times \frac{3}{5}$ (**d**) $3 \times \frac{3}{10}$ (**e**) $5 \times \frac{2}{9}$ (**f**) $4 \times \frac{5}{7}$

(**g**) $3 \times \frac{7}{8}$ miles (**h**) $7 \times \frac{5}{6}$ kg (**i**) $6 \times \frac{3}{5}$ km (**j**) $9 \times \frac{3}{8}$ m (**k**) $10 \times \frac{2}{3}$ cm (**l**) $2 \times \frac{9}{10}$ kg

2 (**a**) A bottle of wine holds $\frac{7}{10}$ of a litre. What is the volume of 5 bottles?

(**b**) A packet of fish fingers weighs $\frac{4}{5}$ of a kilogram. What is the weight of 6 packets?

(**c**) A can of Iron Brew holds $\frac{2}{7}$ of a litre. What is the volume of 6 cans?

(**d**) The width of a desk top is $\frac{7}{8}$ of a metre. What is the total width of 5 desks placed side by side?

(**e**) John trains in the gym for $\frac{3}{4}$ of an hour each day. How long is this each week?

Review exercise 4

1 What fraction of liquorice is in this sweet?

2 What fraction of this packet of wine gums is
  (**a**) blackcurrant
  (**b**) raspberry?

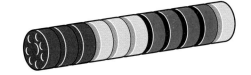

3 (**a**) How many fifths of a pizza are in 2 pizzas?
  (**b**) How many tenths of a gingerbread are in $2\frac{1}{2}$ gingerbreads?

4 Copy and complete:
  (**a**) $\dfrac{5}{8} = \dfrac{\ }{16}$ (**b**) $\dfrac{1}{5} = \dfrac{\ }{45}$ (**c**) $\dfrac{7}{9} = \dfrac{35}{\ }$ (**d**) $\dfrac{5}{12} = \dfrac{10}{\ }$

5 Copy and complete:
  (**a**) $\dfrac{1}{7} = \dfrac{\ }{21} = \dfrac{\ }{42}$ (**b**) $\dfrac{2}{9} = \dfrac{6}{\ } = \dfrac{\ }{45}$ (**c**) $\dfrac{3}{10} = \dfrac{\ }{40} = \dfrac{15}{\ }$

6 Express these fractions in simplest form.
  (**a**) $\dfrac{7}{14}$ (**b**) $\dfrac{15}{35}$ (**c**) $\dfrac{9}{12}$ (**d**) $\dfrac{18}{27}$ (**e**) $\dfrac{72}{81}$ (**f**) $\dfrac{150}{200}$

7 In a packet of Jelli Babes there are 7 red, 6 green, 8 yellow
  and 5 black. What fraction of the Jelli Babes are black?

8 How many $\frac{1}{4}$ litre tumblers of orange juice can be filled from a bottle which holds:

  (**a**) 1 litre   (**b**) 3 litres   (**c**) $2\frac{1}{2}$ litres?

9 Calculate:
  (**a**) $\dfrac{1}{3}$ of a class of 27 pupils   (**b**) $\dfrac{1}{7}$ of 56 passengers.

10 Calculate:
  (**a**) $\dfrac{3}{8}$ of 24 eggs in a container   (**b**) $\dfrac{5}{6}$ of the 36 people on the eight o'clock train.

11 27 birds were feeding on the garage roof.
  If $\frac{4}{9}$ of the birds were sparrows, how many of the birds were sparrows?

12 Calculate the total weight of eight $\frac{1}{4}$ kg bags of sweets.

13 There are 4 runners in a relay race; each runs $\frac{1}{3}$ of a mile. What is the length of the race?

14 Calculate:
  (**a**) the volume of 7 bottles of shampoo each holding $\frac{3}{10}$ of a litre

  (**b**) the total length of 8 sections of pipe each $\frac{8}{9}$ of a metre long.

Summary

Understanding fractions

$\dfrac{2}{5}$

2 sections are red – the **numerator**

total of 5 equal sections – the **denominator**

$\dfrac{2}{5}$ of the shape is red

Equivalent fractions – multiply numerator and denominator by the same number.

$$\dfrac{2}{5} \overset{\times 2}{=} \dfrac{4}{10} \overset{\times 5}{=} \dfrac{20}{50}$$

$\dfrac{2}{5}$, $\dfrac{4}{10}$ and $\dfrac{20}{50}$ are equivalent fractions

Simplest form – divide numerator and denominator by the same number.

$$\dfrac{24}{84} \overset{\div 12}{=} \dfrac{2}{7} \quad \text{or} \quad \dfrac{24}{84} \overset{\div 4}{=} \dfrac{6}{21} \overset{\div 3}{=} \dfrac{2}{7}$$

$$\dfrac{24}{84} = \dfrac{2}{7} \text{ in simplest form}$$

Calculating a fraction of a quantity

To find $\frac{1}{4}$ of £32 divide by 4

$\frac{1}{4}$ of £32 = £8

To find $\frac{5}{8}$ of £24 first divide by 8 then multiply by 5

$\frac{1}{8}$ of £24 = £3

$\frac{5}{8}$ of £24 = 5 × £3

$= £15$

Multiplying a fraction by a whole number

$$7 \times \dfrac{2}{5} = \dfrac{14}{5}$$
$$= 2\dfrac{4}{5}$$

$\dfrac{5}{5} = 1 \quad \dfrac{10}{5} = 2$

5 Angles

Angles are used in many everyday situations, from buildings to games.
In this chapter you will learn to work with angles.

5.1 Naming Angles

An angle is formed where two **arms** meet at a **vertex**.

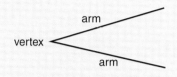

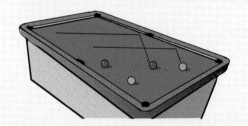

Look at this diagram.
How many angles are there at point B?

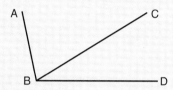

There are several angles.

All the angles cannot be called B – you would not know to which angle you were referring.
A better method is needed. Each different angle needs a different name.

The red angle is called ∠ABC or ∠CBA.
The blue angle is called ∠CBD or ∠DBC.
The green angle is called ∠ABD or ∠DBA.

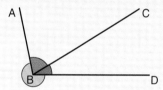

Exercise 5.1

1 Name each marked angle in two ways.

(**a**)

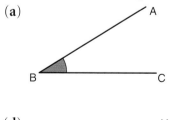

(**b**)

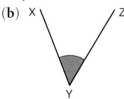

(**c**)

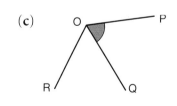

(**d**)

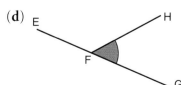

(**e**)

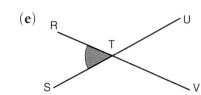

2 The diagram shows a trapezium PQRS. Name the
   (**a**) red angle   (**b**) blue angle
   (**c**) green angle   (**d**) yellow angle

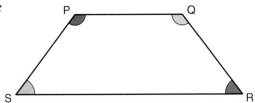

3 In triangle ABC name the angle marked
   (**a**) o   (**b**) ✶   (**c**) □

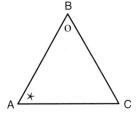

4 Copy these diagrams and shade each of the angles given.
   (**a**) ∠ABC   (**b**) ∠RTV   (**c**) ∠PQR   (**d**) ∠XYZ

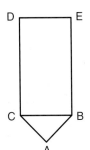 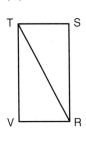 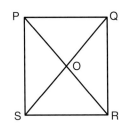 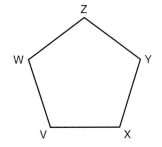

5 Name the marked angles in these diagrams.
   (**a**)

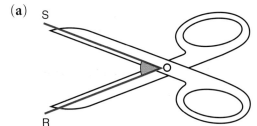

   (**b**)

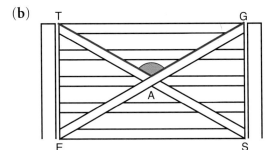

   (**c**)

   (**d**)

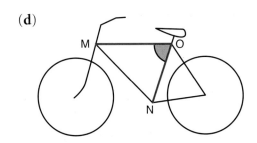

5.2 Drawing angles

Draw ∠ABC = 42°

Step 1 Draw line AB 6 cm long.

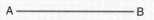

Step 2 Place the centre of the protractor on B with the base line on AB as shown.

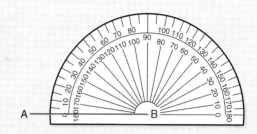

Step 3 Find the zero which is on the line AB, count up the number of degrees and put a dot at 42°.

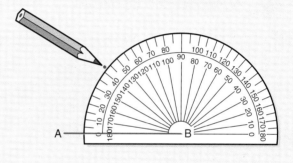

Step 4 Draw a line from B through the dot and mark C.

Step 5 Label your angle as shown.

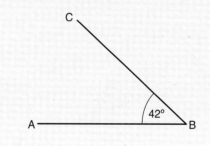

Exercise 5.2

You need a ruler and a protractor.

1 Draw accurately the following angles:
  (**a**) ∠ABC = 50°   (**b**) ∠ABC = 30°   (**c**) ∠ABC = 45°   (**d**) ∠ABC = 85°

2 Draw accurately the following angles:
  (**a**) ∠XYZ = 60°   (**b**) ∠DEF = 10°   (**c**) ∠GHI = 65°   (**d**) ∠JKL = 90°
  (**e**) ∠MNO = 110°   (**f**) ∠PQR = 145°   (**g**) ∠STU = 180°   (**f**) ∠VWX = 135°
  (**g**) ∠SFA = 23°   (**h**) ∠DAT = 157°   (**i**) ∠ANG = 38°   (**j**) ∠KOP = 168°

5.3 Measuring angles

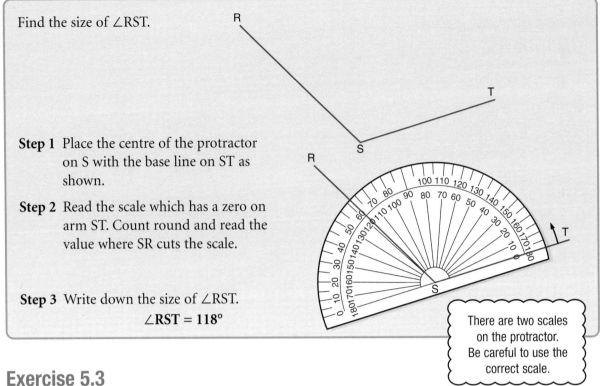

Find the size of ∠RST.

Step 1 Place the centre of the protractor on S with the base line on ST as shown.

Step 2 Read the scale which has a zero on arm ST. Count round and read the value where SR cuts the scale.

Step 3 Write down the size of ∠RST.
$$∠RST = 118°$$

There are two scales on the protractor. Be careful to use the correct scale.

Exercise 5.3

1 Read the size of the angles in each diagram.

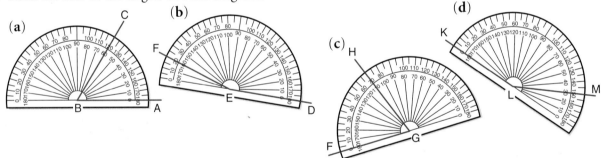

(a) (b) (c) (d)

W You may use worksheet 5.1 for this question.

2 Measure the size of each angle.

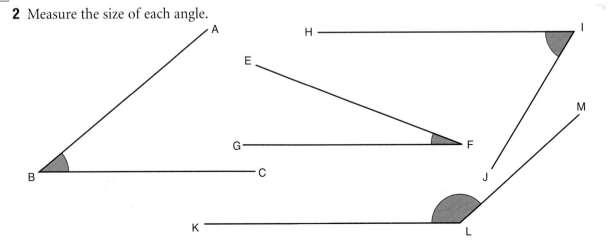

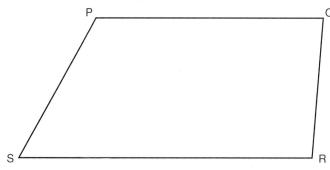

N **3** You may use worksheet 5.1 or trace this trapezium into your jotter.

    (**a**) Join P to R in shape PQRS.

    (**b**) What shapes have you formed?

    (**c**) Measure the angles

       (**i**) ∠PQR

       (**ii**) ∠QRP

       (**iii**) ∠RPQ.

    (**d**) What do you notice about the sum of the angles in (**c**)?

    (**e**) Measure the angles

       (**i**) ∠PSR

       (**ii**) ∠SRP

       (**iii**) ∠RPS.

    (**f**) What do you notice about the sum of the angles in (**e**)?

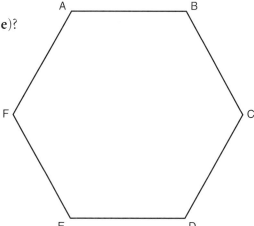

N **4** You may use worksheet 5.1 or trace this hexagon into your jotter.

    (**a**) Join A to C, A to D and D to F.

    (**b**) Measure all the angles in

       (**i**) triangle ABC   (**ii**) triangle CAD

       (**ii**) triangle ADF and   (**iv**) triangle DEF

    (**c**) What do you notice about the sum of the angles in each triangle?

5.4 Types of angles

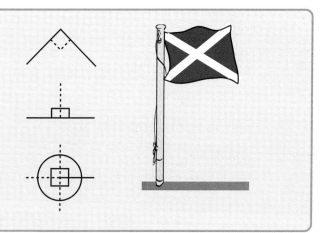

One right angle is 90°
Any two lines which form a right angle are said to be **perpendicular**.

Two right angles added together make a **straight angle**.
A straight angle is 180°.

Four right angles added together make a **complete turn**.
One complete turn is 360°.

Exercise 5.4

1 Fold a piece of paper in half. You have formed a straight angle. Now fold it again. You have now formed a right angle. Use your right angle to check that the corners of your jotter are right angled.

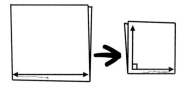

2 Make a list of objects in the classroom or elsewhere which contain a
   (**a**) right angle   (**b**) straight angle.

3 Through how many degrees would the minute hand of a clock move in
   (**a**) 15 minutes   (**b**) 30 minutes   (**c**) 1 hour?

4 (**a**) Write down two times when the hands of a clock form a right angle.
   (**b**) Do the hands of a clock form a right angle at 0930? Explain your answer.
   (**c**) Write down a time when the hands of a clock form a straight angle.
   (**d**) Do the hands of a clock form a straight angle at 1230? Explain your answer.

5 Name all the right angles in these diagrams.
   (**a**)

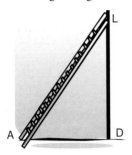

   (**b**)

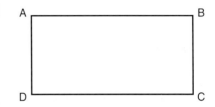

   (**c**)

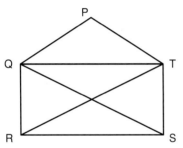

   (**d**)

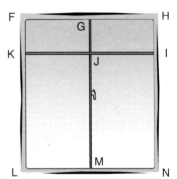

6 (**a**) How many right angles are there in the corner of a room?
   (**b**) Name these angles.

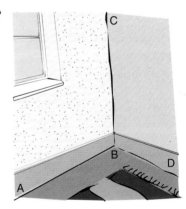

7 Name the straight angles in these diagrams.

(**a**)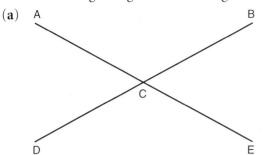

(**b**)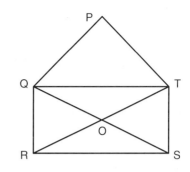

(**c**)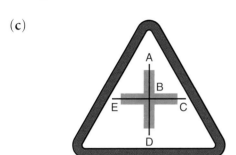

(**d**)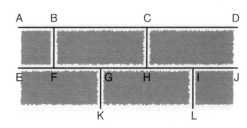

5.5 Calculating angles

Example

Calculate the size of the missing angle in each diagram.

(**a**)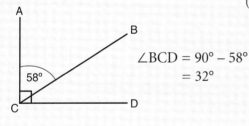

$\angle BCD = 90° - 58°$
$\qquad = 32°$

(**b**)

$\angle EFG + \angle GFH = 105° + 155°$
$\qquad\qquad\qquad = 260°$
$\angle EFH = 360° - 260°$
$\qquad = 100°$

Exercise 5.5

1 Calculate the sizes of the coloured angles in these diagrams.

(**a**)

(**b**)

(**c**)

(**d**)

(**e**)

(**f**)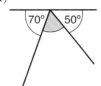

(**g**)

(**h**)

(**i**)

2 Calculate the shaded angles in these diagrams.

(a)

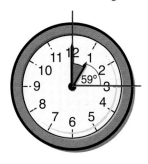

(b)

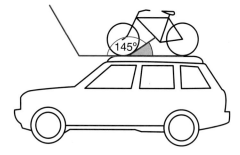

(c)

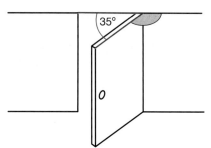

(d)

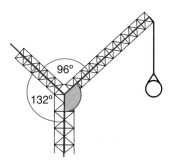

(e)

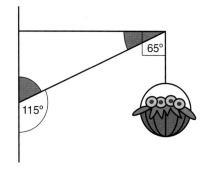

3 (a) Calculate ∠ACB when ∠BCD is (i) 35° (ii) 68° (iii) 17°.
  (b) If ∠BCD increases by 15°, what happens to ∠ACB?
  (c) If ∠BCD decreases by 20°, what happens to ∠ACB?
  (d) What is the least possible value of ∠ACB?
  (e) What is the greatest possible value of ∠ACB?

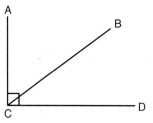

4 (a) Calculate ∠PQR when ∠PQS is (i) 140° (ii) 125° (iii) 115°
  (b) If ∠PQS increases by 15°, what happens to ∠PQR?
  (c) If ∠PQS decreases by 20°, what happens to ∠PQR?
  (d) What is the least possible value of ∠PQR?
  (e) What is the greatest possible value of ∠PQR?

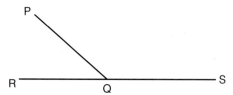

5.6 More types of angles

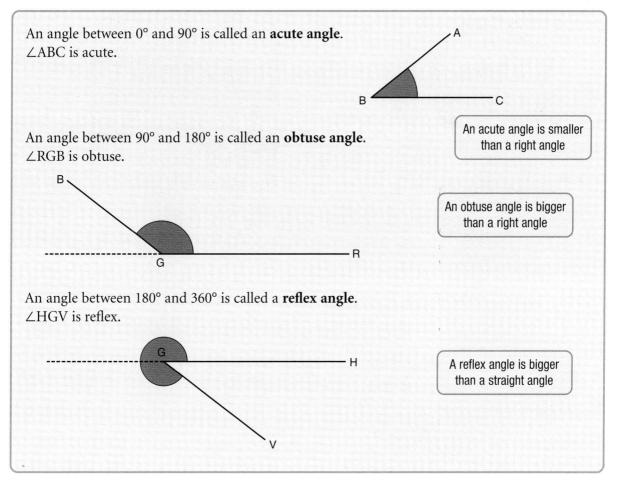

An angle between 0° and 90° is called an **acute angle**.
∠ABC is acute.

An acute angle is smaller than a right angle

An angle between 90° and 180° is called an **obtuse angle**.
∠RGB is obtuse.

An obtuse angle is bigger than a right angle

An angle between 180° and 360° is called a **reflex angle**.
∠HGV is reflex.

A reflex angle is bigger than a straight angle

Exercise 5.6

1 Name (**a**) an acute angle
     (**b**) an obtuse angle
     (**c**) a straight angle.

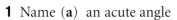
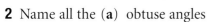

2 Name all the (**a**) obtuse angles
        (**b**) right angles
        (**c**) straight angles
        (**d**) acute angles.   (There are 10)

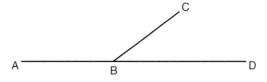

3 Name all the angles in the diagrams and state whether each is acute, obtuse or reflex.

(**a**)   (**b**)   (**c**)   (**d**)

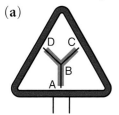
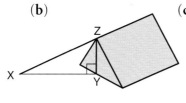
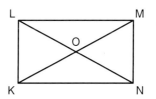
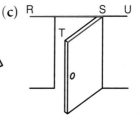
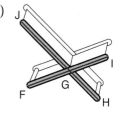

4 From this diagram name the following:
  (**a**) two acute angles (**b**) one obtuse angle
  (**c**) one reflex angle (**d**) four right angles.

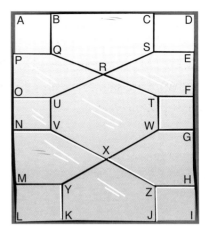

5.7 Related angles

In the diagram ∠ABD is a right angle.
∠ABC and ∠CBD fit together to equal 90°.
∠ABC and ∠CBD are said to be **complementary angles**.
∠ABC is the **complement** of ∠CBD.

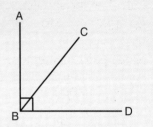

Example
Find the complement of 20°.

The complement is 90° − 20° = 70°.

Exercise 5.7

1 Calculate the complement of:
  (**a**) 30° (**b**) 40° (**c**) 89° (**d**) 71° (**e**) 18° (**f**) 3°

2 Name pairs of complementary angles in each of these diagrams.

(**a**)
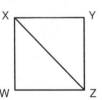

(**b**)
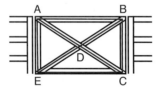

(**c**)
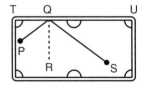

3 For each diagram (**a**) name a pair of complementary angles and (**b**) calculate the size of each complement.

(**i**)
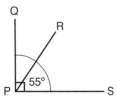

(**ii**)
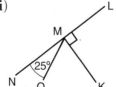

(**iii**)
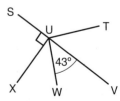

4 If an angle has size x, write down an expression for the complement of the angle.

5.8 Supplementary angles

In the diagram ∠XYZ is a straight angle. ∠XYW and ∠WYZ fit together to equal 180°.
∠XYW and ∠WYZ are said to be **supplementary angles**.
∠XYW is the **supplement** of ∠WYZ.

Example
Find the supplement of 25°.
The supplement is 180° − 25° = 155°

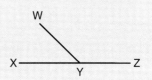

Exercise 5.8

1 Calculate the supplement of
(**a**) 120°   (**b**) 145°   (**c**) 179°   (**d**) 73°   (**e**) 12°   (**f**) 9°

2 Name pairs of supplementary angles in each of these diagrams.

(**a**)    (**b**) 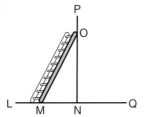   (**c**)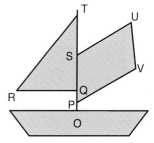

3 For each diagram (**a**) name a pair of supplementary angles and
(**b**) calculate the size of each supplementary angle.

(**i**) 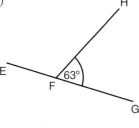   (**ii**) 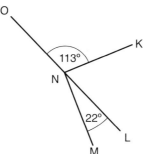   (**iii**)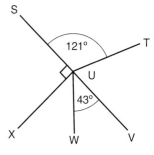

4 If an angle has size *x*, write down an expression for the supplement
of the angle.

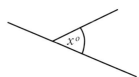

5.9 Crossing lines

Exercise 5.9

1 (**a**) Draw two lines, each about 12 cm long, crossing as shown.
(**b**) Measure the four marked angles and write their sizes.
(**c**) Which pairs of angles are equal?
(**d**) Draw another two lines at different angles.
(**e**) Which angles are equal?
(**f**) Explain why you have found pairs of equal angles.

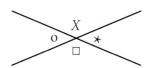

5.10 Vertically opposite angles

a and *b* fit together to make a straight angle. $a + b = 180°$
a and *d* also fit together to make a straight angle. $a + d = 180°$
Hence $b = d$.

b and *d* are called **vertically opposite** angles and are equal.
a and *c* are also **vertically opposite** and are also equal.

> **Vertically opposite angles are equal.**

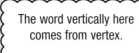

The word vertically here comes from vertex.

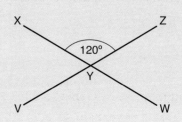

Find the size of each angle.
∠VYW is vertically opposite ∠XYZ.   Hence ∠VYW = 120°
∠ZYW and ∠XYZ are supplementary.   Hence ∠ZYW = 180° − 120° = 60°
∠XYV is vertically opposite ∠ZYW.   Hence ∠ZYW = 60°

Exercise 5.10

1 Write down the size of each coloured angle.

(a) 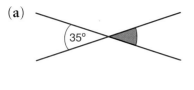   (b) 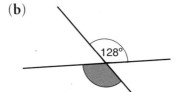   (c)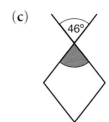

2 Two railway lines cross as shown in the diagram.
   Calculate the sizes of all missing angles.

3 Calculate the size in degrees of each coloured angle.

    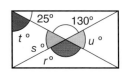

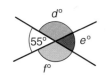

4 Calculate the size of all marked angles in the following diagrams.

(**a**)

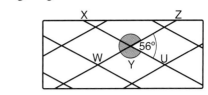

(**b**)

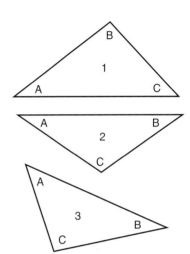

5 Explain why it is impossible to have only one pair of vertically opposite angles in any diagram.

5.11 Angles in a triangle

Exercise 5.11

You may use worksheet 5.2 for questions 1 and 2.

1 Take a large plain sheet of A4 paper.
Draw 3 large triangles as shown in this diagram.
(**a**) Cut out triangle 1.
(**b**) Tear out the angles marked A, B and C.
(**c**) Try to fit the angles together. Stick this into your jotter.
(**d**) Write down anything you notice.

2 Repeat question 1 for triangles 2 and 3.
3 Draw your own triangle. Repeat question 1 with your triangle.

5.12 Sum of angles in a triangle

When the angles of a triangle ABC are fitted together
they form a straight angle.
The angles fit together to make 180°.
$a° + b° + c° = 180°$

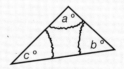
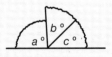

The sum of the angles of a triangle is 180°.

Example
Find the size of ∠ABC.
$∠BAC + ∠ACB = 50° + 60° = 110°$

$∠ABC = 180° − 110°$
$∠ABC = 70°$

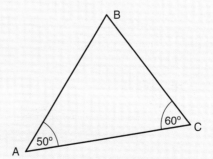

Exercise 5.12

1 Find the size of ∠ABC in each triangle.

(a)

(b)

(c)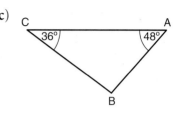

2 Calculate the size of each blue angle.

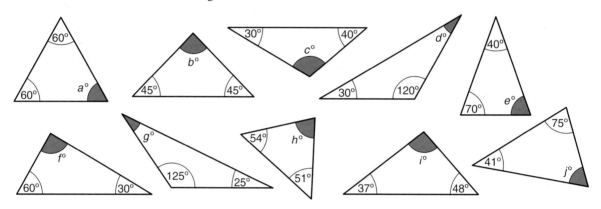

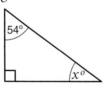

3 Calculate the value of *x* in each triangle.

(a)

(b)

(c)

4 Calculate the missing angles in each diagram.

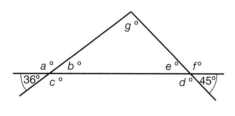
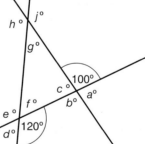

5 Calculate the size of a and b in this diagram of a crane.

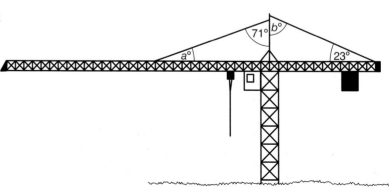

5.13 Compass points

Compass points may be used to give directions.

From Inverness, Portree is west. However, from Portree, Inverness is east.

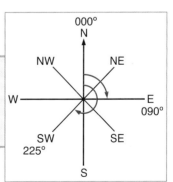

Exercise 5.13

1 From Perth what town lies to the
(**a**) north   (**b**) west
(**c**) south   (**d**) northwest
(**e**) southwest   (**f**) northeast   (**g**) southeast?

2 What is the direction of Perth from
(**a**) Dunfermline   (**b**) Aberdeen   (**c**) Stranraer
(**d**) Thurso   (**e**) Oban   (**f**) Portree?

3 If you fly north from Glasgow, until you reach a town, then turn to the west, over what town would you next fly?

4 What is the size of the smaller angle between
(**a**) N and E   (**b**) S and SW   (**c**) W and N
(**d**) NE and SW   (**e**) N and SE   (**f**) N and SW?

5 If you were facing north and turned in a clockwise direction, in which direction would you be facing if you turned through each of the following angles?
(**a**) 90°   (**b**) 180°   (**c**) 45°   (**d**) 225°   (**e**) 270°   (**f**) 315°

6 If you were facing south and turned in a clockwise direction through each of the angles in question 5, in what direction would you be facing in each case?

5.14 Bearings

Bearings are angles which are used to give directions. Three-figure bearings are measured clockwise from north.

The bearing of north is 000°, east is 090°, southwest is 225°.

Exercise 5.14

1 Write these directions as bearings.
(**a**) S   (**b**) E   (**c**) SE   (**d**) NE   (**e**) NW

2 Use the map of Scotland above to give the bearing of each of the following from Perth.
(**a**) Thurso   (**b**) Aberdeen   (**c**) Dunfermline
(**d**) Oban   (**e**) Portree   (**f**) Stranraer

You need a protractor for questions 3 and 4.

3 The map shows the route taken by a girl in an orienteering competition.
Copy and complete this table to give the bearing of each stage.

Stage	Bearing
Start to 1	
1 to 2	
2 to 3	
3 to 4	
4 to 5	
5 to finish	

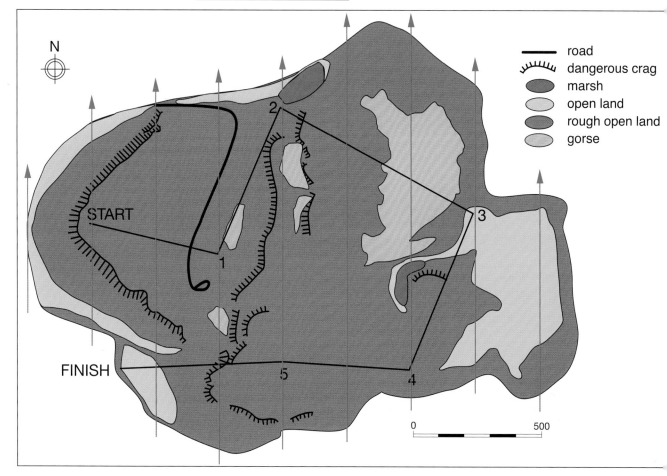

road
dangerous crag
marsh
open land
rough open land
gorse

N

START

FINISH

0   500

4 This table gives the bearings of the landmarks from the viewpoint at the top of Moray Mount.
Copy and complete the diagram using the bearings given in the table.

Landmark	Bearing
Ard Tor	060°
Ben Dearg	098°
Cad Beag	153°
Dun Add	230°
Edin Hill	305°

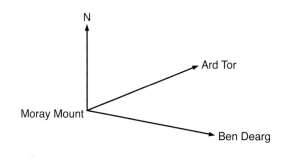

N

Ard Tor

Moray Mount

Ben Dearg

Review exercise 5

You need a protractor for questions 3, 4 and 14.

1 Name each marked angle in two ways.

(a)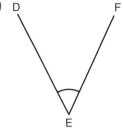

(b)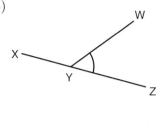

(c)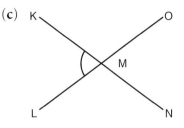

2 Name the marked angles in these diagrams.

(a)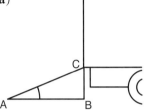

(b)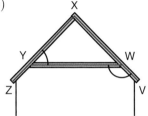

(c)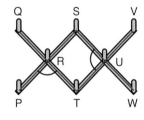

3 Measure the size of each angle.

(a)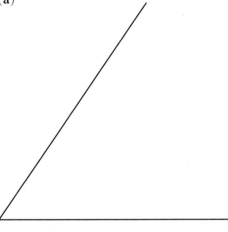

(b)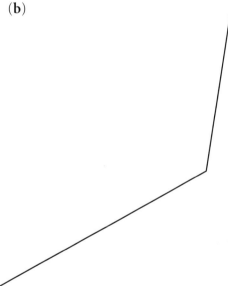

4 Draw accurately the following angles.

(a) ∠ABC = 60°   (b) ∠HIJ = 135°   (c) ∠XYZ = 245°

5 Name the right angles in these diagrams.

(**a**) STUR is a rectangle.

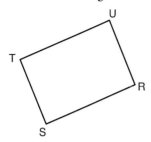

(**b**) DF is horisontal.
FH is vertical.

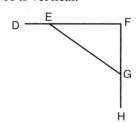

6 Name all the straight angles in these diagrams.

(**a**)

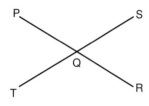

(**b**)

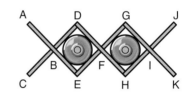

7 Calculate the sizes of the missing angles in these diagrams.

(**a**)

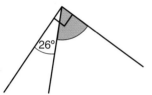

(**b**)

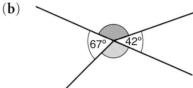

8 Name all the angles in the diagrams and state whether each is acute, obtuse or reflex.

(**a**)

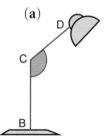

(**b**)

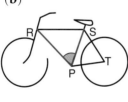

(**c**)

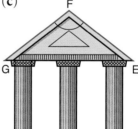

(**d**)

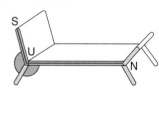

9 In the diagrams below (**a**) name a pair of complementary angles and calculate the size of each complement (**b**) name 4 pairs of supplementary angles and calculate the size of each supplement.

(**i**)

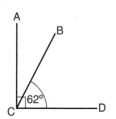

(**ii**)

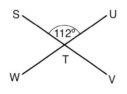

(**iii**)

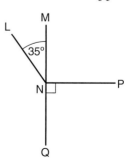

10 Copy each diagram and calculate the size of all angles in the following.

(**a**)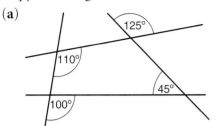

(**b**)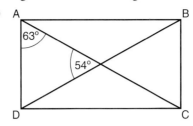

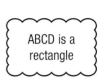
ABCD is a rectangle

11 Calculate the value of *x* in each diagram.

(**a**)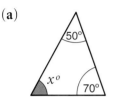

(**b**)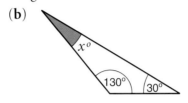

(**c**)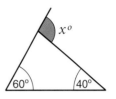

(**d**)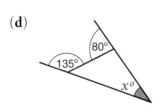

(**e**)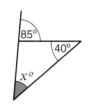

(**f**)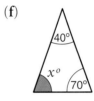

12 From Checkpoint 1 which checkpoint lies to the
(**a**) north   (**b**) west   (**c**) south
(**d**) northwest   (**e**) southwest   (**f**) northeast
(**g**) southeast?

13 What is the direction of Checkpoint 1 from
(**a**) Checkpoint 2   (**b**) Checkpoint 3
(**c**) Checkpoint 4   (**d**) Checkpoint 7
(**e**) Checkpoint 8   (**f**) Checkpoint 9?

14 Surveyors use theodalites to measure angles on building sites. The plan shows the posts laid out in a new housing estate. Measure the bearing of each post from the theodalite.

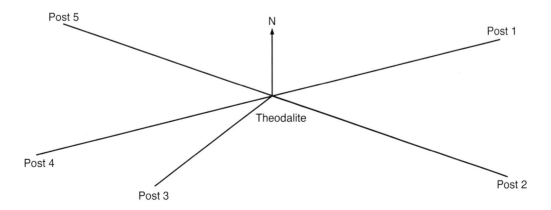

Summary

Naming angles

An angle is formed where **two** arms meet at a **vertex**.

The red angle is called ∠ABC or ∠CBA.
The blue angle is called ∠CBD or ∠DBC.
The green angle is called ∠ABD or ∠DBA.

Drawing angles

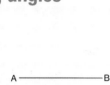
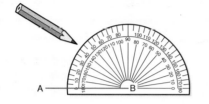
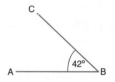

Measuring angles

Remember there are two scales on the protractor
Be careful to use the correct scale.
∠RST = 118°

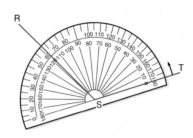

Types of angles

A **right angle** is 90°. Any two lines which form a right angle are said to be **perpendicular**.

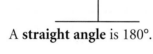

A **straight angle** is 180°.

A **complete turn** is 360°.

An **acute angle** lies between 0° and 90°.

An **obtuse angle** lies between 90° and 180°.

A **reflex angle** lies between 180° and 270°.

Related angles

Complementary angles add to give 90°.
Supplementary angles add to give 180°.
Vertically opposite angles are equal.

Angles in a triangle add to give 180°.
a + b + c = 180°.

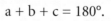

Compass points and bearings

A direction may be described using **compass points** or **bearings**.

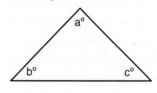
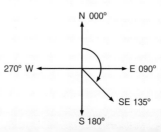

6 Decimals

In this chapter you will revise and extend your knowledge of decimal fractions.

6.1 Place value

Remember the number system is built like this:

Thousands	Hundreds	Tens	Units	·	tenths	hundredths
Th	H	T	U	·	t	h

7 3 2 1 ● 4 5   represents the number

seven **Th**ousands, three **H**undreds, two **T**ens, one **U**nit, four **t**enths and five **h**undredths

Exercise 6.1

1 Write these numbers in words:

(a) 8 7 6 5 ● 4 3

(b) 1 0 5 2 ● 7 3

(c) ⬤ 7 2 ● 1 6

(d) ⬤ 5 0 ● 3 ⬤

2 Write these numbers in words:

(a) 123·82   (b) 34·71   (c) 23·04   (d) 150·2
(e) 2·01   (f) 20·13   (g) 1010·01   (h) 0·1

6.2 Rounding to the nearest whole number

The arrow lies between 3 and 4.

The units figure is 3.

The arrow is 4 tenths along from 3.

It points to 3·4.

3·4 is nearer to 3 than 4.

3·4 rounded to the nearest whole number is 3.

Example 15·7 rounded to the nearest whole number is 16.

Exercise 6.2

1 Write the number indicated by each arrow.

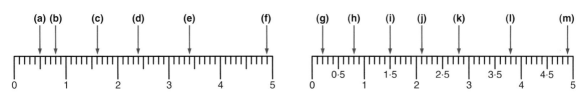

2 Round each answer in question **1** to the nearest whole number.

3 Write the number indicated by each arrow.

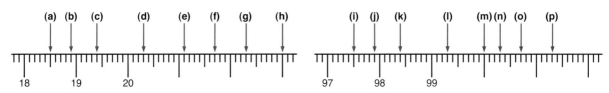

4 Round each answer in question **3** to the nearest whole number.

5 Round each of the following to the nearest whole number.

(**a**) 3·9	(**b**) 6·1	(**c**) 7·2	(**d**) 0·8	(**e**) 11·2
(**f**) 15·7	(**g**) 0·5	(**h**) 92·7	(**i**) 0·4	(**j**) 100·3
(**k**) 31·5	(**l**) 23·4	(**m**) 0·6	(**n**) 9·5	(**o**) 99·5

6 Round each length to the nearest whole number.
Use the rounded figures to estimates the total lengths.

(**a**) 9·8 cm + 3·1 cm + 7·2 cm   (**b**) 12·6 m + 9·9 m + 2·4 m

(**c**) 1·3 km + 8·5 km + 3·1 km   (**d**) 10·5 mm + 29·6 mm + 99·5 mm

7 By rounding each distance to the nearest whole number, estimate the total
length of the car journey from A to B.

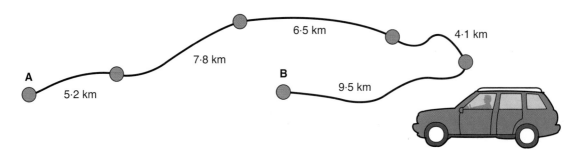

6.3 Rounding to one decimal place

The arrow lies between 0·2 and 0·3.

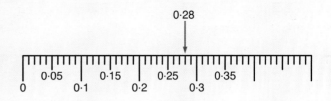

It points to 0·28.
0·28 is nearer 0·3 than 0·2.

0·28 rounded to one decimal place (the nearest tenth) is 0·3.

Example   6·23 rounded to one decimal place is 6·2

Exercise 6.3

1 Write the number indicated by each arrow.

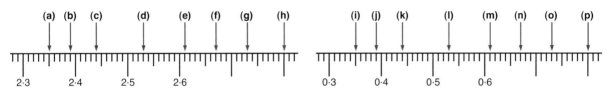

2 Round each answer in question 1 to one decimal place.

3 Write the number indicated by each arrow.

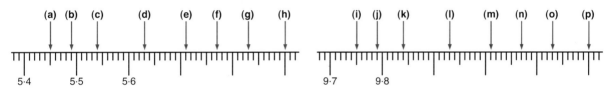

4 Round each answer in question 3 to one decimal place.

5 Round each number to one decimal place.
   (**a**)   3·91   (**b**)   6·19   (**c**)   7·21   (**d**)   0·83   (**e**)   11·26
   (**f**) 15·74   (**g**) 23·47   (**h**) 92·73   (**i**) 154·11   (**j**) 100·39
   (**k**) 31·65   (**l**)   0·55   (**m**) 0·65   (**n**)   0·95   (**o**)   9·95

N You may use worksheet 6.1 for supplementary questions 6 to 9.

6.4 Adding and subtracting

When adding or subtracting decimals, figures with the same place value must be in line with each other.

Example   (a) Find $3·72 + 1·2$ (b) Find $6·2 − 3·16$

$$
\begin{array}{r}
3·72 \\
+\ 1·20 \\
\hline
4·92 \\
\hline
\end{array}
\qquad
\begin{array}{r}
6·20 \\
-\ 3·16 \\
\hline
3·04 \\
\hline
\end{array}
$$

Decimal points **must** be in line

Decimal points are in line.

Exercise 6.4

1 Copy and complete:

(a) $\begin{array}{r} 2·60 \\ +\ 1·63 \\ \hline \end{array}$ (b) $\begin{array}{r} 8·70 \\ +3·42 \\ \hline \end{array}$ (c) $\begin{array}{r} 23·26 \\ +39·80 \\ \hline \end{array}$ (d) $\begin{array}{r} 123·40 \\ +\ 45·55 \\ \hline \end{array}$ (e) $\begin{array}{r} 0·02 \\ +\ 0·08 \\ \hline \end{array}$

(f) $\begin{array}{r} 123·55 \\ -\ 45·41 \\ \hline \end{array}$ (g) $\begin{array}{r} 1·02 \\ -\ 0·08 \\ \hline \end{array}$ (h) $\begin{array}{r} 23·26 \\ -\ 19·80 \\ \hline \end{array}$ (i) $\begin{array}{r} 4·60 \\ -\ 1·63 \\ \hline \end{array}$ (j) $\begin{array}{r} 8·70 \\ -\ 3·42 \\ \hline \end{array}$

2 Find:

(a) $3·6 + 2·3$ (b) $8·2 + 3·9$ (c) $21·6 + 5·7$
(d) $11·2 + 2·52$ (e) $40·31 + 8·7$ (f) $0·4 + 1·62$
(g) $5·67 − 1·13$ (h) $12·3 − 1·12$ (i) $34·7 − 12·61$
(j) $123·45 − 23·5$ (k) $10·06 − 0·1$ (l) $100·01 − 0·02$
(m) $12·06 + 12·6$ (n) $11·1 − 9·01$ (o) $3·56 + 4·44$
(p) $1·5 − 1·06$ (q) $99·6 + 0·4$ (r) $123·4 − 24·41$
(s) $13·01 + 9·6$ (t) $11·34 + 23·1$ (u) $141·71 + 34·5$
(v) $55·55 + 55·55$ (w) $11·11 − 2·22$ (x) $0·06 + 0·04$

3 Find:

(a) $18 + 5·6$ (b) $20 − 8·2$ (c) $15 + 25·64$
(d) $21 − 14·5$ (e) $52 + 56·79$ (f) $57 − 29·62$
(g) $132 − 21·9$ (h) $33·87 − 21$ (i) $21 − 20·07$
(j) $52·1 − 21·3$ (k) $20·2 − 14·61$ (l) $100·1 − 9·99$

4 Find:

(a) $3·6 + 2·7$ (b) $5·1 + 8·9$ (c) $23·4 + 2·25$
(d) $1·4 + 2·3 + 3·1$ (e) $8·3 + 2·6 + 1·1$ (f) $12·2 + 3·7 + 5·6$
(g) $7·4 + 2·5 − 6·3$ (h) $5·5 + 6·6 − 7·7$ (i) $18·3 + 11·9 − 20·02$

5 Find the total edge length of each shape.

(a)

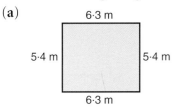

6·3 m

5·4 m   5·4 m

6·3 m

(b)

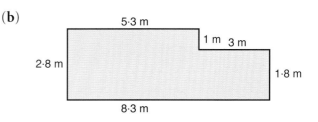

5·3 m

1 m   3 m

2·8 m

1·8 m

8·3 m

6 Three competitors run a 3 lap race.
Their lap times in seconds are shown in the table.

(a) Find the total race time in seconds for
each competitor.

(b) Write the name of the race winner.

(c) What was the time difference
between first and second place?

	Lap 1	Lap 2	Lap 3
Bart	23·6	21·12	20·07
Pete	21·21	21·43	20·5
Mary	20·37	22·3	20·44

7 Pamela pours 1·1 litres of cola, 1·25 litres of lemonade and
2 litres of orange into a large bowl to make punch for her party.
Unfortunately, the bowl only holds 3·5 litres.
How much of the punch will overflow onto the table?

8 Each day Jason sprints 200 m. His times in seconds are as follows

   Mon: 25·32   Tue: 26·41   Wed: 24·6   Thu: 21·78   Fri 21·6

(a) Find the difference between the sprint times for
   (i) Monday and Tuesday
   (ii) Wednesday and Thursday
   (iii) his fastest and slowest times.

(b) On Saturday, Jason was 0·71 seconds **faster** than on Friday.
Write his sprint time on Saturday.

(c) On Sunday, Jason was 1·2 seconds **slower** than Thursday.
Write his sprint time for Sunday.

(d) List all the sprint times in order from fastest to slowest.

9 Here are the times, in seconds, for the six finalists in the 50 metre freestyle.

Ruth	Meg	Arlene	Seonaid	Stephanie	Katy
28·61	27·31	26·51	26·22	27·43	26·55

(a) List the finalists in order, starting with the winner.

(b) What was the time difference between first and last place?

(c) Katy beat the club record by 1·04 seconds. What was the previous record?

(d) Which others also beat the previous record?

(e) What is the new club record? Who is the new holder?

6.5 Multiplying and dividing

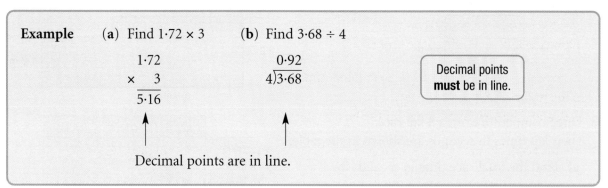

Example (a) Find 1·72 × 3   (b) Find 3·68 ÷ 4

```
   1·72
×     3
───────
   5·16
```

```
      0·92
4)3·68
```

Decimal points **must** be in line.

Decimal points are in line.

Exercise 6.5

1 Copy and complete:

(a)   3·4   (b)   6·1   (c)   4·21   (d)   6·36   (e)   18·4
     × 2   × 2   × 3   × 2   × 4

(f) 2)8·4   (g) 2)12·6   (h) 3)12·9   (i) 2)24·28   (j) 4)16·84

(k)   14·62   (l)   23·51   (m) 31·01   (n) 40·45   (o) 10·06
    ×   2   ×   4   ×   6   ×   5   ×   5

(p) 2)7·4   (q) 3)7·2   (r) 2)13·36   (s) 5)16·25   (t) 7)57·33

2 Find:

(a) 3·2 × 3   (b) 5·3 × 2   (c) 8·1 × 3   (d) 6·4 × 3   (e) 7·6 × 5
(f) 8·4 ÷ 2   (g) 9·63 ÷ 3   (h) 12·15 ÷ 3   (i) 31·6 ÷ 4   (j) 44·05 ÷ 5
(k) 12·3 × 4   (l) 14·6 × 3   (m) 42·78 × 2   (n) 33·34 × 4   (o) 9·99 × 6
(p) 2·8 ÷ 2   (q) 3·15 ÷ 3   (r) 23·82 ÷ 6   (s) 34·16 ÷ 7   (t) 100·02 ÷ 3

3 Bob the joiner is making shelves 1·62 metres long.
Calculate the length of (a) three shelves
                        (b) seven shelves.

4 Bob has a plank of wood 4·32 metres long.
He cuts four 0·72 metre lengths from the plank.
How much of the plank is left?

5 A bag of flour weighs 1·5 kilogrammes.
(a) What is the total weight of 8 bags?
(b) A recipe states that one bag contains enough
    flour to make 6 cakes.
    How much flour is used in each cake?

6 Paul has a 2 litre bottle of juice.
He pours five full glasses of juice.
Each glass holds 0·35 litres.
How much juice is left in the bottle?

7 A large packet of sweets weighs 1·28 kilogrammes.
Nine packets are put into a box.
Calculate the weight of sweets in the box.

8 Sparks & Marks are selling a special
presentation pack of toiletries.
The pack contents are shown. Find:
(a) the total weight of each pack
(b) the weight of 4 packs
(c) the weight of 9 packs.

Presentation pack contents

Item	Weight
Soap	35·25 g
Shampoo	44·7 g
Deodorant	32·33 g
Talc	21·93 g

9 A boat travels 6·24 kilometres in one hour.
How far will the boat travel in four hours at the same speed?

10 A chef distributes ingredients equally among **eight** pies.
Mushrooms : 0·48 kg   Cheese : 1·6 kg   Onion : 0·568 kg
Find the weight of each ingredient in one pie.

11 A truck company buys a 50 litre drum of oil.
Four trucks are given 9·83 litres each.
Calculate how much oil remains in the drum.

12 Six small loaves of bread weigh a total of 1·02 kilogrammes.
Calculate the weight of (a) one small loaf
                                            (b) four small loaves.

13 A waiter uses 10·5 litres of wine to fill five
carafes equally.
(a) How much wine is in each carafe?
(b) Seven people share a carafe.
    How much wine will each person drink?

14 Joan buys 8 cans of cola. Find:
(a) the total cost of the cola if each can costs 45 p.
(b) the total weight if each can weighs 0·35 kilogrammes.
(c) the total volume if each can contains 0·33 litres.

6.6 Multiplying by 10

When multiplying by 10 all the figures move **one** place to the **left**.

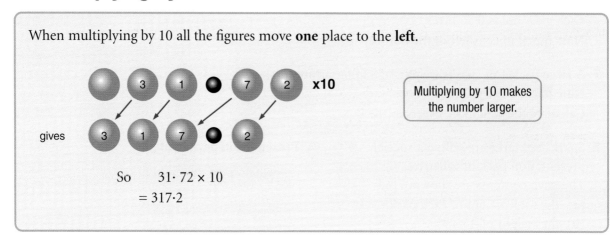

So   31·72 × 10
      = 317·2

Multiplying by 10 makes
the number larger.

Exercise 6.6

1 Multiply each number by 10:

(**a**)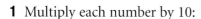

(**b**)

(**c**)

(**d**)

(**e**)

(**f**)

(**g**)

(**h**)

(**i**)

(**j**)

2 Multiply each number by 10:

(**a**) 32·34	(**b**) 21·76	(**c**) 18·91	(**d**) 23·2	(**e**) 29·03
(**f**) 10·37	(**g**) 50·01	(**h**) 2·41	(**i**) 0·5	(**j**) 0·02
(**k**) 123·21	(**l**) 321·91	(**m**) 100·51	(**n**) 143·2	(**o**) 100·01

3 A traffic light at a busy road changes every 1·25 minutes.
How long would it take for the lights to change ten times?

4 A jet takes 5·32 seconds to fly a kilometre. How long would
it take the jet to fly 10 kilometres at the same speed?

5 Alan's computer takes 0·06 seconds to complete a calculation.
How long would it take the computer to calculate ten similar calculations?

6 The table shows the times taken by each cyclist to complete a lap.
Cyclist 1 is given a target of 126·2 seconds to complete ten laps.
Write the targets for the other cyclists.

Lap times (seconds)

Cyclist 1	12·62
Cyclist 2	18·08
Cyclist 3	9·34
Cyclist 4	10·6

6.7 Multiplying by 100

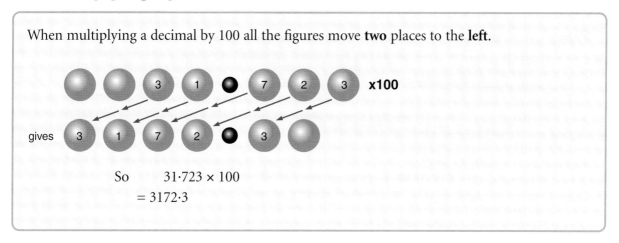

When multiplying a decimal by 100 all the figures move **two** places to the **left**.

So   31·723 × 100
= 3172·3

Exercise 6.7

1 Multiply each number by 100:

(a)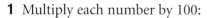

(b)

(c)

(d)

(e)

(f)

(g)

(h)

2 Multiply each number by 100:

(a)	32·341	(b)	1·762	(c)	18·901	(d)	23·25	(e)	2·03
(f)	10·375	(g)	50·01	(h)	0·413	(i)	0·51	(j)	0·02
(k)	123·21	(l)	321·901	(m)	100·511	(n)	143·22	(o)	100·19
(p)	5·001	(q)	100·12	(r)	10·01	(s)	4·3	(t)	2·1

3 A jet takes 6·41 seconds to fly a kilometre. How long would it take the jet to fly 100 km at the same speed?

4 A computer takes 0·063 seconds to complete a calculation. How long would it take the computer to complete one hundred similar calculations?

5 The thickness of a piece of card is 2·3 millimetres.
Find the thickness of 100 pieces.

6 A short plank is 5·61 centimetres thick.
How thick is a pile of 100 planks?

7 £1 is worth 1·52 Euros. How many Euros is £100 worth?

6.8 Dividing by 10 and 100

When dividing by 10 all the figures move **one** place to the **right**.

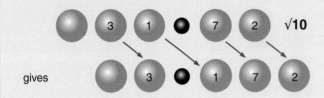

Dividing by 10 makes the number smaller

gives

So   31·72 ÷ 10
    = 3·172

When dividing by 100 all the figures move **two** places to the **right**.

Example   642·3 ÷ 100
    =   6·423

Exercise 6.8

1 Divide each number by 10:

(a)

(b)

(c)

(d)

(e)

(f)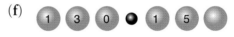

(g)

(h)

2 Divide each number by 10:

(a) 15·2	(b) 26·3	(c) 5·4	(d) 6·89	(e) 10·5
(f) 123·4	(g) 12·51	(h) 0·6	(i) 10·04	(j) 100·1
(k) 0·52	(l) 53	(m) 204	(n) 0·02	(o) 111·1

3 Divide each number by 100:

(a) 15·2	(b) 126·3	(c) 25·4	(d) 76·8	(e) 10·5
(f) 1123·4	(g) 12·51	(h) 3410·6	(i) 0·3	(j) 100·1
(k) 56	(l) 90	(m) 0·21	(n) 8	(o) 0·02

4 Jay takes 100 paces and covers 98·5 metres.
   What length is each pace?

5 Bill has 532 millilitres of concentrated orange juice for
the half-time break of the five-a-side football match.
He pours 10 equal cupfuls.
Calculate the amount in each cup.

6 A machine produces a chocolate drink
at a rate of 234 millilitres every 100 seconds.
How much chocolate drink does the machine produce in
(**a**) 10 seconds
(**b**) 1 second?

7 A food depot supplies a chain of restaurants.
The food is distributed equally
among 100 restaurants.
Calculate the weight of each item that a
restaurant will receive.

Depot Item	Total Weight
Potatoes	4560 kg
Carrots	825 kg
Turnip	641·5 kg
Peas	59 kg

8 A computer takes 0·6 seconds to complete 100 calculations.
How long would it take to complete   (**a**) 10 similar calculations
(**b**) 1 calculation?

6.9 Multiples of 10 and 100

Example 1
6·3 × 20   6·3 × 2 = 12·6 → 12·6 × 10 = 126
So 6·3 × 20 = 126

Example 2
96 ÷ 300   96 ÷ 3 = 32 → 32 ÷ 100 = 0·32
So 96 ÷ 300 = 0·32

Exercise 6.9

1 Calculate:
(**a**) 5·2 × 20 (**b**) 12·3 × 20 (**c**) 21·4 × 30 (**d**) 36·8 × 30 (**e**) 10·5 × 40
(**f**) 123·4 × 50 (**g**) 12·51 × 50 (**h**) 10·62 × 80 (**i**) 0·3 × 70 (**j**) 100·15 × 60

2 Calculate:
(**a**) 56·9 × 200 (**b**) 9·09 × 200 (**c**) 0·07 × 300 (**d**) 0·59 × 400 (**e**) 0·86 × 600
(**f**) 2·3 × 800 (**g**) 12·3 × 300 (**h**) 20·1 × 400 (**i**) 32·03 × 900 (**j**) 1·5 × 800

3 Calculate:
(**a**) 23·4 ÷ 20 (**b**) 12·64 ÷ 40 (**c**) 10·65 ÷ 50 (**d**) 0·9 ÷ 30 (**e**) 100·15 ÷ 50
(**f**) 56·8 ÷ 80 (**g**) 0·09 ÷ 90 (**h**) 9·06 ÷ 60 (**i**) 0·77 ÷ 70 (**j**) 0·99 ÷ 90

4 Calculate:
(**a**) 345 ÷ 500 (**b**) 264 ÷ 200 (**c**) 42·7 ÷ 700 (**d**) 26·1 ÷ 300
(**e**) 8·04 ÷ 400 (**f**) 9·65 ÷ 500 (**g**) 5·12 ÷ 800 (**h**) 0·8 ÷ 200

6.10 Calculations with a calculator

Exercise 6.10

You may use a calculator for this exercise.

1 Calculate:
   (a) $23{\cdot}6 + 12{\cdot}83$ (b) $34{\cdot}61 + 23{\cdot}9$ (c) $125{\cdot}02 + 100{\cdot}09$
   (d) $12{\cdot}7 - 9{\cdot}32$ (e) $37{\cdot}52 - 28{\cdot}96$ (f) $162{\cdot}3 - 99{\cdot}02$
   (g) $15{\cdot}6 \times 12$ (h) $45{\cdot}62 \times 16$ (i) $17{\cdot}09 \times 23$
   (j) $408 \div 32$ (k) $4141{\cdot}26 \div 27$ (l) $1081{\cdot}08 \div 12$

2 Round each answer to 1 decimal place.
   (a) $137{\cdot}51 \div 18$ (b) $23{\cdot}89 \div 31$ (c) $33{\cdot}3 \div 66$
   (d) $11{\cdot}11 \div 12$ (e) $53{\cdot}1 \div 29$ (f) $989{\cdot}901 \div 99$

3 Mary earns £199·08 for working 36 hours in a week.
How much does Mary earn per hour?

4 A crate contains 24 small bottles of ginger beer.
Each bottle holds 35·8 millilitres.
Calculate how many millilitres of ginger beer there are in the crate.

5 A large barrel contains 1280 litres of liquid soap.
The soap is poured into 400 bottles.
Calculate the amount of soap in each bottle.

6 Petrol is sold at a price of 74·5 pence per litre.
Find the cost for each person below.
   (a) Jill buys 50 litres
   (b) Apu buys 42 litres
   (c) Andy buys 12 litres

7 Gasco charge 3·65 pence per unit of gas used.
Calculate how much each person will pay for
the gas they have used.

	Units used
Mr Sobel	2440
Mrs Gray	3700
Mr Trent	3220

8 A cola container can hold 400 litres of cola.
   (a) How many 1·5 litre bottles will this fill?
   (b) How many litres will be left over?

6.11 Decimal calculations involving money

Answers to calculations involving money **must** have **two** numbers after the decimal point.

Example 1   What is £31 × 1·5?
The calculator gives an answer of 46·5
This is written as **£46·50**

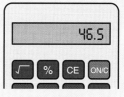

Example 2   What is £10 ÷ 3?
The calculator gives an answer of 3·33333333
This is written as **£3·33**

Exercise 6.11

You need a calculator for this exercise.
Round each answer to the nearest penny where appropriate.

1 Find:
(**a**) £35 × 1·5   (**b**) £45 × 0·5   (**c**) £11 × 2·5   (**d**) £21 × 0·5
(**e**) £21 ÷ 2   (**f**) £15 ÷ 2   (**g**) £10 ÷ 6   (**h**) £20 ÷ 6
(**i**) £30 ÷ 7   (**j**) £100 ÷ 8   (**k**) £44 ÷ 9   (**l**) £1 ÷ 11
(**m**) £5 × 5·5   (**n**) £9 × 4·3   (**o**) £0·80 ÷ 3   (**p**) £0·30 ÷ 25

2 A lottery win of £5000 is shared equally among 3 people.
How much will each person receive to the nearest penny?

3 John and seven friends buy £3·60 worth of sweets.
How much should each pay?

4 (**a**) For each bottle of shampoo
calculate the cost of 1 millilitre.
(**b**) Which bottle is the best
value for money?

6.12 Expressing decimals as fractions

U $\cdot$ t h

represents the number

four tenths and five hundredths **or** 45 hundredths.

Example (a) $0.5 = \frac{5}{10}$

(b) $0.45 = \frac{45}{100}$

(c) $0.314 = \frac{314}{1000}$

Exercise 6.12

1 Express each decimal as a fraction:
- (a) 0·9
- (b) 0·3
- (c) 0·5
- (d) 0·21
- (e) 0·99
- (f) 0·7
- (g) 0·2
- (h) 0·05
- (i) 0·25
- (j) 0·75
- (k) 0·17
- (l) 0·11
- (m) 0·01
- (n) 0·90
- (o) 0·001
- (p) 0·52
- (q) 0·97
- (r) 0·12
- (s) 0·45
- (t) 0·005

2 Calculate and express each answer as a fraction:
- (a) $0.88 \div 4$
- (b) $0.21 \div 7$
- (c) $5.2 \div 4$
- (d) $1.86 \div 6$
- (e) $20.7 \div 3$
- (f) $30.36 \div 4$
- (g) $0.015 \div 5$
- (h) $0.001 \div 1$
- (i) 0.045×6
- (j) 0.055×8
- (k) 0.05×6
- (l) 0.01×1

Review exercise 6

1 Write each number in words using the terms hundreds, tens, units, tenths and hundredths.
- (a) 5·6
- (b) 23·57
- (c) 0·8
- (d) 5·02
- (e) 100·03

2 Round to the nearest whole number:
- (a) 8·1
- (b) 12·9
- (c) 1·5
- (d) 56·199
- (e) 99·51

3 Round to one decimal place:
- (a) 5·61
- (b) 18·88
- (c) 29·52
- (d) 99·16
- (e) 199·95

4 Copy and complete:

(**a**)   4·5
       + 3·1
	(**b**) 6·6
	       + 3·8
		(**c**) 17·8
		       + 1·52
			(**d**) 29·38
			       + 4·8
				(**e**) 130·55
				       + 51·46

(**f**)   3·6
       − 2·2
	(**g**) 5·1
	       − 3·7
		(**h**) 18·7
		       − 9·4
			(**i**) 22·34
			       − 3·8
				(**j**) 110·3
				       − 21·61

5 Calculate:

(**a**) 3·6 + 2·7   (**b**) 2·6 + 5·72   (**c**) 18·64 + 3·5   (**d**) 16·25 + 18·76
(**e**) 3·6 − 2·5   (**f**) 6·6 − 3·92   (**g**) 8·64 − 3·7   (**h**) 16·25 − 11·76

6 Copy and complete:

(**a**)   4·3
       × 2
	(**b**) 6·1
	       × 3
		(**c**) 4·41
		       × 3
			(**d**) 6·36
			       × 4
				(**e**) 18·43
				       × 5

(**f**) 2)6·4   (**g**) 3)12·6   (**h**) 4)12·72   (**i**) 6)24·18   (**j**) 4)16·08

7 Calculate:

(**a**) 1·54 × 10   (**b**) 6·82 × 20   (**c**) 16·01 × 40
(**d**) 0·15 × 60   (**e**) 0·02 × 90   (**f**) 2·89 × 80

8 Calculate:

(**a**) 1·62 × 100   (**b**) 3·125 × 300   (**c**) 13·67 × 400
(**d**) 0·05 × 500   (**e**) 0·01 × 700   (**f**) 0·02 × 900

9 Calculate:

(**a**) 15·4 ÷ 10   (**b**) 6·2 ÷ 20   (**c**) 19·02 ÷ 30
(**d**) 0·12 ÷ 40   (**e**) 0·04 ÷ 80   (**f**) 0·06 ÷ 50

10 Calculate:

(**a**) 15·6 ÷ 100   (**b**) 26·8 ÷ 200   (**c**) 1·02 ÷ 300
(**d**) 0·15 ÷ 500   (**e**) 8 ÷ 400   (**f**) 16·1 ÷ 700

11 Find the total edge length of the shapes shown.

(**a**)

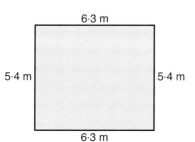

6·3 m
5·4 m   5·4 m
6·3 m

(**b**)

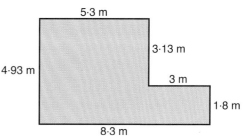

5·3 m
3·13 m
4·93 m   3 m
1·8 m
8·3 m

12 Jill's dad buys a large carton of juice for her party.
Jill's mum buys a medium carton.

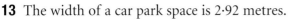

   (**a**) How much juice in total is there for the party?

   (**b**) How much more juice is in the larger carton?

   (**c**) Jill's brother bought 3 medium cartons of juice.
      How many litres has Jill's brother bought in total?

   (**d**) Jill's brother paid £8·73 for 3 cartons of juice.
      How much did he pay for each carton?

   (**e**) Jill pours 7·2 litres into a large container and shares
      the juice equally among 6 people.
      How much juice should each person receive?

13 The width of a car park space is 2·92 metres.
Calculate the width of   (**a**) 10 spaces
                              (**b**) 100

14 The total length of 100 car spaces is 472 metres.
Calculate the length of   (**a**) 1 space
                              (**b**) 10 spaces

 You need a calculator for question **15**.

15 Find:

   (**a**) £10 ÷ 4   (**b**) £5 ÷ 8   (**c**) £9 × 1·5   (**d**) £11 × 2·5   (**e**) £0·33 ÷ 6

16 Express each decimal as a fraction:

   (**a**) 0·9   (**b**) 0·2   (**c**) 0·57   (**d**) 0·25   (**e**) 1·5

Summary

Place value

324·21 represents the number
three hundreds, two tens, four units, two tenths and one hundredth.

Rounding

5·2 is 5 rounded to the nearest whole number
4·56 is 4·6 rounded to one decimal place (the nearest tenth)

Calculations

Decimal points **must** be in line.

$$
\begin{array}{r}
3{\cdot}72 \\
+\,1{\cdot}19 \\
\hline
4{\cdot}91
\end{array}
\qquad
\begin{array}{r}
5{\cdot}30 \\
-\,2{\cdot}47 \\
\hline
2{\cdot}83
\end{array}
\qquad
\begin{array}{r}
1{\cdot}72 \\
\times\ 3 \\
\hline
5{\cdot}16
\end{array}
\qquad
\begin{array}{r}
0{\cdot}92 \\
4\overline{)3{\cdot}68}
\end{array}
$$

$$4{\cdot}21 \times 10 \qquad\qquad 6{\cdot}8 \times 100 \qquad\qquad 23{\cdot}4 \div 10 \qquad\qquad 312{\cdot}6 \div 100$$
$$= 42{\cdot}1 \qquad\qquad = 680 \qquad\qquad = 2{\cdot}34 \qquad\qquad = 3{\cdot}126$$

$$21{\cdot}34 \times 20 \qquad\qquad 13{\cdot}1 \times 300 \qquad\qquad 57{\cdot}5\ \div 50 \qquad\qquad 3{\cdot}4 \div 200$$
$$= 42{\cdot}68 \times 10 \qquad = 39{\cdot}3 \times 100 \qquad = 11{\cdot}5\ \div 10 \qquad = 1{\cdot}7 \div 100$$
$$= 426{\cdot}8 \qquad\qquad = 3930 \qquad\qquad = 1{\cdot}15 \qquad\qquad = 0{\cdot}017$$

Money

Decimal calculations involving money must **always**
have two numbers after the decimal point.

20·4 is written as £20.40.

Express a decimal as a fraction

$$0{\cdot}3 = \tfrac{3}{10} \qquad\qquad 0{\cdot}51 = \tfrac{51}{100}$$

7 Measurement

In this chapter you will use different units of measurements, particularly metric units.

7.1 Length

A variety of units have been used in the past. In Europe most people use the metric system.

Metric length

Remember:

1000 millimetres (mm) = 1 metre (m)   10 millimetres (mm) = 1 centimetre (cm)

1000 metres (m) = 1 kilometre (km)   100 centimetres (cm) = 1 metre (m)

Estimating measurements using common objects as a guide is a useful start before measuring accurately.

- The height of most doors is about 2 metres.
- The length of the Forth Bridge is about 1 kilometre.
- The thickness of a fingernail is about 1 millimetre.
- The thickness of this book is about 1 centimetre.

Exercise 7.1

1 Estimate your height in (**a**) feet and inches and (**b**) metres.

2 Which of the following gives the best estimate of the distance between Edinburgh and Glasgow?

10 miles	20 miles	50 miles	90 miles	200 miles
16 kilometres	32 kilometres	80 kilometres	144 kilometres	320 kilometres

3 Which of the following gives the best estimate of the distance between Inverness and Glasgow?

(**a**) 5 miles	40 miles	80 miles	150 miles	300 miles
(**b**) 16 kilometres	32 kilometres	80 kilometres	240 kilometres	480 kilometres

4 Which metric unit – kilometre, metre, centimetre or millimetre – would you use to measure the following?

(**a**) a book   (**b**) a room   (**c**) a pencil point

(**d**) a CD   (**e**) a motorway   (**f**) the distance around the Earth

5 Estimate the sizes of each of the following using metric measures.

(**a**) The length of   (**i**) your classroom   (**ii**) your foot   (**iii**) an eye lash

(**b**) The height of   (**i**) your classroom   (**ii**) your school building   (**iii**) Ben Nevis

(**c**) The width of   (**i**) your thumb   (**ii**) the classroom door   (**iii**) the Tay Bridge

(**d**) The distance

(**i**)   from your town to Edinburgh   (**ii**) from your desk to the door

(**iii**)   around your school building

6 Estimate the length of each of these lines   1 cm

(**a**) ———————

(**b**) ——————————————

(**c**) ————————————————————

(**d**) ——————————

7 The sketches of these mountains are drawn to scale. The height of Ben Nevis is approximately 1300 metres. Estimate the height of the other mountains.

Ben   Ben   Matterhorn   Mount   Mount
Lomond   Nevis   McKinley   Everest

8 Find out the distance between your home and your school.
Give your answer in (**a**) miles and (**b**) kilometres.

7.2 Measuring length

Accuracy in many situations is essential.
The length of this picture is 4 centimetres 6 millimetres or
4·6 centimetres or 46 millimetres.

4 cm 6 mm = 4·6 cm = 46 mm

The height of table is 104 centimetres or
1 metre 4 centimetres or 1·04 metres.

104 cm = 1 m 4 cm = 1·04 m

Exercise 7.2

1 Draw horizontal lines in your jotter of length:

   (**a**) 6 cm   (**b**) 5 cm 4 mm   (**c**) 75 mm   (**d**) 4·3 cm   (**e**) 10·5 cm

2 Measure the length of each of the following expressing the answer in
   (**i**) centimetres and millimetres (**ii**) centimetres and (**iii**) millimetres.

   (**a**)   (**b**)   (**c**)

  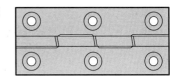

   (**d**)   (**e**)   (**f**)

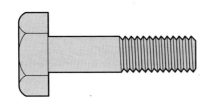

3 Measure accurately the lines in Exercise 7.1 question 6, giving your
   answer in centimetres and millimetres.

4 Write each of the following in centimetres:

(**a**) 5 cm 8 mm   (**b**) 19 cm 3 mm   (**c**) 49 cm 1 mm

(**d**) 99 cm 9 mm   (**e**) 0 cm 5 mm   (**f**) 25 mm

(**g**) 2 mm   (**h**) 455 mm   (**i**) 625 mm

5 Write each of the following in millimetres:

(**a**) 6·9 cm   (**b**) 27·5 cm   (**c**) 65·6 cm

(**d**) 87·4 cm   (**e**) 0·8 cm   (**f**) 5 cm 8 mm

(**g**) 15 cm   (**h**) 25 cm 6 mm   (**i**) 1 m 20 cm

6 Work with a partner. You need a tape measure, metre stick
or trundle wheel for this question. Measure (**a**) to (**f**)
expressing the answer in

(**i**) metres and centimetres   (**ii**) metres   (**iii**) centimetres.

Make sure that for each item you make an estimate before you
measure accurately:

(**a**) your height   (**b**) your partner's height

(**c**) the width of the classroom   (**d**) the height of the door

(**e**) the length of the corridor   (**f**) the length of 10 paces

(**g**) How many paces would you take for 1 kilometre?

7 Write each of the following in metres:

(**a**) 5 m 25 cm   (**b**) 42 m 45 cm   (**c**) 67 m 83 cm

(**d**) 9 m 5 cm   (**e**) 12 m 345 mm   (**f**) 18 m 23 mm

(**g**) 5 m 3 mm   (**h**) 4 m 25 cm 9 mm   (**i**) 325 cm

(**j**) 485 cm   (**k**) 35 cm   (**l**) 9 cm

(**m**) 4000 mm   (**n**) 700 mm   (**o**) 50 mm

8 Write each of the following in centimetres:

(**a**) 6 m   (**b**) 12·6 m   (**c**) 10·31 m

(**d**) 87·54 m   (**e**) 8 m 50 cm   (**f**) 900 mm

(**g**) 4 m 850 mm   (**h**) 6 m 8 cm   (**i**) 3 m 10 mm

9 Write each of the following in kilometres:

(**a**) 3000 m   (**b**) 600 m   (**c**) 20 m

(**d**) 8 m   (**e**) 4567 m   (**f**) 65 890 m

(**g**) 37 009 m   (**h**) 200 000 m   (**i**) 2 400 000 m

10 Round each of the following measurements to the nearest centimetre:

(**a**) 7·8 cm   (**b**) 3·2 cm   (**c**) 2 m 16 mm

(**d**) 5·018 m   (**e**) 0·6 cm   (**f**) 87 mm

(**g**) 7 mm   (**h**) 344 mm   (**i**) 1·672 m

11 Round each of the following measurements to the nearest metre:

(**a**) 5·8 m   (**b**) 46·2 m   (**c**) 83·6 m

(**d**) 9·55 m   (**e**) 8 m 45 cm   (**f**) 19 m 99 mm

(**g**) 6 m 533 mm   (**h**) 8 m 299 mm   (**i**) 5 m 49 cm 9 mm

7.3 Calculating length

Example 1   Find the perimeter of this rectangle.

length   = 5 cm 4 mm = 5·4 cm
breadth   = 3 cm 7 mm = 3·7 cm

Perimeter = 5·4 cm + 3·7 cm + 5·4 cm + 3·7 cm
          = 18·2 cm

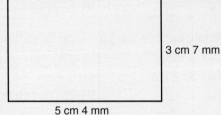

3 cm 7 mm

5 cm 4 mm

Example 2   A car has a length of 2 metres 56 centimetres.
What is the total length of 6 identical cars?

Length of 1 car = 2 m 56 cm = 2·56
Total length   = 2·56 m × 6
          = 15·36 m

Exercise 7.3

1 (**a**) Draw a rectangle 6 centimetres long and 4 centimetres broad.
   (**b**) Calculate its perimeter.

2 Measure the length and breadth of each rectangle to the nearest millimetre and
calculate its perimeter.

(**a**)

(**b**)

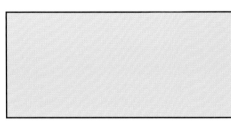

(**c**)

(**d**)

3 (**a**) Draw a square of side 5 centimetres 3 millimetres.

  (**b**) Calculate its perimeter.

4 Find the length of the perimeter of each square.

  (**a**)

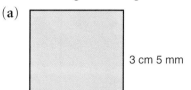

3 cm 5 mm

  (**b**)

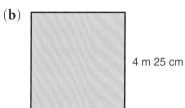

4 m 25 cm

5 (**a**) Collect the heights, in metres, of a group of 10 pupils in your class.

  (**b**) Calculate their average height in metres.

6 The following plan shows the outline of flowerbeds being built. Each bed is the same size.

  (**a**) Calculate the total perimeter of all four flower beds.

  (**b**) Round this perimeter to the nearest metre.

  (**c**) The edging for the beds costs £3·50 per metre. Find the cost of edging the four flower beds.

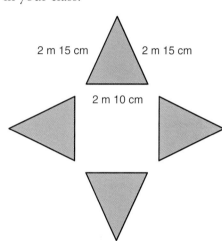

2 m 15 cm   2 m 15 cm

2 m 10 cm

7 A hillwalker follows the route shown on the map. Calculate the total distance covered for his entire route.

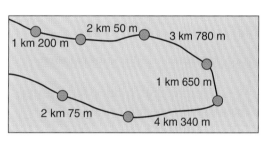

2 km 50 m   3 km 780 m

1 km 200 m

1 km 650 m

2 km 75 m

4 km 340 m

8 Tom's garden path is rectangular in shape. It is 30 metres long and 1.5 metres broad. He is planning to pave the area with square slabs of side 50 cm. (The diagram is not drawn to scale.)

  (**a**) How many slabs can be placed along the length?

  (**b**) How many slabs would be placed across the path?

  (**c**) How many slabs are required altogether?

  (**d**) What would be the total cost if one slab costs £2·50?

30 m

1.5 m

9 A joiner requires to cut a piece of wood into 6 equal pieces. How long will each piece be if the original length of wood to be cut is 1·5 metres?

10 A queue of traffic on the road to the Forth Road Bridge stretches for 5 kilometres. The average length of a vehicle is 3 metres. If the cars are 1 metre apart how many vehicles are there in the queue?

7.4 Weight

Remember:
> 1000 milligrammes (mg) = 1 gramme (g)
> 1000 gramme (g)   = 1 kilogramme (kg)
> 1000 kilogramme (g)   = 1 tonne

Estimating weights using common objects as a guide is a useful start before measuring accurately.

- The weight of a headache pill is about 100 milligrammes.
- The weight of an A4 sheet of paper is about 1 gramme.
- The weight of a bag of sugar is about 1 kilogramme.
- The weight of a bus is about 3 tonnes.
- The weight of an average man is about 100 kilogrammes.

Exercise 7.4

1 Estimate your weight. Give your answer in kilogrammes.

2 Match the estimated weights with objects given.

   (**a**) A dinghy   (**b**) A leaf   (**c**) A CD   (**d**) A car   (**e**) A litre of juice

   1 kilogramme   **100 kilogrammes**   **10 grammes**   **10 milligrammes**   **1 tonne**

3 Which metric unit, tonnes, kilogrammes, grammes or milligrammes, would you use to measure the weight of the following?

   (**a**) a book   (**b**) sweet wrapper   (**c**) a pencil
   (**d**) a CD   (**e**) you   (**f**) an oil tanker

4 Estimate the weights of each of the following using metric measures.

   (**a**) A chocolate bar   (**b**) A lorry   (**c**) An eagle   (**d**) 2 litres of cola

7.5 Measuring weight

The weight of this person is
63 kilogrammes 523 grammes
or 63·523 kilogrammes

63 kg 523 g = 63·523 kg

The weight of this chemical
compound is 3500 milligrammes
or 3·5 grammes

3500 mg = 3·5 g

Exercise 7.5

You need a set of bathroom scales for question 2.

1 Write down the weights shown on each scale in kilogrammes.

(a)    (b)    (c)    (d)

2 Work with a partner. You need a set of bath room scales. Measure:
(a) your weight   (b) your partner's weight   (c) the weight of ten textbooks.

3 Write each of the following in grammes:
(a) 6 g 500 mg   (b) 8 g 256 mg   (c) 4 g 28 mg   (d) 10 g 25 mg
(e) 25 g 750 mg   (f) 268 mg   (g) 95 mg   (h) 5 mg

4 Write each of the following in milligrammes:
(a) 3 g   (b) 8·953 g   (c) 4·5 g   (d) 5·98 g
(e) 8 g 250 mg   (f) 2 g 58 mg   (g) 65 g 5 mg   (h) 0·8 g

5 Write each of the following in kilogrammes:
(a) 5 kg 500 g   (b) 12 kg 45 g   (c) 58 kg 250 g   (d) 8 kg 5 g
(e) 800 g   (f) 90 g   (g) 1 g   (h) 2140 g

6 Write each of the following in grammes:
(a) 8 kg   (b) 5·7 kg   (c) 12·007 kg   (d) 25·05 kg
(e) 1 kg 50 g   (f) 4 kg 9 g   (g) 0·75 kg   (h) 0·003 kg

7 Write each of the following in tonnes:
(a) 5000 kg   (b) 300 kg   (c) 50 kg   (d) 2 kg
(e) 5982 kg   (f) 6870 kg   (g) 10 002 kg   (h) 67 090 kg

8 Round each of the following measurements to the nearest gramme:
(a) 6·2 g   (b) 5·499 g   (c) 2899 mg   (d) 497 mg
(e) 1200 mg   (f) 4 g 786 mg   (g) 45 g 99 mg   (h) 78 g 5 mg

9 Round each of the following measurements to the nearest kilogramme:

(**a**) 8·9 kg   (**b**) 6·52 kg   (**c**) 83·299 kg   (**d**) 2·499 kg

(**e**) 6 kg 450 g   (**f**) 45 kg 550 g   (**g**) 26 kg 90 g   (**h**) 8 kg 490 g 99 mg

10 Round each of the following measurements to the nearest tonne:

(**a**) 8·9 tonnes   (**b**) 6·52 tonnes   (**c**) 83·299 tonnes   (**d**) 2·499 tonnes

(**e**) 8 tonnes 589 kg   (**f**) 24 tonnes 200 kg   (**g**) 25 tonnes 3 kg   (**h**) 125 tonnes 493 kg

7.6 Calculating weight

Example 1   Find the difference in weight between these bags.

Weight of red bag   = 8 kg 500 g = 8·5 kg

Weight of blue bag   = 7 kg 125 g = 7·125 kg

Difference in weight = 8·5 kg – 7·125 kg

                = 1·375 kg

$$\begin{array}{r} 8\cdot500 \\ -7\cdot125 \\ \hline 1\cdot375 \end{array}$$

Example 2   A tanker weighs 3 tonnes 625 kilogrammes.

What is the total weight of 8 tankers?

Weight of 1 tanker = 3 tonnes 625 kilogrammes = 3·625 tonnes

Total weight   = 3·625 tonnes × 8

                 = 29 tonnes

$$\begin{array}{r} 3\cdot625 \\ \times \qquad 8 \\ \hline 29\cdot000 \end{array}$$

Exercise 7.6

1 Find the total weight of each group of bags.

(**a**)

(**b**)

(**c**)

(**d**)

2 The weight of a saloon car is 1 tonne 578 kg. Find the weight of 6 such cars.

3 The average weight of a 16 year old boy is 72 kilogrammes 890 grammes.
Find the total weight of 6 average boys.

4 The total weight of 5 girls is 150 kilogrammes 560 grammes.
Find the average weight of the girls.

5 (a) Collect the weights in kilogrammes of a group of 10 pupils in your class.
   (b) Calculate their average weight in kilogrammes.

6 The Kyle Rhea ferry can carry a maximum
   of 6 cars. If the average weight of a car is
   1 tonne 250 kilogrammes, what is the
   maximum weight which the ferry can carry?

7 A garden designer has drawn a plan of a new garden.
   He has estimated the amount of compost needed for
   each part of the garden and included them in his plan.
   (a) Calculate the total weight of compost required.
   (b) Compost is sold at £3.50 per kilogramme.
        Find the total cost of the compost.

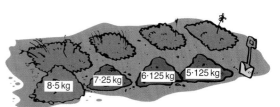

8 A concrete mix requires 2 tonnes 598 kilogrammes of cement and
   4 tonnes 672 kilogrammes of sand. Find the total weight of the mix.

9 Abby's patio is rectangular in shape. It is 20 metres long
   and 12 metres broad. She is planning to pave the area
   with square slabs of side 0·5 metres.
   (a) How many slabs can be placed along the length?
   (b) How many slabs would be placed across the patio?
   (c) How many slabs are required altogether?
   (d) Each slab weighs 15 kilogrammes.
        What is the total weight of all the slabs in tonnes?

10 A lift states that it can carry a maximum of 8 people. If the total weight
    that the lift can carry is 0·7 tonne, what is the average weight of 1 person
    in kilogrammes?

11 A builder's lorry can carry a maximum of 3 tonnes.
    He would like to load the items shown onto the lorry.
    Can this be safely done? Explain your reasons clearly.

Scaffolding	1·15 tonne
Planks	0·225 tonne
Mixer	0·350 tonne
Sand bags	5 × 250 kg
Cement	3 × 50 kg

12 A hotel kitchen has a bin containing 6·4 kilogrammes of flour.
    A recipe uses 160 grammes of flour. How many times can the recipe be made?

13 The healthy weight for a man of height 1·73 metres lies between
    65 kilogrammes and 75 kilogrammes. Jim is overweight at 90 kilogrammes.
    He would like to lose enough to become healthy in 6 months. How much
    would he have to lose each month to reach his target weight?

7.7 Measuring volume

Remember:

1 cubic centimetre (cm^3)	= 1 millilitre (ml)
1000 cubic centimetres (cm^3)	= 1000 millilitres (ml) = 1 litre (l)
1000 litres (l)	= 1 cubic metre (m^3)

Estimating volumes using common objects as a guide is a useful start before measuring accurately.

- A teaspoon contains about 5 millilitres
- A large bottle of cola is 2 litres
- A 50 metre long school swimming pool contains about 3000 cubic metres

The volume of liquid in this measuring jug is
0 litre 525 millilitres or 0·525 litres

525 ml = 0·525 l

Exercise 7.7

1 Write down the volumes shown in each jug. Give your answer in millilitres and litres.

(a)   (b)   (c)   (d)

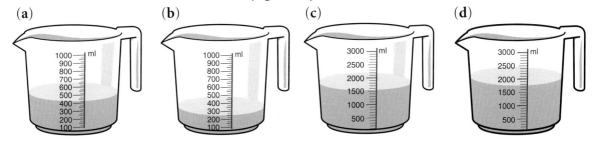

2 Write each of the following in litres:
   (a) 8l 500 ml   (b) 9l 375 ml   (c) 2l 28 ml   (d) 120l 25 ml
   (e) 750 ml   (f) 2275 ml   (g) 75 ml   (h) 5 ml

3 Write each of the following in millilitres:
   (a) 4l (b) 6·275l (c) 8·5l (d) 6·52l
   (e) 2l 750ml   (f) 5l 675 ml   (g) 8l 75 ml   (h) 10l 5 ml

4 Write each of the following in cubic centimetres:
   (a) 6l 500 ml   (b) 1l 325 ml   (c) 0·275l (d) 5l 5 ml
   (e) 5l 750 ml   (f) 3l 75 ml   (g) 2l 15 ml   (h) 6l 2 ml

5 Write each of the following in cubic metres:
   (a) 5m^3 750l (b) 2m^3 250l (c) 1m^3 625l (d) 870l
   (e) 5200l (f) 6245l (g) 15672l (h) 1 000 000l

6 Write each of the following in litres:

(a) $2\,m^3\,500\,l$ (b) $6\,m^3\,760\,l$ (c) $10\,m^3\,545\,l$ (d) $100\,m^3$

(e) $4{\cdot}525\,m^3$ (f) $2{\cdot}56\,m^3$ (g) $8{\cdot}5\,m^3$ (h) $0{\cdot}005\,m^3$

7 Round each of the following measurements to the nearest litre:

(a) $6{\cdot}7\,l$ (b) $4{\cdot}54\,l$ (c) $8{\cdot}499\,l$ (d) $6{\cdot}009\,l$

(e) $5\,l\,450\,ml$ (f) $27\,l\,560\,ml$ (g) $42\,l\,99\,ml$ (h) $8\,l\,99\,ml$

7.8 Calculating volume

Example 1 Find the total volume of these jugs

Volume of blue jug = $2\,l\,400\,ml = 2{\cdot}4\,l$

Volume of brown jug = $725\,ml = 0{\cdot}725\,l$

Total volume = $2{\cdot}4\,l + 0{\cdot}725\,l$

      = $3{\cdot}125\,l$

Example 2 A garage sold a total of 172 litres 500 millilitres of petrol to 5 customers. What was the average amount of petrol sold to each customer?

Total volume   = 172 litres 500 millilitres = $172{\cdot}5\,l$

Average volume = $172{\cdot}5\,l \div 5$

      = $34{\cdot}5\,l$

Exercise 7.8

1 Find the total volume in litres of each group of jugs.

(a)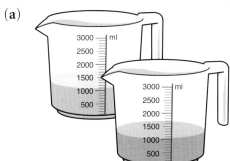

(b)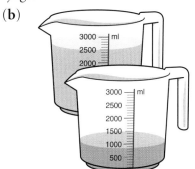

(c)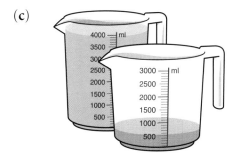

(d)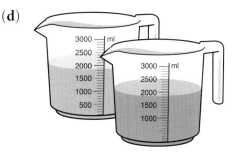

2 Find the total volume of petrol taken from these pumps.

3 The petrol tank of a car can hold 64 litres. Moira fills her tank.
If she put in 45 litres 250 millilitres, how much petrol was in
the tank prior to filling?

4 Aimee is having a party for her six friends. She thinks that each friend will drink
three 250 millilitre glasses of juice and plans to buy several 2 litre bottles.
  (**a**) What is the total volume of juice required?
  (**b**) How many bottles will she need?
  (**c**) If each bottle costs £1·75, how much will Aimee have to spend on juice?

5 A cup of tea holds 200 millilitres. A flask holds 1·2 litres.
Tasnim normally drinks 4 cups of tea in one day, while Mhairi normally
drinks 3 cups. Does the flask hold enough to satisfy their daily needs?
Explain your answer clearly.

6 The engine capacity of a small car is given as 1500 cubic centimetres.
What is this capacity in litres?

7 A bottle of cola contains 2 litres. How many glasses of 250 millilitres
could be filled from this?

8 A 2·5 litre bottle of orange juice costs £1·99.
A bottle containing 500 cubic centimetres costs 39 pence.
Which is the better value? Explain your answer clearly.

9 The tank of a car holds 34 litres of petrol. The car uses 125 millilitres
to travel 1 mile. How far can it travel on a full tank of petrol?

10 Coffee Central sells coffee in large mugs, small mugs and cups.
Each holds the following volume:
        large mug 500 millilitres
        small mug 350 millilitres
        cup 200 millilitres
In a normal day they estimate that they will sell 250 large mugs,
500 small mugs and 300 cups of coffee.
  (**a**) What is the total volume of coffee sold in one day?
  (**b**) A large mug costs £1.50, a small mug costs £1.25 and a cup costs £1.10.
The cost of making 1 litre of coffee is 40 pence. How much profit will
Coffee Central make in one day?

Review exercise 7

1 Find the perimeter of each rectangle.

(a)
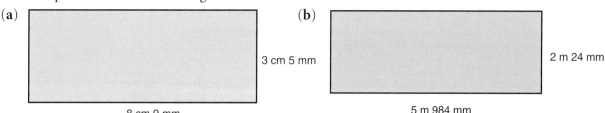
3 cm 5 mm

8 cm 9 mm

(b)
2 m 24 mm

5 m 984 mm

2 How many pieces of string 12 centimetres long can be cut from a ball 48 metres long?

3 An athlete runs each morning for a week. Each time he trains he completes 20 laps of a 400 metre track. How many kilometres does he run in a full week?

4 The average car is 3 metres long. How many cars would there be in a traffic jam 3·5 kilometres long assuming that there is a gap of 50 centimetres between each car?

5 A rectangular gift box is 15·5 centimetres long, 3·5 centimetres broad and 5 millimetres high.
What length of ribbon is required to tie the box as shown assuming that the bow requires 20 centimetres?

6 The weight of a lorry is 3 tonne 475 kg. Find the weight of 6 such lorries.

7 Find the total weight of the contents of this shopping basket.

8 A lift can safely carry a total of 720 kilogrammes.
Could it safely carry the following people?

9 A pedestrian bridge can safely hold a weight of 4 tonnes. If the average weight of a person is 80 kilogrammes, how many average pedestrians can safely use the bridge at one time?

10 A large bakery bakes 5000 loaves each morning.
They require 800 grammes of flour for each loaf.
(a) Calculate the total weight of flour required each day.
(b) The bakery buys flour at £60 per tonne.
Find the total cost of the flour required for a week's baking.

11 Every time a car is serviced it requires 4 litres 600 millilitres of engine oil. What is the total volume of oil required for 5 such services?

12 For health reasons Rupa drinks 375 millilitres of bottled water four times each day.
   (**a**) What volume of water does she drink in one week?
   (**b**) If a 1·5 litre bottle costs £1.25, how much does the water cost Rupa each week?

13 The average healthy woman should drink 2 litres of fluid each day. How many cubic metres of water should be drunk by a healthy woman who lives to be 80 years old?

Summary

Length

1000 millimetres (mm) = 1 metre (m)	10 millimetres (mm) = 1 centimetre (cm)
1000 metres (m) = 1 kilometre (km)	100 centimetres (cm) = 1 metre (m)

Weight

1000 milligrammes (mg) = 1 gramme (g)
1000 grammes (g) = 1 kilogramme (kg)
1000 kilogrammes (g) = 1 tonne

Volume

1 cubic centimetre (cm^3) = 1 millilitre (ml)
1000 cubic centimetres (cm^3) = 1000 millilitres (ml) = 1 litre (l)
1000 litres (l) = 1 cubic metre (m^3)

8 Coordinates

In this chapter you will learn how to read and plot coordinates.

8.1 Reading coordinates

On a coordinate diagram the horizontal line is called the *x*-axis and the vertical line is called the *y*-axis.

The point where the *x*-axis and *y*-axis meet is called the **origin, O**.

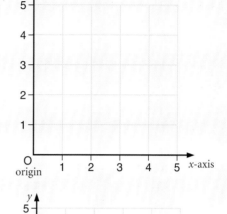

The location of a point is described by its **coordinates**.

From the origin, the point A is 3 lines along then 1 line up.

This is written as **A (3,1)**.

(3,1) are the coordinates of A.

The coordinates of B are (2,5).
The origin has coordinates (0,0).

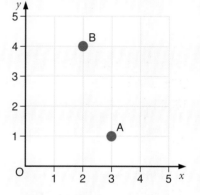

Exercise 8.1

For questions 1 to 6 write the coordinates of each point.

1
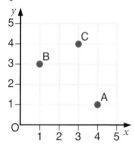

2
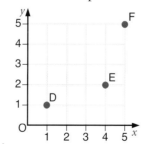

3
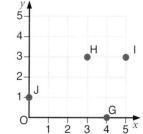

4

5

6

8.2 Using coordinates

P has coordinates (3,5)

The *x*-coordinate is 3.
The *y*-coordinate is 5.

Exercise 8.2

1 (**a**) Write the coordinates of each point from A to J.
  (**b**) Write the *x*-coordinate of:
    (**i**) D   (**ii**) E   (**iii**) F
    (**iv**) G   (**v**) H   (**vi**) J
  (**c**) Write the *y*-coordinate of:
    (**i**) J   (**ii**) H   (**iii**) G
  (**d**) Which two points have the
    same *x*-coordinate?
  (**e**) Which two points have the
    same *y*-coordinate?
  (**f**) Which point has the same
    x and *y*-coordinate?
  (**g**) The point K has the same
    x-coordinate as E and the
    same *y*-coordinate as D.
    Write the coordinates of K.

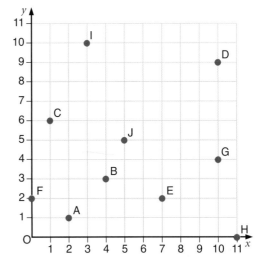

2 Look at the map of Pirate Island.

(**a**) Write the coordinates of the
   (**i**) harbour
  (**ii**) village
 (**iii**) rock.

(**b**) What landmark is at (2,5)?

(**c**) T marks the spot where the treasure is buried. Write the coordinates of the treasure.

(**d**) Pirate Paddy is at the Swamp. He moves along 4 to the right then up 5.
   (**i**) What is Paddy standing next to?
  (**ii**) Write Paddy's coordinates.

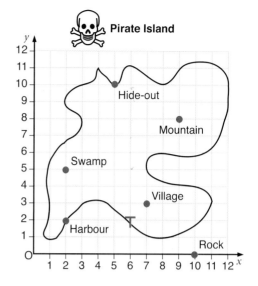

3 (**a**) Write the coordinates of A, B and C.

(**b**) Write the coordinate of D so that ABCD is a rectangle.

(**c**) Point E is exactly halfway between points B and C. Write the coordinates of E.

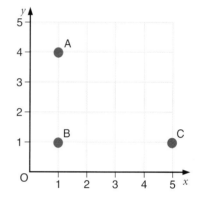

4 (**a**) Write the coordinates of E and F.

(**b**) Write the coordinates of G and H so that EFGH is a square.

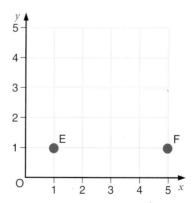

W You may use worksheet 8.1 for supplementary questions 5 and 6.

8.3 Plotting coordinates

Marking a point on a coordinate diagram is called **plotting** a point.

Before plotting a point, draw the axes with numbers on the lines.

To plot (4,6) from the origin, count along 4 lines then up 6 lines.

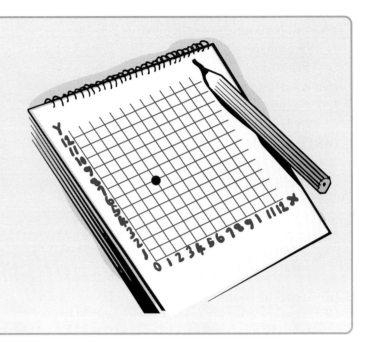

Exercise 8.3

W You may use worksheet 8.2 for questions 1 to 4.

1 (**a**) Draw an x-axis with numbers 0 to 12. Draw a y-axis with numbers 0 to 10. Label your axes.

(**b**) Plot these points on your diagram:

A(3,1) B(1,5) C(7,0) D(0,3)

2 (**a**) Draw another diagram with the same axes as in question 1.

(**b**) Plot these points on your new diagram:

E(3,6) F(1,9) G(5,0) H(6,6) I(0,8) J(12,9) K(4,1)

3 Draw a coordinate diagram with x and y-axis numbered up to 10. Plot the points, join them in order, and name the object.

(0,2) (10,2) (8,0) (2,0) (0,2) STOP
(6,2) (6,9) (0,3) (6,3) STOP

4 The diagram shows points
A(5,9) B(2,4) C(4,4) D(4,1) and E(5,1).
The red line is an axis of symmetry.

(**a**) Copy and complete the diagram.

(**b**) List the coordinates of the image points.

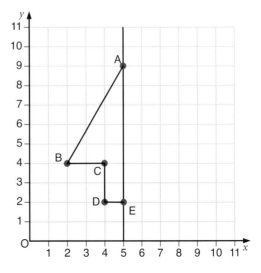

5 Draw a coordinate diagram with *x*- axis and *y*-axis numbered up to 6
for each set of coordinates.
Plot the points and join them in order.
(**a**) (2,4) (0,0) (4,3) (0,3) (4,0) (2,4)
(**b**) (1,0) (5,0) (1,4) (5,4) (3,5) (1,4) (1,0) (5,4) (5,0)

6 Draw a coordinate diagram with *x*-axis and *y*-axis numbered up to 10.
Plot the points, join them in order, and name the object.
(4,0) (4,2) (0,2) (2,3) (0,3) (2,4) (1,4) (3,5) (1,5) (3,6) (2,6) (4,8)
(6,6) (5,6) (7,5) (5,5) (7,4) (6,4) (8,3) (6,3) (8,2) (4,2) STOP

W You may use worksheet 8.3 for question 7.

7 Draw a coordinate diagram with *x*-axis numbered up to 29 and *y*-axis numbered up to 35.
Plot the points, join them in order and name the well-known character.

Head: (12,4) (5,4) (0,7) (2,15) (1,17)
(1,19) (3,20) (8,34) (9,32) (10,34)
(11,31) (13,34) (14,31) (16,33) (16,30)
(18,32) (19,29) (21,31) (21,28) (23,29)
(23,27) (26,28) (25, 26) (27,26) (25,24)
(19,9) (20,8) (20,6) (19,5) (18,5)
(18,2) (16,0) (11,0) (7,4) STOP

Eyes: (6,11) (4,12) (3,13) (3,14) (4,15)
(6,15) (7,14) (8,12) (10,11) (12,11)
(15,13) (10,16) (7,16) (5,18) (3,18)
(1,17) (3,14) STOP

Extras: (5,18) (5,17) (6,17) STOP
(9,18) (7,16) STOP
(14,17) (15,16) (15,13) STOP
(12,15) (12,14) (13,14) STOP
(18,8) (19,9) (18,6) STOP
(7,16) (7,14) STOP

8 Draw a coordinate diagram with *x*-axis numbered up to 55 and *y*-axis numbered up to 35. Plot the points, join them in order and name the well-known character.

 Arm: (2,0) (2,9) (0,11) (4,11) (4,13)
(5,14) (6,14) (7,12) (9,13) (11,11)
(11,9) (13,9) (13,7) (10,5) (10,0)
(12,1) (13,3) (18,5) (20,8) (21,9)
(21,7) STOP
(7,12) (6,10) (7,9) (8,9) (10,11)
(11,11) STOP

 Arm: (50,0) (51,2) (52,6) (51,11) (53,12)
(54,13) (53,14) (50,14) (51,17) (50,18)
(48,16) (45,16) (44,15) (44,12) (43,11)
(41,12) (40,11) (40,10) (43,9) (44,8)
(43,4) (40,4) (39,6) (34,6) (33,8)
(32,9) (32,7) (29,6) (27,2) (25,5)
(20,8) STOP
(45,15) (46,15) (47,13) (49,13) (48,16) STOP
(33,8) (32,7) (32,11) STOP

 Mouth: (21,9) (21,14) (22,16) (25,18) (25,17)
(26,16) (27,16) (28,17) (28,18) (31,16)
(32,13) (32,11) (31,9) (28,7) (25,7)
(22,9) (21,11) STOP
(26,10) (26,11) (27,11) (27,10) (26,10) STOP

 Eye: (33,18) (31,17) (30,17) (28,18) (27,20)
(27,22) (28,23) (30,24) (31,24) (33,23)
(34,22) (34,20) (33,18) (34,17) (34,16)
(33,15) (32,15) STOP
(31,18) (31,19 (32,19) (32,18) (31,18) STOP

 Eye: (20,18) (22,17) (23,17) (25,18) (26,20)
(26,22) (25,23) (23,24) (22,24) (20,23)
(19,22) (19,20) (20,18) (19,18) (19,16)
(20,15) (21,15) STOP
(21,18) (21,19) (22,19) (22,18) (21,18) STOP

 Head: (19,22) (20,27) (21,30) (22,31) (25,32)
(28,32) (31,31) (32,30) (33,27) (34,22) STOP
Hint: (38,20) (38,25) (39,25) (40,24) (40,22)
(39,20) (38,20) STOP

8.4 Drawing coordinate diagrams

When drawing a coordinate diagram, use the largest coordinate to decide the length of each axis.

To plot A(**8**,1) and B (**2**,**9**):

draw the *x*-axis numbered up to **8** and draw the *y*-axis numbered up to **9**.

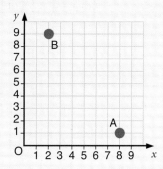

Exercise 8.4

Draw separate coordinate diagrams for each question. Look at the coordinates in each question to decide the length of each axis.

1 (**a**) Plot the points A(1,0), B(5,0), C(5,3) and D(1,3)
  (**b**) Join up the points ABCD in order. What shape is ABCD?

2 (**a**) Plot the points and join them in order:
     K(3,3), L(5,3), M(5,7) and N(3,7)
  (**b**) What shape is KLMN?

3 (**a**) Plot the points A(1,0), B(5,0) and C(5,2).
  (**b**) Plot the point D so that ABCD is a rectangle.
  (**c**) Write the coordinates of E, where the diagonals of the rectangle meet.

4 (**a**) Plot the points A(2,1) and B(5,1).
  (**b**) If ABCD is a square, plot the points C and D and write their coordinates.
  (**c**) Write the coordinates of E, where the diagonals cross.

5 Draw a line joining the points P(6,3) and R(1,5).
PR is a diagonal of rectangle PQRS.
Plot and write the coordinates of Q and S.

6 (**a**) Plot the points A(2,1), B(0,6), C(2,8) and D(4,6).
  (**b**) Join up the points ABCD in order. What shape is ABCD?
  (**c**) Plot the point P(7,0).
  (**d**) Plot the points Q, R and S so that PQRS is the same shape as ABCD.
  (**e**) Write down the coordinates of Q, R and S.

Review exercise 8

1 (**a**) Write the coordinates of all the points in the diagram.
  (**b**) Which points that have the same *x*-coordinates?
  (**c**) ABDF is a square. Write the coordinates of F.
  (**d**) Write the coordinates of M, where the diagonals of
     ABDF would meet.

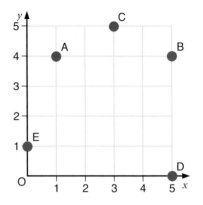

2 (**a**) Draw a coordinate diagram and plot the points:
     J(3,4), K(6,1), L(1,4), M(0,2), N(4,0), P(1,2) and Q(5,5)
  (**b**) The point R is halfway between L and P. Write the coordinates of R.

3 (**a**) Plot the points V(3,4) and W(3,0) on a coordinate diagram.
  (**b**) T has an *x*-coordinate of 7. STWV is a rectangle. Write the
     coordinates of T and S.

Summary

The position of a point is described by its **coordinates**.

The horizontal axis is called the ***x*-axis**.
The vertical axis is called the ***y*-axis**.
The axes meet at the **origin, O**.

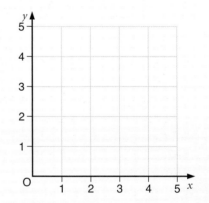

A has coordinates (3,1).
3 is the *x*-coordinate, 1 is the *y*-coordinate.
B has coordinates (2,5).

Marking points on a coordinates diagram is
called **plotting** points.

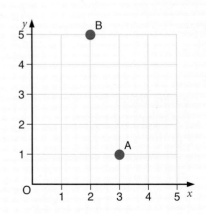

9 Percentages

In this chapter you will revise and extend your knowledge of percentages.

9.1 Percentages, fractions and decimals

Percent (%) means **out of 100**.
71% means 71 out of 100.
This can be written as $\frac{71}{100}$ or 0·71
71%, $\frac{71}{100}$ and 0·71 are **equivalent**.

$$= \frac{71}{100} = 71\%$$

Exercise 9.1

1 Write each percentage as a fraction and as a decimal.

(**a**) 33%   (**b**) 41%   (**c**) 17%   (**d**) 11%   (**e**) 83%   (**f**) 69%   (**g**) 9%

$51\% = \frac{51}{100} = 0·51$

2 Write each fraction as a percentage and as a decimal.

(**a**) $\frac{21}{100}$ (**b**) $\frac{19}{100}$ (**c**) $\frac{61}{100}$ (**d**) $\frac{93}{100}$ (**e**) $\frac{43}{100}$ (**f**) $\frac{31}{100}$ (**g**) $\frac{7}{100}$

$\frac{13}{100} = 13\% = 0·13$

3 Write each decimal as a percentage and as a fraction.

(**a**) 0·37   (**b**) 0·57   (**c**) 0·67   (**d**) 0·77   (**e**) 0·81   (**f**) 0·29   (**g**) 0·03

$0·23 = 23\% = \frac{23}{100}$

4 Copy and complete the table of equivalent percentages, fractions and decimals.

Percentage	Fraction	Decimal
51%		
49%		
	$\frac{53}{100}$	
	$\frac{19}{100}$	
		0·23
		0·99
79%		
	$\frac{27}{100}$	
		0·47
	$\frac{59}{100}$	
		0·63
73%		
89%		
		0·39
	$\frac{1}{100}$	

9.2 Simplest form

88% may be written as $\frac{88}{100}$

To write $\frac{88}{100}$ in simplest form divide numerator and denominator by 4.

So 88% is equivalent to $\frac{22}{25}$

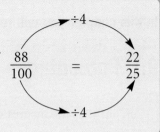

$$\frac{88}{100} = \frac{22}{25}$$
(÷4, ÷4)

Exercise 9.2

1 For each percentage write the equivalent fraction in simplest form.

(**a**) 40% (**b**) 20% (**c**) 50% (**d**) 60% (**e**) 75% (**f**) 4% (**g**) 12%

(**h**) 52% (**i**) 16% (**j**) 80% (**k**) 35% (**l**) 95% (**m**) 55% (**n**) 64%

2 Write each ingredient of the tomato sauce as a fraction in simplest form.

Tomato sauce

Water 30%   Tomato 54%
Oil 10%   Spices 6%

3 From the coleslaw label, change the percentage of each nutritional element to a fraction in simplest form.

COLESLAW

Total fat 24%
Saturated fat 15%
Cholesterol 2%
Sodium 8%

4 In a survey of tourists' activities the results were:

Sunbathing	22%	Swimming	14%
Shopping	26%	Scuba diving	15%
Sport	25%	Sightseeing	36%

Change each percentage to a fraction in simplest form.

5 A weather station in Fife has predicted the chance of rain in three months of the year.

May 65%   June 58%   July 56%

Change each percentage to a fraction in simplest form.

6 A bank charges variable interest rates for different accounts.

Savings account 6%   Current account 4%   Credit card 18%

Change each percentage to a fraction in simplest form.

9.3 Common percentages

Some percentages are used very frequently.

It is useful to **know** these as fractions and decimals.

For example, 50% is equivalent to $\frac{1}{2}$ ($\frac{50}{100}$) and 0·5.

10% OFF

20% interest

25% extra

Exercise 9.3

1 Copy and complete the table of common percentages.

Percentage	Fraction	Decimal
50%		
25%		
75%		
1%		
10%		
20%		
$33\frac{1}{3}$%	$\frac{1}{3}$	0·333
$66\frac{2}{3}$%		

$$33\frac{1}{3}\% = \frac{33\frac{1}{3}}{100} = \frac{1}{3}$$

2 Without looking at your table, write each fraction or decimal as a percentage.

(a) $\frac{1}{2}$ (b) 0·25   (c) $\frac{3}{4}$ (d) $\frac{1}{3}$ (e) 0·2   (f) $\frac{1}{10}$

(g) 0·1   (h) $\frac{2}{3}$ (i) 0·333   (j) 0·75   (k) $\frac{1}{5}$ (l) $\frac{1}{100}$

9.4 Percentage of a quantity without a calculator

Example 1
Calculate 25% of £340

25% of 340

= $\frac{1}{4}$ of 340

= $\frac{1}{4}$ × 340 = **£85**

To find $\frac{1}{4}$ divide by 4

Example 2
Calculate $66\frac{2}{3}$% of 630 g

Find $\frac{1}{3}$ of 630

= $\frac{1}{3}$ × 630 = 210

So, $\frac{2}{3}$ of 630 = 2 × 210 = **420 g**

$66\frac{2}{3}$% is equivalent to $\frac{2}{3}$

Exercise 9.4

1 Without a calculator, calculate:

(a) 50% of £84   (b) 25% of £1000   (c) 20% of £8

(d) 10% of 40 g   (e) 1% of 6400 kg   (f) $66\frac{2}{3}$% of £4.50

(g) 50% of 45 km   (h) 20% of £45   (i) 10% of 52 ml

(j) $33\frac{1}{3}$% of 93 kg   (k) 75% of £64   (l) $66\frac{2}{3}$% of £24

9.5 Using one percent

Example

Calculate how many grams of fat there are in the lasagne.

$$1\% \text{ of } 300\,g$$
$$= \tfrac{1}{100} \times 300 = 3\,g$$

> 1% is equivalent to $\tfrac{1}{100}$

Lasagne 300 g
8% fat

So, 8% of 300 g = 8 × 3 g = **24 g**

Exercise 9.5

1 Calculate 6% of:

  (**a**) 500 g (**b**) 800 km (**c**) 400 m (**d**) £700 (**e**) 820 cm (**f**) 440 kg

2 Calculate:

  (**a**) 11% of 200 ml (**b**) 8% of £420 (**c**) 4% of 1200 g
  (**d**) 3% of 840 mm (**e**) 7% of 2400 km (**f**) 9% of £324

3 The workers in a factory have won an 8% wage rise.
  Find the rise in each person's weekly pay.

  (**a**) Sue, £230 (**b**) John, £180 (**c**) Gwen, £320 (**d**) Alan, £480

4 A diet brand of food plans to reduce the fat content of all its products by 9%.
  Calculate the reduction in fat content for each product.

  (**a**) biscuits, 80 g (**b**) cake, 70 g (**c**) lasagne, 120 g (**d**) chocolate, 220 g

9.6 Using ten percent

Example

Calculate the profit on a £524 sale.

$$10\% \text{ of } £524$$
$$= \tfrac{1}{10} \times 524 = £52.40$$

> 10% is equivalent to $\tfrac{1}{10}$

30% profit on all sales

So, 30% of 524 = 3 × 52.40 = **£157.20**

Exercise 9.6

1 Calculate 40% of:

  (**a**) £860 (**b**) 550 cm (**c**) 2400 m (**d**) £843 (**e**) £6540 (**f**) 645 ml

2 Calculate:

  (**a**) 60% of £340 (**b**) 90% of 560 g (**c**) 30% of 94 m
  (**d**) 70% of £45 (**e**) 80% of 500 g (**f**) 40% of 670 ml

3 Michael is offered 40% of £600 or 30% of £720.
  Which offer should he take?

9.7 Percentage – increase and decrease

To find the sale price of a coat costing £85:

10% of £85

$= \frac{1}{10} \times 85 = £8.50$

10% is equivalent to $\frac{1}{10}$

The sale price is £85 – £8.50 = **£76.50**

SALE
10% off

Exercise 9.7

1 Calculate the sale price of each item.

(**a**) jacket, £56   (**b**) shoes, £62

(**c**) shirt, £35   (**d**) jeans, £29

SALE
10% off

SALE
$33\frac{1}{3}$% off

2 Calculate the sale price for each vehicle.

(**a**) estate car, £5700   (**b**) saloon car, £8400

(**c**) 4 wheel drive, £9570

3 A textile factory has awarded a 20% wage rise to all employees.
Calculate the new wage for each grade of employee.

(**a**) technician, £280   (**b**) researcher, £460   (**c**) designer, £590

4 A sweet manufacturer plans to make its range of chocolate bars larger.
The bars are advertised as 25% bigger.
Find the weight of the new, bigger bars.

(**a**) 20 g   (**b**) 40 g   (**c**) 80 g   (**d**) 150 g   (**e**) 300 g

5 Prices change over time.
Find the current price for each item.

	Item	Old price	Change in price
(a)	Car	£4200	10% decrease
(b)	House	£34 500	$33\frac{1}{3}$% increase
(c)	Computer	£1200	5% decrease
(d)	Holiday	£480	25% increase
(e)	Fridge	£390	20% increase

6 The Slimma food company makes low fat foods for slimmers.
Each type of food has less fat than the normal version.
Calculate the amount of fat in each Slimma food.

	Food	Normal fat content	Percentage less in Slimma
(a)	Crisps	8 g	25%
(b)	Pizza	10 g	20%
(c)	Ice cream	15 g	$33\frac{1}{3}$%
(d)	Pasta sauce	3 g	10%

9.8 Percentages using a calculator

Example   Calculate 17% of £350

| 0·17 | × | 350 | = | 59·5 |

17% is equivalent to 0·17

So 17% of £350 is **£59.50**

Exercise 9.8

1 Calculate:
(**a**) 12% of 640 ml   (**b**) 23% of £220   (**c**) 35% of 54 ml   (**d**) 64% of £128
(**e**) 33% of 150 m   (**f**) 85% of £95   (**g**) 19% of £3400   (**h**) 7% of 42 kg

2 Find the weight of each ingredient in a 250 g packet of biscuits.

Starch 28%   Sugar 7%
Fat 16%   Fibre 11%

3 Calculate the volume of each ingredient in a 1.5 *l* carton of fruit juice.

1.5 *l* = 1500 ml

Water 72%   Orange juice 8%
Grape juice 11%   Apple juice 9%

9.9 Percentage increase and decrease using a calculator

Example
Find the sale price of a camera which costs £480.
    35% of £480

| 0·35 | × | 480 | = | 168 |

35% is equivalent to 0·35

SALE 35% off

    Sale price is £480 − £168 = **£312**

Exercise 9.9

1 Find the sale price of each item if prices are reduced by 35%.
(**a**) coat £124   (**b**) dress £96   (**c**) shoes £65   (**d**) jeans £58

2 The Fern restaurant adds a 12% service charge to every bill. Add the service charge to each bill.
(**a**) £32   (**b**) £24.50   (**c**) £65   (**d**) £86   (**e**) £124

3 A shop gives a 22% discount to its staff. Find the staff price for each item.
(**a**) weedkiller £12   (**b**) lawnmower £146   (**c**) greenhouse £235

Discount means money off

4 Each customer in a cash and carry has a different discount.
Find the price each person will pay.
(**a**) 14% off £95   (**b**) 22% off £254   (**c**) 28% off £445

9.10 Fractions to percentages using a calculator

In his French exam Alex scored $\frac{54}{60}$.

What is this as a percentage?

$\frac{54}{60} = 0{\cdot}9 = \mathbf{90\%}$

Exercise 9.10

1 Change each fraction to a percentage.

(**a**) $\frac{7}{20}$ (**b**) $\frac{12}{40}$ (**c**) $\frac{11}{50}$ (**d**) $\frac{7}{25}$ (**e**) $\frac{3}{10}$ (**f**) $\frac{9}{30}$ (**g**) $\frac{72}{80}$

(**h**) $\frac{33}{60}$ (**i**) $\frac{34}{85}$ (**j**) $\frac{12}{15}$ (**k**) $\frac{81}{90}$ (**l**) $\frac{21}{25}$ (**m**) $\frac{36}{90}$ (**n**) $\frac{93}{150}$

2 Frosini has listed her test results.

(**a**) Change each result to a percentage.

(**b**) In which subject did she do best?

Maths	$\frac{81}{90}$	French	$\frac{64}{80}$
English	$\frac{54}{75}$	Science	$\frac{90}{120}$

9.11 Percentage of a total

A travel company has booked its clients into 5 hotels. What percentage is staying at the Hotel Sol e Mar?

Hotel Sol e Mar: 27 out of 150 people

$= \frac{27}{150} = 0{\cdot}18 = \mathbf{18\%}$

Hotel	Number of clients
Sol e Mar	27
Mirabar	45
Guadelupe	12
Costa Azur	60
Grande	6
Total	150

Exercise 9.11

1 Calculate the percentage staying in each hotel on the list above.

2 The table shows the final destinations for a plane load of passengers travelling to Majorca. Calculate the percentage travelling to each resort.

Magaluf	36
Palma	72
Cala D'Or	45
Santa Ponsa	27
Total	180

3 A holiday rep has listed the activity choices for a group of tourists.

(**a**) Calculate the total number of tourists.

(**b**) Calculate the percentage choosing each activity.

Boat trip	27
market	9
Beach party	18
castle	6

4 S2 pupils have chosen social subjects as shown. Calculate the percentage choosing each subject.

History	75
Geography	80
Modern Studies	45

Review exercise 9

1 Copy and complete the table for equivalent percentages, fractions and decimals.

Percentage	Fraction	Decimal
50%		
10%		
	$\frac{1}{4}$	
		0·75
20%		
	$\frac{1}{100}$	

2 For each percentage write the equivalent fraction in simplest form.
   (**a**) 82%   (**b**) 45%   (**c**) 48%   (**d**) 12%

3 Write each percentage as an equivalent decimal.
   (**a**) 13%   (**b**) 77%   (**c**) 8%   (**d**) $33\frac{1}{3}$%

4 Find:
   (**a**) 10% of £240   (**b**) 25% of 80 kg   (**c**) $33\frac{1}{3}$% of 96 ml

5 Calculate:
   (**a**) 6% of £340   (**b**) 11% of 850 g   (**c**) 9% of 34 kg

6 In a sale all prices are reduced by 30%.
   Find the sale price of a briefcase which normally costs £140.

7 A company awards a wage rise of 7%.
   Calculate the new weekly wage for each employee.
   (**a**) Frank, old wage £340   (**b**) Rachael, old wage £465

8 Michael scored $\frac{18}{25}$ in his science test.

   What is this as a percentage?

9 A school surveyed the teachers on how they travel to work.
   From the results, what percentage
   (**a**) drive   (**b**) walk   (**c**) do not cycle?

Drive	42
Cycle	3
Walk	12
Bus	3

Summary

Percentage means **out of 100**.

A percentage may be written as an equivalent fraction and decimal.

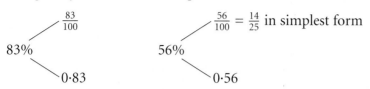

$$83\% \quad \begin{array}{c} \frac{83}{100} \\ 0{\cdot}83 \end{array}$$

$$56\% \quad \begin{array}{c} \frac{56}{100} = \frac{14}{25} \text{ in simplest form} \\ 0{\cdot}56 \end{array}$$

Some percentages are in common usage.

Percentage	Fraction	Decimal
1%	$\frac{1}{100}$	0·01
10%	$\frac{1}{10}$	0·1
20%	$\frac{1}{5}$	0·2
25%	$\frac{1}{4}$	0·25
50%	$\frac{1}{2}$	0·5
75%	$\frac{3}{4}$	0·75
$33\frac{1}{3}\%$	$\frac{1}{3}$	0·33
$66\frac{2}{3}\%$	$\frac{2}{3}$	0·67

To calculate a percentage use $\quad 1\% = \frac{1}{100} \quad$ or $\quad 10\% = \frac{1}{10}$

To find 7% of £160:

$$1\% \text{ of } 160 = \frac{1}{100} \times 160 = £1.60$$

So 7% of $160 = 7 \times 1{\cdot}60 = $ **£11.20**

To find 40% of £48:

$$10\% \text{ of } 48 = \frac{1}{10} \times 48 = £4.80$$

So 40% of $48 = 4 \times 4{\cdot}80 = £19.20$

Using a calculator

56% of 130 ml

To change a fraction to a percentage:

$$\frac{45}{60} = 0{\cdot}75$$
$$= \textbf{75}\%$$

10 2D Shape

In this chapter you will revise and extend your knowledge of some common 2D shapes.

10.1 Words to remember

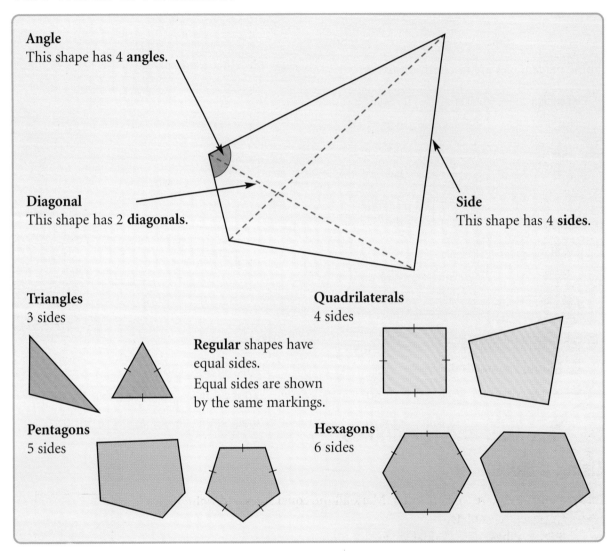

Angle
This shape has 4 **angles**.

Diagonal
This shape has 2 **diagonals**.

Side
This shape has 4 **sides**.

Triangles
3 sides

Quadrilaterals
4 sides

Regular shapes have equal sides.
Equal sides are shown by the same markings.

Pentagons
5 sides

Hexagons
6 sides

Exercise 10.1

1 Write the meaning of each word.

(**a**) triplet   (**b**) quadrilateral   (**c**) pentathlon   (**d**) hexagon
(**e**) tricycle   (**f**) quadruplet   (**g**) pentagon   (**h**) bicycle
(**i**) decade   (**j**) decathlon   (**k**) octopus   (**l**) heptathlon

2 A prefix is the start of a word. Write the number these prefixes stand for.

(**a**) quad   (**b**) hexa   (**c**) tri   (**d**) penta   (**e**) octa

3 You may use worksheet 10.1 for this question. Copy and complete the table.

Shape	Name	Regular or not regular	Number of sides	Number of angles
(a)	triangle	regular	3	3
(b)				
(c)				
(d)				
(e)				
(f)				
(g)				
(h)				
(i)				

10.2 Squares and rectangles

Exercise 10.2

1 (**a**) Sketch a square in your jotter. Mark all the equal sides and right angles.

   (**b**) Copy and complete:

   A square has _____ equal sides.

   A square has _____ right angles.

2 (**a**) Sketch a rectangle in your jotter. Mark all the equal sides and right angles on it.

   (**b**) Copy and complete:

   The opposite sides of a rectangle are _____ .

   A rectangle has _____ right angles.

3 (**a**) On your sketches of the square and rectangle draw all axes of symmetry using dotted lines.

   (**b**) Copy and complete:

   A square has _____ axes of symmetry.

   A rectangle has _____ axes of symmetry.

10.3 Properties of squares and rectangles

The diagonals have been drawn on this square and this rectangle.

Square   **Rectangle**

A square has
- 4 equal sides
- 4 right angles
- equal diagonals
- diagonals which **bisect** each other
- diagonals which are **perpendicular**

| Bisect means cut in half |

A rectangle has
- 2 pairs of equal, opposite sides
- 4 right angles
- equal diagonals
- diagonals which **bisect** each other

| Perpendicular means meet at right angles |

Exercise 10.3

You need a ruler and protractor for this exercise.

1 (a) Draw accurately the following squares and rectangles.

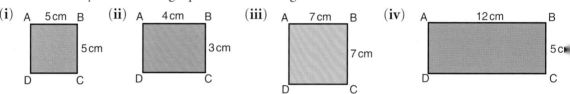

(i) A 5cm B, 5cm, D C
(ii) A 4cm B, 3cm, D C
(iii) A 7cm B, 7cm, D C
(iv) A 12cm B, 5cm, D C

(b) Draw and measure the diagonals.
(c) Mark E where the diagonals intersect.
(d) Measure and mark the lengths AE, BE, CE and DE.

2 (a) Draw accurately the following square and rectangle.

(i) P 8cm Q, 8cm, S R
(ii) P 12cm Q, 7cm, S R

(b) Draw the diagonals and mark the point of intersection T.
(c) Measure and mark ∠PTQ, ∠QTR, ∠RTS and ∠STP.

3 Say whether each of the following is true or false.
(a) The sides of a rectangle are equal.
(b) The angles of a square are equal.
(c) There are two axes of symmetry for a rectangle.
(d) In a rectangle the diagonals are axes of symmetry.
(e) The diagonals of a square are perpendicular.
(f) The diagonals of a rectangle bisect each other.
(g) A tracing of a rectangle fits its outline 4 times in one turn.
(h) A square has 4 axes of symmetry.
(i) The diagonals of a square bisect each other at right angles.
(j) The diagonals of a square make two angles of 45° at each vertex.

10.4 Types of triangles

Equilateral triangle	Isosceles triangle	Scalene triangle
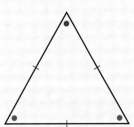	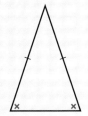	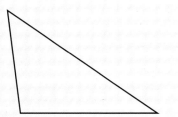
3 equal sides	2 equal sides	no equal sides
3 equal angles	2 equal angles	no equal angles
all angles are 60°		

Exercise 10.4

1 Use the letters to list the triangles which are

    (**i**) scalene
    (**ii**) isosceles
    (**iii**) equilateral.

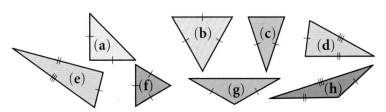

2 Write the number of axes of symmetry for
  (**a**) an equilateral triangle   (**b**) an isosceles triangle   (**c**) a scalene triangle.

3 (**a**) How many equilateral triangles can you see in this design?
  (**b**) How many axes of symmetry does it have?

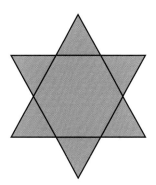

4 For each triangle find (**i**) the length of the red side
                        (**ii**) the size of the angle marked by the red dot

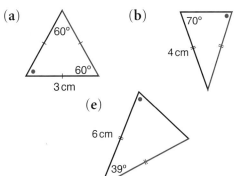

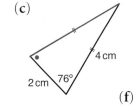

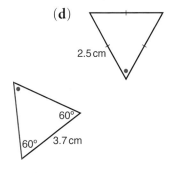

10.5 Angles in triangles

An **acute-angled** triangle has every angle acute.

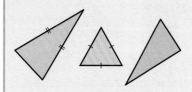

A **right-angled** triangle has one right angle.

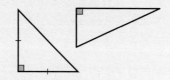

An **obtuse-angled** triangle has one obtuse angle.

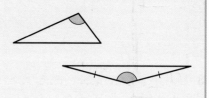

Exercise 10.5

1 Use the letters to list the triangles which are

(**a**) acute-angled   (**b**) right-angled   (**c**) obtuse-angled.

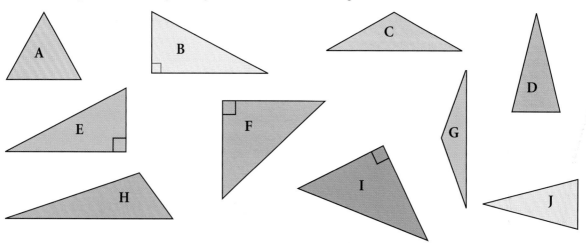

10.6 Angles and sides

Triangles can be described by both angles and sides. This triangle is both **right-angled** and **isosceles**.

Exercise 10.6

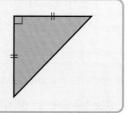

1 Use the letters to list the triangles which are

(**a**) obtuse-angled
(**b**) isosceles
(**c**) both obtuse-angled and isosceles.

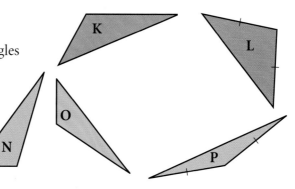

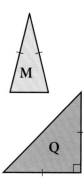

2 Use the letters to list the triangles which are

(**a**) acute-angled

(**b**) scalene

(**c**) acute-angled and scalene.

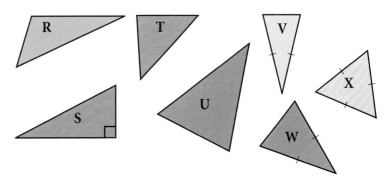

3 A diagonal divides each of these quadrilaterals into two identical triangles. What type of triangle makes each quadrilateral?

(**a**)

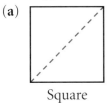

Square

(**b**)

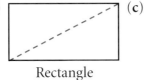

Rectangle

(**c**)

Rhombus

(**d**)

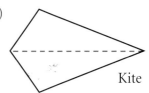

Kite

(**e**)

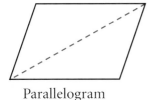

Parallelogram

(**f**)

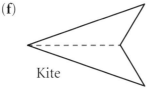

Kite

(**g**)

Rhombus

4 (**a**) Plot the following sets of points on squared paper.
Use separate coordinate diagrams for each set of points.
In each case join the points to make a triangle.

Triangle L	$(1, 1), (6, 2), (4, 3)$
Triangle M	$(1, 1), (1, 3), (8, 2)$
Triangle N	$(8, 2), (5, 5), (2, 2)$
Triangle T	$(2, 0), (5, 6), (6, 0)$
Triangle P	$(2, 7), (4, 4), (2, 1)$
Triangle Q	$(1, 3), (3, 5), (7, 1)$
Triangle R	$(1, 1), (3, 4), (8, 6)$
Triangle S	$(0, 0), (5, 0), (0, 5)$

(**b**) Copy the table. Enter the letters of the triangles in the correct space in the table.

	Acute-angled	Right-angled	Obtuse-angled
Isosceles			
Scalene			L

10.7 Perimeter and area

Perimeter
is the **total distance** around the outside edge of a shape.

The units for perimeter are millimetres, centimetres, metres and kilometres.

Area
is the **surface** covered by a shape.

The **units** for area are square millimetres, square centimetres, square metres and square kilometres.

Example

Calculate the perimeter and area of the rectangular painting.

Perimeter = length + breadth + length + breadth
$$= 35 + 25 + 35 + 25$$
$$= 120 \, cm$$

Area $\quad$ = length × breadth
$$= 35 \times 25$$
$$= 875 \, cm^2$$

25 cm

35 cm

Exercise 10.7

1 Calculate the perimeter and area of each shape.

(a)
8 cm
12 cm

(b)
9 cm
9 cm

(c) 7 mm
15 mm
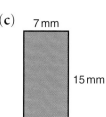

(d) 25 mm
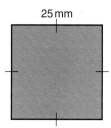

2 Measure each side in centimetres, then calculate the perimeter and area of each shape.

(a)

(b)
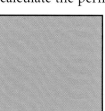

(c)

(d)
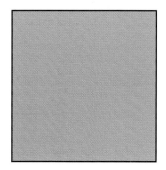

(e)

10.8 Area of a right-angled triangle

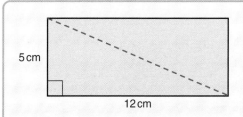
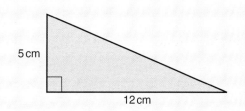

Area of rectangle = length × breadth
= 12 × 5
= 60 cm²

Area of triangle = ½ of the area of the rectangle
= ½ × 60
= 30 cm²

Example Calculate the area of the triangle.
Area of rectangle = 8 × 10 = 80 cm²
So, area of triangle = ½ × 80
= **40 cm²**

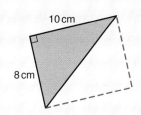

Exercise 10.8

1 Calculate the area of each right-angled triangle.

(**a**)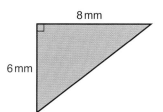

b)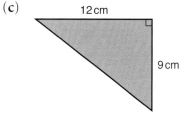

(**c**)

(**d**)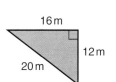

(**e**)

(**f**)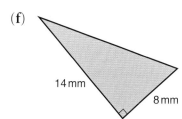

2 Calculate the perimeter and area of each triangle.

(**a**)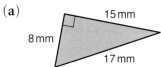

(**b**)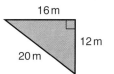

(**c**)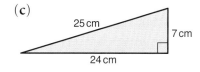

(**d**)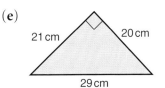

(**e**)

(**f**)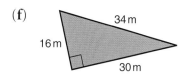

10.9 Areas of composite shapes

More complicated shapes can be split into section to find the area.

Example Calculate the total area of this shape.

Area of red rectangle $= 5 \times 4 = 20\,cm^2$
Area of green rectangle $= 3 \times 2 = 6\,cm^2$
Area of blue square $= 2 \times 2 = \underline{4\,cm^2}$

Total area $= \mathbf{30\,cm^2}$

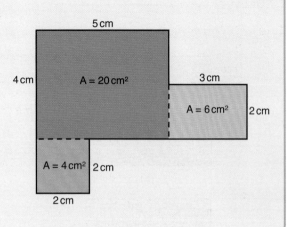

Exercise 10.9

1 Calculate the total area of each shape.

(a)

(b)

(c)

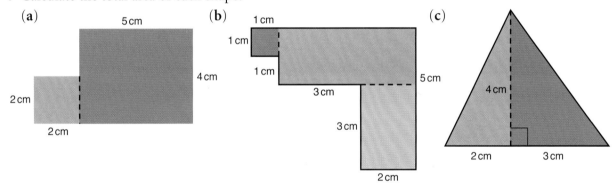

2 (a) Sketch each shape.
  (b) Use dotted lines to divide the shape into rectangles, squares or triangles.
  (c) Calculate the total area of each.

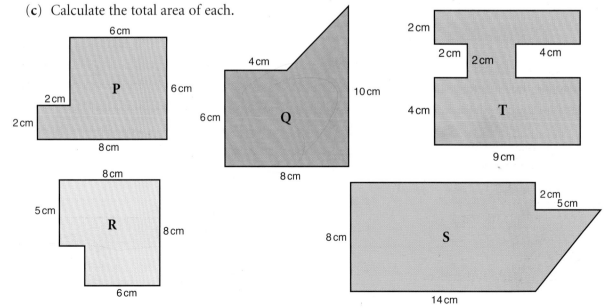

10.10 Conservation of area

Exercise 10.10

1 (**a**) Calculate the area of each shape.

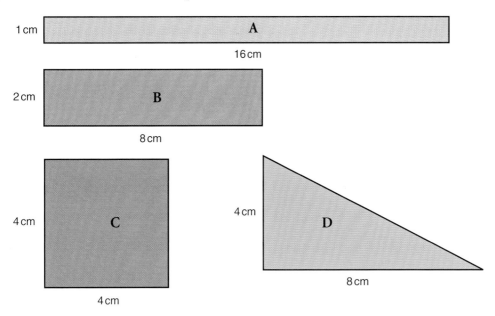

(**b**) What do you notice about your answers?

2 (**a**) Make a sketch of each shape and calculate its area.
    (**i**) Rectangle 4 cm by 9 cm   (**ii**) Rectangle 3 cm by 12 cm
   (**iii**) Square of side 6 cm   (**iv**) Right-angled triangle with base 9 cm and height 8 cm
(**b**) What do you notice about your answers?

3 Sketch four different rectangles with an area of 24 cm². The side lengths must be whole numbers.

4 (**a**) Calculate the area of this rectangle.
(**b**) What size of square has the same area as this rectangle?

5 The square and the rectangle have the same area.
(**a**) Calculate the area of the square.
(**b**) Calculate the length of the rectangle.

6 The triangle, square and rectangle have the same area. Calculate
(**a**) the side length of the square
(**b**) the breadth of the rectangle.

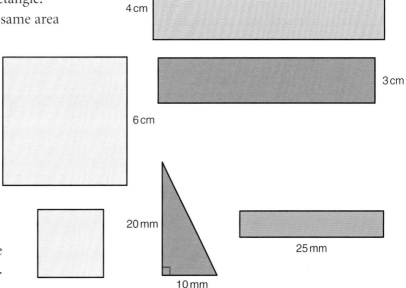

Review exercise 10

1 Copy and complete the table.

	Shape	Name	Regular or not	Number of sides	Number of angles	Number of diagonals
(a)						
(b)						
(c)						

2 Which of the following statements are true for **(a)** a rectangle **(b)** a square?
  (i) All sides are equal.
 (ii) All angles are equal.
(iii) The shape has 4 axes of symmetry.
 (iv) The diagonals are equal.
  (v) The diagonals bisect each other.
 (vi) The diagonals are perpendicular.

3 Describe each triangle in two ways.

  (a)   **(b)**   **(c)**   **(d)**

4 Calculate the perimeter and area of each shape.

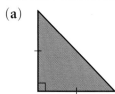
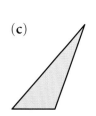
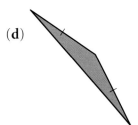
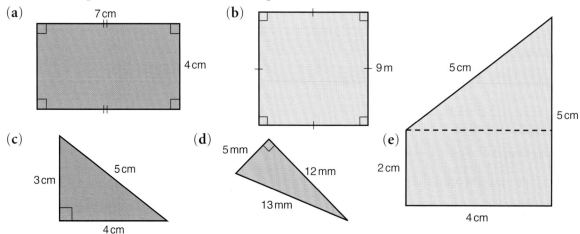

Summary

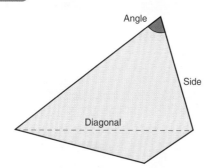

Regular shapes have equal sides.

Properties

Rectangle   **Square**

Types of triangles

By sides   **By angles**

Equilateral   Acute-angled

Isosceles   Right-angled

Scalene   Obtuse-angled

Perimeter

The total distance around the outside edge of a shape.

$$P = 6 + 5 + 5 + 4$$
$$= 20 \, \text{cm}$$

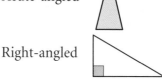

Area

Rectangle   **Square**   **Triangle**
Area = length × breadth   Area = length × length   Area = $\frac{1}{2}$ of area of surrounding rectangle

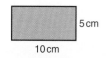   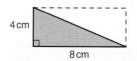

Area = 10 × 5 = 50 cm^2 Area = 6 × 6 = 36 cm^2 Area = $\frac{1}{2}$ × 32 = 16 cm^2

11 Time

In this chapter you will use 12 hour and 24 hour time in everyday situations.

11.1 Measuring time

When measuring time a number of different units may be used:

Remember

60 seconds = 1 minute

60 minutes = 1 hour

24 hours = 1 day

7 days = 1 week

52 weeks = 1 year (approximately)

12 months = 1 year

365 days = 1 year

366 days = 1 leap year

30 days have September, April, June and November.
All the rest have 31, except February alone
With 28 days clear and 29 in each leap year.

Example 1

(**a**) How many hours are in 4 days?

   4 days = 4 × 24 hours

   = 96 hours

(**b**) How many minutes are in 2 days?

   2 days = 2 × 24 hours

   = 48 hours

   = 48 × 60 minutes

   = 2880 minutes

Example 2

How many days are there from 23rd August to 12th October including both dates?

   23rd August to 31st August = 9 days

   September = 30 days

   1st October to 12th October = 12 days

   Total = 9 + 30 + 12

   = 51 days

Exercise 11.1

1 How many:
  (**a**) months are in 3 years   (**b**) weeks are in 2 years
  (**c**) months are in $5\frac{1}{2}$ years   (**d**) minutes are in 4 hours
  (**e**) hours are in 5 days   (**f**) days are in 5 weeks?

2 How many:
  (**a**) minutes are in one week   (**b**) hours are in one year
  (**c**) seconds are in one day   (**d**) minutes are in 3 days
  (**e**) hours are in 5 years   (**f**) minutes are in 3 weeks?

3 If 1st August is a Friday, what day of the week is:
  (**a**) 12th August   (**b**) 15th September   (**c**) 2nd October?

4 If the 12th November is a Tuesday, what day of the week is:
  (**a**) 4th December   (**b**) 25th December   (**c**) 6th January?

5 Carole goes on holiday on 18th August for 3 weeks. On what date should she return?

6 **Including** both dates, how many days are there from:
  (**a**) 3rd July to 18th July   (**b**) 24th May to 5th June
  (**c**) 22nd January to 10th February   (**d**) 28th November to 2nd January
  (**e**) 25th October to 5th December   (**f**) 9th April to 18th August?

7 The first day of summer camp is 10th June and the last day is 4th July.
How many days did the camp last?

8 How many days are between 4th August and 1st November **excluding** both dates?

9 If the 20th June was a Friday, what was the date of the first Wednesday in June?

11.2 Telling the time

We can use the 12 hour clock or the 24 hour clock to tell the time.

12 hour clock

Is 5 o'clock in the morning or the evening? It could be either.

5 a.m. is in the morning.
5 p.m. is in the afternoon or evening.

a.m. means *ante meridiem*
p.m. means *post meridiem*

24 hour clock

There is no need to use a.m. or p.m.
5 a.m. becomes 0500 hours and 5 p.m. becomes 1700 hours.

Example 1 Write 2.15 p.m. in 24 hour clock time and in words.
2.15 p.m. = 1415 hours = quarter past two in the afternoon

Example 2 Write 0450 in 12 hour clock time and in words.
0450 = 4.50 a.m. = ten to five in the morning

Exercise 11.2

1 Write these times in 12 hour time:
   (**a**) quarter past one in the afternoon
   (**b**) quarter to nine in the morning
   (**c**) twenty five past eleven at night
   (**d**) ten to seven in the evening
   (**e**) five minutes before midnight
   (**f**) twenty minutes after noon

2 Write these times in 12 hour time and words.

(**a**) 0345 hours   (**b**) 2020 hours   (**c**) 1625 hours

(**d**) 1100 hours   (**e**) 1330 hours   (**f**) 0920 hours

(**g**) 2300 hours   (**h**) 0115 hours   (**i**) 0030 hours

3 Write these times in 24 hour time.

(**a**) 6 a.m.   (**b**) 2 p.m.   (**c**) 8 p.m.   (**d**) 10.45 p.m.

(**e**) 11.15 a.m.   (**f**) 3.17 a.m.   (**g**) 3.45 p.m.   (**h**) 12.05 p.m.

4 Write these times using 12 hour and 24 hour time.

(**a**) 25 minutes after 10.25 p.m.

(**b**) 20 minutes after 1.40 p.m.

(**c**) three quarters of an hour after 2.30 p.m.

(**d**) 20 minutes before 12.15 p.m.

(**e**) 20 minutes before ten to six in the evening

(**f**) 10 minutes before 11.05 a.m.

11.3 Calculating time intervals

Example 1

Calculate the length of time between (**a**) 9.15 a.m. and 3.05 p.m.

                                                     (**b**) 10.15 p.m. and 4.35 a.m.

(**a**)

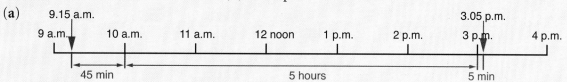

Total time   45 minutes + 5 hours + 5 minutes

                 = **5 hours 50 minutes**

(**b**)

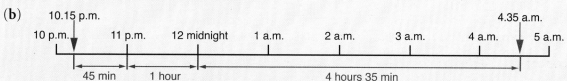

Total time   45 minutes + 1 hour + 4 hours 35 minutes

                 = 5 hours 80 minutes

                 = **6 hours 20 minutes**

Example 2

A plane leaves Glasgow at 2250 hours and arrives in Miami $6\frac{1}{2}$ hours later. At what time did it arrive?

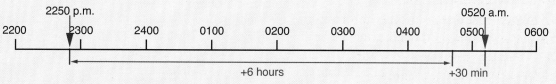

The plane arrived at **0520 hours**.

Exercise 11.3

1 Calculate the length of time between:
- (**a**) 11 a.m. and 6 p.m.
- (**b**) 0800 and 2000 hours
- (**c**) 1530 and 2130 hours
- (**d**) 10 p.m. and 5 a.m.
- (**e**) 2200 and 0400 hours
- (**f**) 11.15 p.m. and 10.15 a.m.
- (**g**) Noon and 3.18 p.m.
- (**h**) 3.25 p.m. and 8.05 p.m.
- (**i**) 10.20 a.m. and 11.30 a.m.
- (**j**) 2048 and 2145 hours
- (**k**) 1520 and 1830 hours
- (**l**) 11.05 p.m. and 5 a.m.
- (**m**) 2250 and 0210 hours
- (**n**) 1724 and 0115 hours
- (**o**) 3.10 p.m. and 8.57 p.m.
- (**p**) 1618 and 0845 hours

2 Supersave have a 3 hour photo developing service.
If Tamiza puts a film in at 11.25 a.m., at what time will it be ready?

3 The train journey from Edinburgh to Newcastle takes 1 hour 45 minutes.
If the early evening train leaves Edinburgh at 1843 hours, at what time
should it arrive in Newcastle?

4 (**a**) What time does the 1845 programme finish?
- (**b**) What time does the last showing finish?
- (**c**) Sarita is going to the cinema to see The Puzzle and has to get the last
  bus home at 10.05 p.m. It will take her 10 minutes to walk to the bus stop.
  What is the latest starting time she could see the film and still catch the bus?

5 (**a**) Prabhu's time for the London marathon in 2003 was 3 hours 50 min.
  He crossed the start line at 9.25 a.m. What time did he finish?
- (**b**) Danielle crossed the start line at 9.20 a.m. and finished at 12.54 p.m.
  How long did she take?

6 Pete, Mike and David are going on holiday.

Pete's dad is driving them to the airport and will have to pick each of them up using the route shown. The diagram shows the time taken for each stage of the journey.

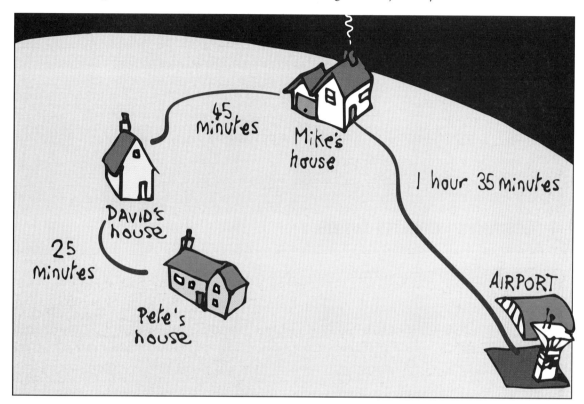

(a) Calculate the total expected travelling time to the airport.
(b) The boys need to be at the airport by 10 p.m.
What is the latest time that Pete's dad should leave his house?
(c) If they actually leave Mike's house at 7.06 p.m.,
  (i) what time should they arrive at the airport
  (ii) how many minutes would they have to spare?

7 Use this bus timetable to answer the following questions.

Edinburgh	1040	1105	1135	1205	1230	1245	1305
South Gyle	1100	1125	1155	1225	—	1305	1325
Kirkliston	1120	1145	1215	1245	—	1325	1345
Linlithgow	1152	1217	1247	1317	—	1357	1417
Stirling	1232	1257	1327	1357	1402	1437	1457

(a) How long does the journey from Edinburgh to Linlithgow take?
(b) Mr Brown lives in Kirkliston and has to be in Stirling for 1.10 p.m.
Which bus should he take?
(c) The next bus leaves Edinburgh at 1.45 p.m.
What time should it arrive in Kirkliston?
(d) The 1230 is an express bus. How long does this bus take to get to Stirling?
(e) How much quicker than the other buses is the express bus?

8 The flight from Glasgow to Rhodes takes 6 hours 20 minutes.

(**a**) Pat's flight was due to leave at 2245 on Monday the 23rd July.
At what time would it arrive in Rhodes?

(**b**) If the flight was delayed by 2 hours 25 minutes at what time did
the flight actually leave?

9 Andrew has made a list of the lectures he wants to go to in the science festival:

The Animal Kingdom	9.15 a.m. – 10.15 a.m.
The Colour of Money	11.40 a.m. – 12.45 p.m.
Number Magic	2.15 p.m. – 3.10 p.m.
Science at the Cinema	7.15 p.m. – 9.05 p.m.

(**a**) Calculate the length of time for each lecture.

(**b**) What is the total time in hours and minutes spent at the lectures?

11.4 Measuring shorter times

> Remember Small periods of time may be measured using minutes and seconds
> 1 minute = 60 seconds
> 2 minutes = 120 seconds
> 3 minutes = 180 seconds
>
> **Example 1** Change 225 seconds into minutes and seconds.
> 225 sec = 180 sec + 45 secs
>   = **3 mins 45 secs**
>
> **Example 2** Two songs on a CD lasted 2 minutes 53 seconds and
> 3 minutes 35 seconds. What was the total playing time?
>
> 2 mins 53 secs + 3 mins 35 secs
> = 5 mins 88 secs
> = **6 mins 28 secs**

Exercise 11.4

1 Change these times to minutes and seconds:

(**a**) 70 seconds   (**b**) 105 seconds   (**c**) 170 seconds

(**d**) 200 seconds   (**e**) 240 seconds   (**f**) 350 seconds

2 It took an athlete 2 minutes 34 seconds to run 1 lap of a track.
If he continued at this speed, how long would it take him to run

(**a**) 2 laps   (**b**) 3 laps   (**c**) 5 laps   (**d**) 10 laps?

3 In a school sports relay race the
A team's times for each lap were:

> Lisa　　1 minute 56 seconds
> Al　　　1 minute 50 seconds
> Joan　　1 minute 25 seconds
> Lee　　 1 minute 32 seconds

(**a**) Who ran the fastest lap?

(**b**) What was the team's total time?

4 In the 400 metre time trials, Ben's three times were 59.21 seconds,
57.03 seconds and 56.80 seconds.
Alf's times were 59.05 seconds, 57.33 seconds and 56.92 seconds.

(**a**) What was the difference between Ben's fastest and slowest time?

(**b**) What was the total time for Alf's 3 races?

(**c**) Who had the fastest total time and by how much?

5

OLYMPIC 100 METRE SPRINT TIMES		
YEAR	WOMEN'S 100M	MEN'S 100M
1928	12·2s	10·8s
2000	10·75s	9·87s

(**a**) How much faster was the men's 1928 time than the women's 1928 time?

(**b**) How much faster was the men's 2000 time than the women's 2000 time?

(**c**) What is the difference between the women's 1928 time and 2000 time?

(**d**) What is the difference between the men's 1928 time and 2000 time?

6 The 1998 women's snowboarding slalom was won by France with a time of
2 minutes 17.34 seconds. Germany came second with a time of 2 minutes 19.17 seconds.
How much faster was the French time?

11.5 Average speed

Example 1

Bob cycled 24 miles in 3 hours. What was his average speed in miles per hour?

	Time	Distance
÷3 ⤵	3	24	÷3
	1	8

Bob's speed is **8 miles per hour**.

Example 2

Maureen can type 20 words in 30 seconds. What is her average speed in words per minute?

	Time	Words
×2 ⤵	30 sec	20	×2
	60 sec	40

Maureen's speed is **40 words per minute**.

Exercise 11.5

Work with a partner for questions 1 and 2.

You need a stopwatch for question 1.

1 Copy out as much of the passage as you can in 30 seconds.
Your partner should time you.

> The small girl smiles. One eyelid flickers.
> She whips a pistol from her knickers.
> She aims it at the creature's head
> And bang bang bang, she shoots him dead.
> A few weeks later, in the wood, I came across Miss Riding Hood.
> But what a change! No cloak of red,
> No silly hood upon her head.
> She said, 'Hello, and do please note
> My lovely furry WOLFSKIN COAT.'
> (Extract from Roald Dahl's Little Red Riding Hood and the Wolf)

(**a**) How many words can you write in 30 seconds?

(**b**) What is your average speed in words per minute?

You need a stopwatch and a trundle wheel or tape measure for question 2.

2 Measure how far you can walk in 10 seconds. Your partner should time you.
   (**a**) How far can you walk in 10 seconds?
   (**b**) What was your average speed in metres per minute?

3 A train travels 120 miles in 2 hours.
   What is its average speed in miles per hour?

4 (**a**) Mr Rigg travels 25 miles in half an hour.
       If he continues at this speed how far will he travel in one hour?
   (**b**) The speed limit on the road is 60 miles per hour.
       Will he break the speed limit?

5 Tim walked 2 kilometres in half an hour.
   What was his average speed in kilometres per hour?

6 It took the Brown family 2 hours to travel the 106 miles from Edinburgh to Newcastle. What was their average speed in miles per hour?

7 Bikram cycled the 24 miles to his grandmother's house in 3 hours.
   What was his average speed in miles per hour?

8 Amy works from home painting Christmas decorations.
   If it takes her six minutes to paint an ornament,
   (**a**) how many will she paint in 1 hour?
   (**b**) how long, in hours and minutes, will it take her to paint
       14 decorations?
   (**c**) how many decorations will she paint in $2\frac{1}{2}$ hours?

Review exercise 11

1 How many minutes are in:
   (**a**) 4 days
   (**b**) 3 weeks?

2 Mina's local library lends books for three weeks. She borrowed a book from the library on the 24th April 2002 and the librarian stamped the book to be returned on 14.5.02. Was this correct? Give a reason for your answer.

DOWNTOWN LIBRARY	
Return date	
16.8.01	14.5.02
27.10.01	
11.11.01	
20.02.02	

3 Summer holidays in Huffingdon High School run from the 27th June to the 15th August including both dates. How many days do the summer holidays last?

4 Write these times using 24 hour time.

(**a**) 7.30 a.m.   (**b**) 9.15 p.m.   (**c**) 5.45 p.m.

(**d**) 12.20 a.m.   (**e**) 12.45 p.m.   (**f**) 10.45 a.m.

5 Write these times using 12 hour time.

(**a**) 1535 hours   (**b**) 1155 hours   (**c**) 2205 hours

(**d**) 0015 hours   (**e**) 0643 hours   (**f**) 1219 hours

6 Paulo is at the shops with his aunt. At 2.45 p.m. Paulo goes to the cinema with some friends and agrees to meet his aunt again at 5.20 p.m. How much time does Paulo have with his friends?

7 The 1825 bus from Aberdeen takes 4 hours 45 minutes to reach Edinburgh. At what time should it arrive?

Aberdeen	dep.	1825
Edinburgh	arr.	

8 The Stensons decided to drive overnight to their hotel. They left home at 10.15 p.m. and arrived at the hotel at 6.45 a.m. the next morning. How long did their journey take?

9 In a local swimming competition Tina's time was 41.36 seconds and Tim's time was 42.08 seconds. Who was faster and by how much?

10 Coral cycles 15 kilometres in 20 minutes. What is her average speed in kilometres per hour?

11 The Patel family took 8 hours to travel from Glasgow to London, a distance of 420 miles. If they stopped for an hour for lunch, what was their average speed?

Summary

There are many units for measuring time.

$$60 \text{ seconds} = 1 \text{ minute}$$
$$60 \text{ minutes} = 1 \text{ hour}$$
$$24 \text{ hours} = 1 \text{ day}$$
$$7 \text{ days} = 1 \text{ week}$$
$$52 \text{ weeks} = 1 \text{ year (approximately)}$$
$$12 \text{ months} = 1 \text{ year}$$
$$365 \text{ days} = 1 \text{ year}$$
$$366 \text{ days} = 1 \text{ leap year}$$

30 days have September, April, June and November.
All the rest have 31 except February alone,
with 28 days clear and 29 in each leap year.

You can use 12 hour or 24 hour clock to tell the time.

Use a.m. for times before 12 noon
and p.m. for times after 12 noon.

Time intervals

A number line can be used to calculate time intervals.

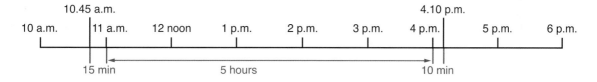

From 10.45 a.m. to 4.10 p.m. is 15 mins + 5 hours + 10 mins
$$= 5 \text{ hours } 25 \text{ minutes.}$$

Average speed

James walked 16 miles in 4 hours. What was his average speed?

Time	Distance
$\div 4 \begin{array}{c} 4 \\ 1 \end{array}$	$\begin{array}{c} 16 \\ 4 \end{array} \div 4$

His average speed was 4 miles per hour.

12 Information handling

In this chapter you will learn how to interpret and display information.

12.1 Interpreting tables

Information is often easier to understand when it is presented in a table.

The table shows the number of first year pupils in Alnwath Academy.

Class	Boys	Girls
1B1	16	12
1B2	15	12
1F1	14	13
1F2	11	15
1W1	12	13
1W2	15	11

Class 1F1 has 14 boys and 13 girls.

Exercise 12.1

1 Look at the table above.
  (**a**) How many boys are there in class 1W1?
  (**b**) Which class has the fewest pupils?
  (**c**) How many more boys than girls are there?

2 The table shows ticket prices for the Alnwath Theatre.

Area of theatre	Day of performance			
	Wed	Thur	Fri	Sat
Stalls	£8	£8	£9	£12
Circle	£9	£9	£11	£15
Upper circle	£5	£5	£6	£6

  (**a**) How much is a ticket for the stalls for the Friday performance?
  (**b**) Which is the most expensive area of the theatre?
  (**c**) Calculate the total cost of three tickets for the upper circle on Saturday.
  (**d**) Children's tickets are half price.
       How much is a child's ticket for the circle on a Friday?

3 Airline seats are designed to fit **average** body dimensions.
  The table shows some of the dimensions in inches.

	Female	Male
Hand length	6.4	8.2
Hand breadth	3.2	4.4
Elbow to wrist	9.6	12.0
Foot breadth	3.2	4.3
Foot length	8.7	11.2
Head breadth	5.4	6.4

  (**a**) What is the average female foot length?
  (**b**) What is the average male hand breadth?
  (**c**) Which female dimension measures 9.6 inches?
  (**d**) On average how much broader is a male head than a female head?
  (**e**) How much longer is a male foot than a female foot?

4 The prices of short break holidays to Helsinki are shown in the table.

Holiday date	Number of nights	Price, £	Number of nights	Price, £	Extra night price, £
Jan–Apr	2	209	3	249	42
May–Aug	2	239	3	279	45
Sept–Dec	2	215	3	255	43

(**a**) How much is a 3 night break in April?

(**b**) How much is a 2 night break in October?

(**c**) What would 4 nights in July cost?

> Find the cost for 3 nights.
> Add on the extra night price.

(**d**) (**i**) Which is cheaper, 3 nights in August or 4 nights in February?

  (**ii**) How much cheaper is it?

5 A number of airlines fly from Chicago to San Francisco.
The flight times and prices are shown in the table.

Flight number	Departs	Arrives	Cost, $
RE1351	1210	1650	346
RE1371	0700	1150	321
AM231	1235	1705	360
AM241	0915	1400	360
AM251	1100	1545	345
GA0035	1220	1715	318
UA0401	1940	0040	306
UA0501	1410	1905	335

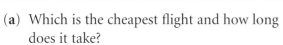

(**a**) Which is the cheapest flight and how long does it take?

(**b**) How long is flight number GA0035?

(**c**) If you had to be in San Francisco by 1pm which flight would you take?

(**d**) Aruna arrived in San Francisco at 5.05pm. How much did she pay for her flight?

6 Age and cholesterol level influence the chances of heart disease.
The table below shows the percentage risk of heart disease based on these factors.

Cholesterol level	Percentage risk of heart disease			
	Age 40–49	Age 50–59	Age 60–69	Age 70–79
less than 160	1	1	1	1
160–199	1	1	1	1
200–239	2	1	1	1
240–279	4	1	1	1
over 279	6	5	1	1

What is the percentage risk of heart disease for each person?

(**a**) Susan: age 45, cholesterol level 260

(**b**) Colin: age 62, cholesterol level 250

(**c**) Sarah: age 69, cholesterol level 150

(**d**) Claire: age 53, cholesterol level 285

12.2 Creating tables

Organising information into a table makes it easier to use.
An ICT company stocks monitors of different sizes and qualities.
The number of each size and type can be recorded in a table.

Size	Quality of resolution		
	Low	Medium	High
12	3	2	
14	1		
15	1		

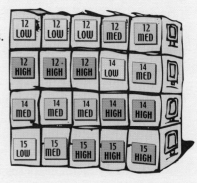

Exercise 12.2

1 Copy the table above and complete it to show the number of each type and size of monitor.

2 Derek has to check the number of pairs of jeans in stock.

(**a**) Copy the table below and complete it for the jeans shown.

Leg length	Jean sizes			
	8	10	12	14
Short (S)				
Medium (M)				
Long (L)				

(**b**) How many size 12 jeans are there?

(**c**) Which leg length is the most common?

3 In a shoe shop Marie-Claire is recording the stock.
She notes down all the sizes for Target trainers.

(**a**) Copy and complete the table.

Width	Size				
	38	39	40	41	42
D					
E					
F					

(**b**) How many trainers are there in an E fitting?

4 Suits come in various chest sizes and sleeve lengths.
Create a table to show how many of each type of suit are in stock.

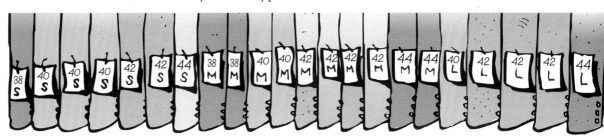

12.3 Bar graphs

Information may be shown on a **bar graph**.
This bar graph shows the average
number of hours of sunshine
per day on the Costa del Sol.

Check the vertical scale carefully when
you read the graph.

Each axis must be labelled.

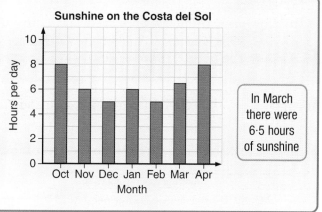

In March
there were
6·5 hours
of sunshine

Exercise 12.3

1 The bar graph shows the percentage of pupils
achieving level E in mathematics over 5 years.
  (**a**) What percentage scored level E in 2000?
  (**b**) Between which two years was there no
    change in the percentage passing?
  (**c**) How much better were the results in
    2002 than in 1999?
  (**d**) Between which two years was there a
    ten percent increase?

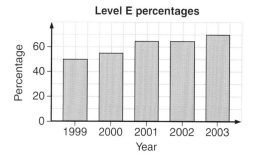

2 The bar graph shows the numbers of pupils
in different classes at Alnwath Academy.
  (**a**) How many girls are there in 2B2?
  (**b**) How many boys are there in 2W1?
  (**c**) How many pupils are there in 2F2?
  (**d**) Which class has the most boys?
  (**e**) Which class has more boys than girls?

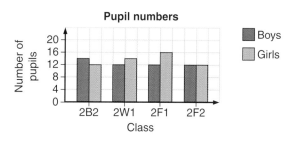

3 Alnwath Academy conducted a one day
survey of food choices in the school canteen.
The bar graph shows the results.
  (**a**) How many pupils chose salad?
  (**b**) Which is more popular, baked potato
    or burgers?
  (**c**) How many more people chose
    pasta than pizza?
  (**d**) Alnwath has been involved in
    a healthy eating campaign.
    Do you think it is working?
    Give a reason for your answer.

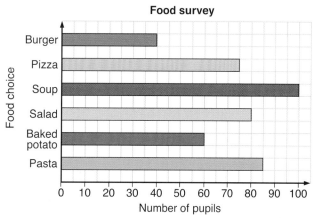

4 The graph shows the number of children under 5
who live on a local housing estate.
   (**a**) How many children under 1 are there?
   (**b**) How many children will be aged 5 next birthday?
   (**c**) Altogether how many children are aged under 3?

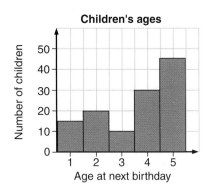

W You may use worksheet 12.1 for questions 5, 6 and 7.

5 (**a**) Use the table below to draw a bar graph of the hours of sunshine in Malaga.

Month	Average winter hours of sunshine in Malaga per day
Oct	8
Nov	7
Dec	6
Jan	6.5
Feb	7.5
Mar	7
Apr	9.5

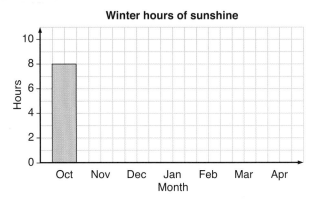

   (**b**) Which is the sunniest month?
   (**c**) Between which two months is there the biggest increase?

6 (**a**) Use the table below to draw a bar graph of baby birthweights.

Birthweight in kg	Number of babies
2.0–2.4	2
2.5–2.9	4
3.0–3.4	9
3.5–3.9	15
4.0–4.4	5
4.5–4.9	3

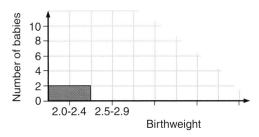

   (**b**) How many babies had a birthweight of less than 3 kg?
   (**c**) How many babies weighed 4 kg or more at birth?

7 (**a**) Use the table of information to draw a
bar graph of where pupils lunch.

Class	Where pupils lunch	
	Dining hall	At home
5A	14	8
5B	12	4
5C	6	10
6A	11	9
6B	9	7

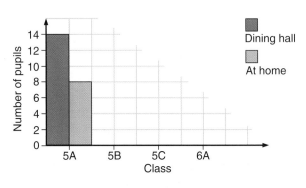

   (**b**) In which class do most pupils prefer to go home for lunch?
   (**c**) Which class uses the dining hall the most?

12.4 Line graphs

Information may be shown on a **line graph**.
The graph shows the air temperature measured over a 24-hour period.
You must read the scale carefully.

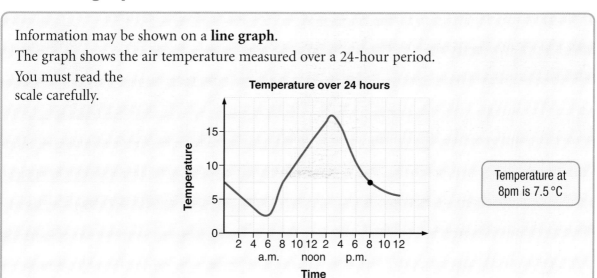

Temperature at 8pm is 7.5 °C

Exercise 12.4

1 From the graph above:
  (**a**) What was the temperature at 2 a.m.?
  (**b**) What was the highest temperature during the day?
  (**c**) How much did the temperature fall between 6 and 8p.m.?

2 The line graph shows the average monthly rainfall at Eskdalemuir weather station.
  (**a**) Which was the driest month of the year?
  (**b**) By how much did the rainfall increase between September and October?
  (**c**) What was the total rainfall in June, July and August?

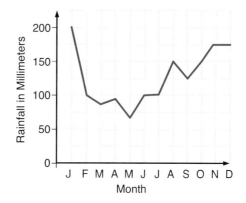

3 Life expectancy in Britain has been rising steadily since 1900. The graph shows the life expectancy for males and females during a 100 year period.
  (**a**) What was the life expectancy for females in 1940?
  (**b**) What was the life expectancy for males in 1980?
  (**c**) By how much did female life expectancy increase from 1950 to 2000?
  (**d**) Life expectancy dropped for males during the 1940s. Can you think of a reason for this?

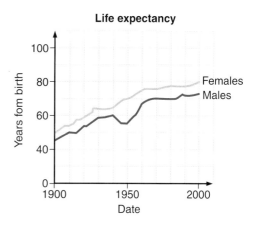

You may use worksheet 12.2 for questions 4, 5 and 6.

4 The table shows the temperature in Glasgow at noon each day for a week.

Day	Mon	Tues	Wed	Thurs	Fri	Sat	Sun
Temperature in °C	15	16	12	18	19	15	14

(a) Draw a graph of the temperature in Glasgow.
(b) On which day was the temperature lowest?
(c) On which days was the temperature the same?
(d) How much did the temperature rise between Wednesday and Friday?

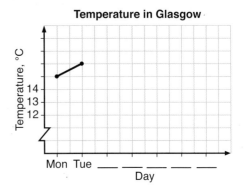

5 The table shows the number of vehicles at a busy junction during the morning rush hour.

Time of day	0700	0715	0730	0745	0800	0815	0830	0845	0900
Number of vehicles	7	9	21	25	31	23	20	11	12

(a) Draw a graph of the number of vehicles during the rush hour.
(b) Which is the busiest time?
(c) Between which two times is the sharpest rise in the number of vehicles?

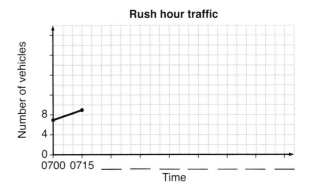

6 The table shows the depth of water in Vigo harbour throughout the day.

Time	6a.m.	7a.m.	8a.m.	9a.m.	10a.m.	12noon	1p.m.	3p.m.	5p.m.	7p.m.
Depth in m	2.4	2	2.4	5.2	8	8.4	6.8	3.6	2	2.4

(a) Draw a graph of the depth of water in Vigo harbour.
(b) How deep was the water at 8am?
(c) At approximately what times was the water 3m deep?
(d) A ship needs a depth of at least 5.2 m. Between which times could the ship enter Vigo harbour?

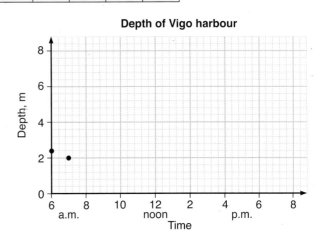

12.5 Frequency tables

Information may be grouped using a **frequency table**.

For each figure make a **tally mark** at the appropriate place.

Count the tally marks to complete the frequency column.

From the table, 9 pupils scored between 10 and 14.

Test scores

15	17	10	10
9	13	14	8
19	3	14	12
13	14	11	16

Test score	Tally marks	Frequency
0–4	\	1
5–9	\\	2
10–14	⊬⊬ \\\\	9
15–19	\\\\	4

Exercise 12.5

W You may use worksheets pages 12.3 and 12.4 for this exercise.

1 Use the frequency table above to draw a bar graph.

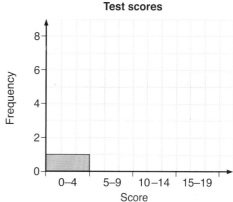

Test scores

2 Here are some football scores for one Saturday last year.

Chelsea 1 Arsenal 2 Nottingham 2 Liverpool 3
Everton 1 Ipswich 1 Southampton 3 Sheffield 2
Leeds Utd 3 Manchester City 0 Stoke City 4 Coventry 0
Leicester 2 Huddersfield 0 Tottenham 4 Wolverhampton 1
Manchester Utd 1 Derby County 0 West Ham 0 Crystal Palace 0
Newcastle 2 West Bromwich 1

(a) Copy and complete the frequency table for the number of goals scored.

Goals scored	Tally marks	Frequency
0		
1		
2		
3		
4		

(b) Draw a bar graph using the information in the frequency table.
(c) How many teams scored 3 goals?

3 These are the weights of pupils in class 1F2.

37   41   28   42   33   38   34   29   41   38   39   35
37   43   29   47   41   30   40   36   33   46   42   40

(a) Copy and complete the frequency table.

Weight interval	Tally marks	Frequency
25–29		
30–34		
35–39		
40–44		
45–49		

(b) How many pupils weigh more than 39 kg?

(c) Draw a bar graph.

4 These are the heights in cm of class 2B1.

138   140   144   152   148   142   136   153   159   143
154   137   139   146   162   165   154   153   172   129

(a) Copy and complete the frequency table.

Height interval	Tally marks	Frequency
120–129		
130–139		
140–149		
150–159		
160–169		
170–179		

(b) Draw a bar graph to display the information from the table.

(c) How many pupils in total are under 160 cm tall?

5 These are the scores in a golf competition:

66   70   69   68   73   74   72   77   77   80   69
66   78   72   78   79   78   71   78   81   78   73

(a) Copy and complete the frequency table for the golf scores.

Golf scores	Tally marks	Frequency
66–68		
69–71		
72–74		
75–77		
78–80		
81–83		

(b) Draw a bar graph from the frequency table.

(c) How many players scored under 75?

6 A set of maximum temperatures across Europe is shown below.

15 23 32 12 24 26 26 23 17 23 32 12 17
14 28 29 30 31 27 28 32 19 28 19 26 27

(**a**) Copy and complete the frequency table.

Temperatures	Tally marks	Frequency
12–16		
17–21		
22–26		
27–31		
32–36		

(**b**) Draw a bar graph from the frequency table.
(**c**) How often was the temperature above 26 °C?

12.6 Pie charts

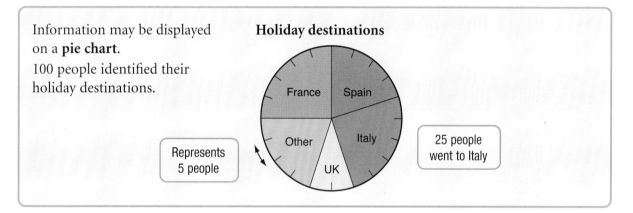

Information may be displayed on a **pie chart**.
100 people identified their holiday destinations.

Holiday destinations

Represents 5 people

25 people went to Italy

Exercise 12.6

1 From the pie chart above:
(**a**) How many people went to
    (**i**) France   (**ii**) Spain?
(**b**) How many chose other destinations?

2 In a survey, 100 pupils identified the most common after school activity.
(**a**) Use the pie chart to copy and complete the table.

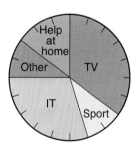

Activity	TV	Sport	IT	Help at home	Other
Number of pupils					

(**b**) How many more people help at home than play sport?

3 60 teachers picked their favourite after-school clubs.
(**a**) How many teachers chose IT?
(**b**) How many teachers picked music?
(**c**) In total, how many picked debating and football?

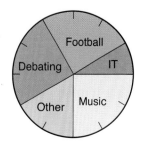

4 Class 1F2 observed the colour of the first 60 vehicles passing the school gate.
The pie chart shows the results.

(a) Which is the most common colour?

(b) How many more red than blue vehicles were there?

(c) In total, how many red, white and blue vehicles were there?

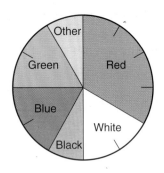

5 The pie chart shows the main government sources of income.

(a) Which is the largest source of income?

(b) List the sources of income in order of importance, from most important to least.

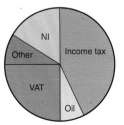

Review exercise 12

1 The table shows the birth month of pupils in sixth year.

Month	Jan	Feb	Mar	Apr	May	Jun	Jul	Aug	Sep	Oct	Nov	Dec
Boys	9	4	4	5	6	6	5	5	7	4	5	2
Girls	5	6	9	2	1	7	4	2	0	7	4	5

(a) How many girls were born in June?

(b) How many pupils were born in February?

(c) In which month were most pupils born?

(d) How many boys are there in sixth year?

2 Kerry is checking the stock of shampoo bottles. Copy and complete the table.

	Size in ml		
	200	300	400
Dry	2		
Normal			
Greasy			

3 The bar chart shows the rainfall in Scotland over a six month period.

(a) Which was the wettest month?

(b) Which two months had the same rainfall?

(c) How much rain fell in May?

(d) Between which two months was there the greatest drop in rainfall?

(e) What was the difference in rainfall between January and June?

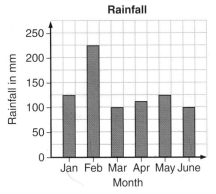

4 During a World Cup competition people were asked
which team they thought would win.
The table shows the result of the survey.

Team chosen	Brazil	Germany	England	Scotland	Italy	France	Argentina
Number of people	24	18	13	12	19	8	21

Copy and complete the bar graph to display this information.

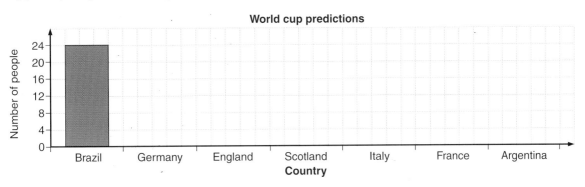

5 The graph shows the cooling curve for naphthalene,
from boiling point to the solid state.

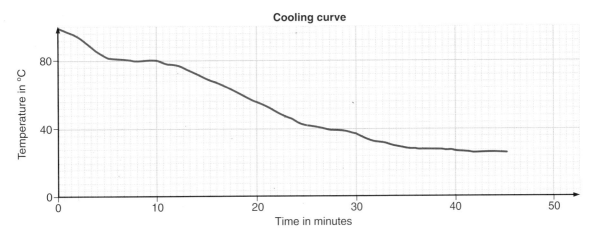

(**a**) After 10 minutes what is the temperature of the naphthalene?

(**b**) What is the temperature after
   (**i**) 17 minutes   (**ii**) 31 minutes   (**iii**) 40 minutes?

(**c**) How long did it take to cool to 56°?

(**d**) How long did it take to reach the solid state?

6 The figures show French test results for class 3F2.

(**a**) Copy and complete the frequency table.

(**b**) How many pupils scored less than 10?

Test score	Tally marks	Frequency
0–4		
5–9		
10–14		
15–19		

10	13	15	15	6	7	12
3	18	7	9	11	13	6
11	12	6	10	8	14	19
19	10	11	4	14	8	13

Summary

Information may be displayed in several ways.

Table

Holiday costs in the Hotel Sol e Mar (£)

Month of travel	Number of nights			
	7	10	14	21
May	299	345	399	499
June	315	369	454	575
July	350	400	495	660

Bar graph

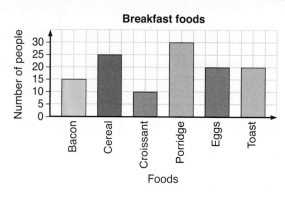

Line graph

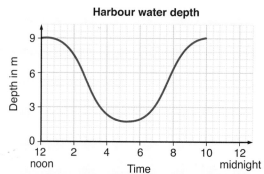

Pie chart

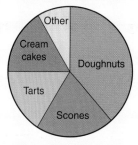

Frequency table

Data may be grouped in a **frequency table**.

```
10    8    12    12    20    5
12    12   18    15    20    6
15    15   10    16    8     16
14    10   16    25    10    20
```

Figure	Tally marks	Frequency
5–9	||||	4
10–14	卌 ||||	9
15–19	卌 ||	7
20–24	|||	3
25–29	|	1

13 Simple algebra

In this chapter you will learn how to solve equations and simplify expressions.

13.1 Letters for numbers

A letter may be used to stand for an unknown number.

Example 1   Find x

$$x + 3 = 7$$
$$\text{✋} + 3 = 7$$
$$x = 4$$

What number plus 3 equals 7?

Example 2   Find a

$$a - 5 = 3$$
$$\text{✋} - 5 = 3$$
$$a = 8$$

What number minus 5 equals 3?

Example 3   Find k

$$6 - k = 4$$
$$k = 2$$

These are examples of **equations**.
Finding an unknown value is called **solving an equation**.
An equation always has an equals sign.

Exercise 13.1

1 Copy and complete to find the unknown number.

(**a**) $x + 2 = 5$
$x =$

(**b**) $y + 4 = 9$
$y =$

(**c**) $b + 2 = 3$
$b =$

(**d**) $p + 5 = 11$
$p =$

(**e**) $x + 9 = 15$
$x =$

(**f**) $y + 14 = 15$
$y =$

(**g**) $c + 2 = 13$
$c =$

(**h**) $q + 5 = 21$
$q =$

(**i**) $h + 12 = 50$
$h =$

(**j**) $z + 14 = 29$
$z =$

(**k**) $e + 22 = 23$
$e =$

(**l**) $p + 15 = 31$
$p =$

(**m**) $x + 20 = 50$
$x =$

(**n**) $k + 24 = 29$
$k =$

(**o**) $y + 21 = 31$
$y =$

(**p**) $d + 8 = 17$
$d =$

(**q**) $x + 23 = 53$
$x =$

(**r**) $y + 41 = 91$
$y =$

(**s**) $b + 12 = 21$
$b =$

(**t**) $p + 55 = 55$
$p =$

2 Find the number for which each letter stands.

(a) $x + 4 = 5$ (b) $y + 7 = 10$ (c) $b + 2 = 7$ (d) $p + 1 = 11$
(e) $y + 7 = 15$ (f) $p + 14 = 19$ (g) $g + 23 = 27$ (h) $j + 21 = 33$
(i) $k + 17 = 25$ (j) $h + 24 = 39$ (k) $v + 34 = 51$ (l) $d + 21 = 21$
(m) $2 + d = 35$ (n) $9 + m = 37$ (o) $23 + k = 127$ (p) $2 + b = 101$
(q) $5 + b = 29$ (r) $11 + f = 4$ (s) $54 + q = 100$ (t) $11 + t = 126$

3 Find each unknown number.

(a) $7 - k = 6$ (b) $5 - k = 3$ (c) $9 - k = 4$ (d) $10 - k = 2$
(e) $8 - c = 1$ (f) $11 - h = 5$ (g) $8 - p = 0$ (h) $12 - s = 2$
(i) $15 - h = 5$ (j) $18 - f = 11$ (k) $22 - q = 10$ (l) $19 - w = 19$
(m) $17 - c = 9$ (n) $31 - g = 15$ (o) $31 - r = 12$ (p) $22 - v = 4$
(q) $27 - c = 17$ (r) $31 - a = 11$ (s) $88 - t = 28$ (t) $52 - c = 27$

4 Find each unknown number.

(a) $a - 2 = 1$ (b) $a - 4 = 3$ (c) $a - 1 = 10$ (d) $a - 3 = 6$
(e) $b - 5 = 2$ (f) $z - 7 = 4$ (g) $w - 2 = 9$ (h) $u - 13 = 2$
(i) $k - 12 = 3$ (j) $d - 9 = 9$ (k) $s - 12 = 8$ (l) $h - 23 = 1$
(m) $m - 35 = 21$ (n) $z - 27 = 1$ (o) $k - 22 = 5$ (p) $p - 23 = 3$

5 Solve:

(a) $b + 5 = 12$ (b) $z - 5 = 2$ (c) $13 - e = 9$ (d) $u - 13 = 2$
(e) $5 - w = 0$ (f) $21 + y = 44$ (g) $w - 7 = 9$ (h) $p - 43 = 11$
(i) $17 + c = 52$ (j) $11 - v = 4$ (k) $m - 32 = 11$ (l) $k - 13 = 54$
(m) $76 + s = 80$ (n) $w - 54 = 6$ (o) $52 - t = 40$ (p) $u - 110 = 8$

6 Solve the equations.

(a) $3 = w + 1$ (b) $15 = 4 + t$ (c) $1 = p - 9$ (d) $11 = 20 - g$
(e) $5 = c - 11$ (f) $7 = 4 + k$ (g) $20 = p - 9$ (h) $29 = 30 - k$
(i) $12 = x + 3$ (j) $15 = 15 - s$ (k) $40 = f + 10$ (l) $20 = z - 5$
(m) $54 = h + 14$ (n) $29 = 33 - x$ (o) $54 = w - 10$ (p) $17 = 25 - c$

13.2 Solving simple equations

Example Solve $2y = 12$

$$2 \times \text{✋} = 12$$

2 times what number equals 12?

$$y = 6$$

Exercise 13.2

1 Copy and complete to find the unknown number.

(a) $2x = 10$ (b) $3a = 18$ (c) $5m = 20$ (d) $4p = 40$
    $x =$ $a =$ $m =$ $p =$

2 Copy and complete:

(**a**) $8y = 24$ (**b**) $6z = 30$ (**c**) $3b = 9$ (**d**) $7y = 21$
   $y =$ $z =$ $b =$ $y =$

(**e**) $5t = 25$ (**f**) $10q = 70$ (**g**) $9s = 81$ (**h**) $4x = 88$
   $t =$ $q =$ $s =$ $x =$

3 Solve the equations.

(**a**) $5y = 50$ (**b**) $3x = 27$ (**c**) $2r = 24$ (**d**) $4s = 32$
(**e**) $11t = 55$ (**f**) $8y = 56$ (**g**) $6a = 42$ (**h**) $7q = 49$
(**i**) $8x = 40$ (**j**) $9m = 45$ (**k**) $4x = 24$ (**l**) $20t = 100$

13.3 Solving equations

Example 1 Solve $2y + 1 = 9$
 $+ 1 = 9$ What number plus 1 equals 9?
$2y = 8$
$y = 4$

Example 2 Solve $3y - 2 = 19$
$- 2 = 19$ What number minus 2 equals 19?
$3y = 21$
$y = 7$

Exercise 13.3

1 Copy and complete to find the unknown number.

(**a**) $2y + 1 = 7$ (**b**) $2y + 3 = 11$ (**c**) $2y + 7 = 9$ (**d**) $2y + 5 = 21$
   $2y =$ $2y =$ $2y =$ $2y =$
   $y =$ $y =$ $y =$ $y =$

(**e**) $3y + 1 = 13$ (**f**) $3y + 5 = 26$ (**g**) $4y + 7 = 27$ (**h**) $4y + 1 = 9$
   $3y =$ $3y =$ $4y =$ $4y =$
   $y =$ $y =$ $y =$ $y =$

(**i**) $2y - 1 = 1$ (**j**) $4y - 5 = 27$ (**k**) $3y - 11 = 1$ (**l**) $5y - 10 = 30$
   $2y =$ $4y =$ $3y =$ $5y =$
   $y =$ $y =$ $y =$ $y =$

(**m**) $6y - 2 = 22$ (**n**) $10y - 4 = 46$ (**o**) $7y - 3 = 25$ (**p**) $3y - 6 = 27$
   $6y =$ $10y =$ $7y =$ $3y =$
   $y =$ $y =$ $y =$ $y =$

2 Solve the equations.

(**a**) $2y + 5 = 9$	(**b**) $2y + 7 = 11$	(**c**) $2y + 17 = 19$	(**d**) $2y + 1 = 21$
(**e**) $3y + 1 = 19$	(**f**) $3y + 3 = 12$	(**g**) $3y + 7 = 16$	(**h**) $3y + 15 = 21$
(**i**) $4y + 1 = 29$	(**j**) $4y + 13 = 57$	(**k**) $5y + 7 = 42$	(**l**) $7y + 9 = 9$

3 Solve the equations.

(**a**) $2y - 1 = 9$	(**b**) $2y - 3 = 11$	(**c**) $2y - 7 = 19$	(**d**) $2y - 1 = 3$
(**e**) $3y - 1 = 8$	(**f**) $3y - 7 = 8$	(**g**) $4y - 7 = 13$	(**h**) $5y - 1 = 29$

4 Solve:

(**a**) $3x + 1 = 10$	(**b**) $5a + 2 = 32$	(**c**) $4a - 5 = 7$	(**d**) $2b - 4 = 10$
(**e**) $5p + 4 = 24$	(**f**) $7q - 3 = 18$	(**g**) $4t + 9 = 41$	(**h**) $3f - 8 = 10$
(**i**) $2s - 9 = 7$	(**j**) $8x + 3 = 11$	(**k**) $9k - 1 = 17$	(**l**) $6w + 5 = 5$

13.4 Forming equations

A bag contains an unknown number of marbles.
Call the number x.

Two marbles are added. The total is six.

This can be written as an equation: $\qquad x + 2 \quad = \quad 6$

Example (**a**) Write an equation for this diagram
(**b**) Solve the equation.

$$
\begin{aligned}
\text{The equation is} \quad 2x + 1 &= 9 \\
2x &= 8 \\
x &= 4
\end{aligned}
$$

There are **4** marbles in each bag.

Exercise 13.4

1 Write an equation for each diagram and solve the equation.

(**a**)

(**b**)

2 Write an equation for each diagram and solve it.

(a)

(b)

(c)

(d)

(e)

(f)

3 I am thinking of a number. If I add twelve the answer is fifteen.

(a) Call the unknown number x. Write an equation to show the problem.

(b) What number was I thinking of?

13.5 Collecting like terms

An **expression** uses letters for numbers.

An **expression** may be simplified.

| **Example** | $w + w + w + w$ can be written as $4w$ |
| | |

$$y + y + y + y + y + y \quad = \quad 6y$$
$$2y + 4y \quad = \quad 6y$$
$$4a + 3a + 2a \quad = \quad 9a$$
$$5t + 3t + t \quad = \quad 9t$$

t is the same as 1t

Exercise 13.5

1 Copy and complete to simplify the expressions.

(a) $a + a =$

(b) $b + b + b =$

(c) $c + c + c =$

(d) $k + k + k + k =$

(e) $m + m + m + m + m + m =$

(f) $f + f + f + f + f + f + f =$

(g) $v + v + v + v + v =$

(h) $z + z + z + z + z + z + z + z =$

(i) $a + a + a + a + a + a =$

(j) $c + c + c + c + c =$

(k) $j + j + j + j + j + j + j + j + j =$

(l) $q + q + q + q + q + q + q + q =$

(m) $m + m + m + m =$

(n) $e + e + e =$

(o) $d + d + d + d + d =$

(p) $i + i + i + i + i + i + i + i =$

(q) $u + u =$

(r) $f + f + f + f + f + f + f + f + f + f + f =$

(s) $g + g + g + g + g + g + g + g + g + g =$

(t) $s + s + s + s + s + s + s + s + s + s + s + s =$

(u) $h + h + h + h + h + h + h + h + h =$

(v) $l + l + l + l + l + l + l + l + l + l + l + l =$

2 Simplify:

(**a**) $2a + 2a$ (**b**) $2b + 2b + 2b$
(**c**) $3c + 3c + 3c$ (**d**) $2k + 2k + k$
(**e**) $2m + 2m + 2m + 2m + 2m + 2m$
(**f**) $3f + 3f + 3f + 3f + 3f + 3f + 3f + 3f$
(**g**) $4v + 4v + 4v$ (**h**) $5z + 5z + 5z + 5z$
(**i**) $2a + 2a + 2a + 2a$ (**j**) $2a + 3a$
(**k**) $3b + 4b$ (**l**) $5g + 3g$
(**m**) $2p + 3p + 2p$ (**n**) $2y + 3y + 4y$
(**o**) $2x + 3x + x$ (**p**) $7y + 3y + 5y$
(**q**) $11k + 2k + 6k$ (**r**) $15t + 10t + 20t$
(**s**) $7y + 3y + 5y$ (**t**) $11k + k + 6k$
(**u**) $15t + 10t + 15t$ (**v**) $9e + 5e + e$

13.6 Simplifying expressions

Different letters cannot be grouped because they stand for different unknown numbers.

$$2a + b \quad \text{cannot be simplified.}$$

To simplify an expression, collect **like terms**.

Example $2a + b + a$ can be written as $3a + b$
$3g + 2k + 2g$ can be written as $5g + 2k$
$a + 3e + 4a + 5e + 6f = 5a + 8e + 6f$

Exercise 13.6

1 Copy and complete to simplify these expressions.

(**a**) $2a + b + 2a =$ (**b**) $2b + 2c + 2b =$
(**c**) $3c + 3d + 2c =$ (**d**) $2k + 5f + 2k =$
(**e**) $2m + 3p + 2m + 3p + 2m =$ (**f**) $3a + 2f + 3a + 4a + 3f =$
(**g**) $4v + 4z + 4v =$ (**h**) $5z + 2a + 5z + 2a + 5z =$
(**i**) $2a + 2b + 2a + 3b =$ (**j**) $2a + 3a + 2b + 5b =$
(**k**) $3b + 4g + 3g + 2b =$ (**l**) $5g + 3g + 2w + 3w + g =$
(**m**) $2p + 3b + 6p + 7b =$ (**n**) $2y + 3w + 4y + 2w + 2y =$
(**o**) $2x + 3x + x + 4y + 2y =$ (**p**) $7y + 3h + 5y + 7h =$
(**q**) $11k + 2s + s + s + 6k =$ (**r**) $15t + 10u + 20t + 10u =$
(**s**) $5e + 8u + 6e + 7u =$ (**t**) $12t + w + 4t + 9t + 5w =$
(**u**) $11h + g + 3g + 7g + 9g + h =$ (**v**) $5m + 3p + 2m + p =$

2 Simplify:

(**a**) $2a + 2b + 2c + 3a + 2b + 4c$

(**b**) $4t + 3s + 2u + 2s + 5t + 4u$

(**c**) $3p + 5r + 3q + 2q + 2r + 6p$

(**d**) $3e + 4i + 2a + 3i + 5e + 2i$

(**e**) $2k + 3g + 2h + 4g + 3k + 2h$

(**f**) $7y + 8j + s + 3y + 2j + s + j$

(**g**) $2w + 3f + t + f + w + 2t + w$

(**h**) $w + 2d + 5k + d + k + 2w$

(**i**) $3r + 2t + 4y + 2t + y + 2r$

(**j**) $a + 2b + 3c + 2a + 3d + 2e$

(**k**) $4u + 8d + e + 2u + d + 6e$

(**l**) $v + a + v + 2v + m + 3a + 4v$

3 Simplify:

(**a**) $w + 2e + w + 3e + e + 2w$

(**b**) $s + t + u + 3s + 4t + 5u$

(**c**) $a + 2b + 3c + 4a + 6b + 8c$

(**d**) $3m + 5y + p + 6y + p + 7m + p$

(**e**) $4k + 5t + 2y + 5k + 5t + 8y + t$

(**f**) $10p + 2p + 8i + 4g + 3i + p + 8g$

(**g**) $a + 2b + 8v + 11a + 12b + 5a$

(**h**) $23k + 34t + u + z + 13t + 17k + 5u$

13.7 Adding and subtracting like terms

Examples

$$5a - 3a \qquad = 2a$$
$$12g - 11g \qquad = g$$
$$3a - a + b \qquad = 2a + b$$
$$5g + 2k - 2g \quad = 3g + 2k$$
$$5a + 3e - 2a - e = 3a + 2e$$

g is the same as 1**g**

Exercise 13.7

1 Copy and complete to simplify these expressions.

(**a**) $5a - 3a =$

(**b**) $6b - 2b =$

(**c**) $4c - 2c =$

(**d**) $8d - 7d =$

(**e**) $5y - 3y =$

(**f**) $3w - 2w =$

(**g**) $7u - 6u =$

(**h**) $9t - 7t =$

(**i**) $15h - 5h =$

(**j**) $12m - 7m =$

(**k**) $2q - q =$

(**l**) $23p - 15p =$

(**m**) $6b - 6b =$

(**n**) $45s - 22s =$

(**o**) $23x - 8x =$

(**p**) $63k - 27k =$

(**q**) $11z - 8z =$

(**r**) $34v - 34v =$

(**s**) $145w - 45w$

(**t**) $312y - 300y =$

2 Simplify:

(**a**) $3c + 5c - 2c$

(**b**) $4d + 3d - 5d$

(**c**) $2e + 7e - 3e$

(**d**) $7k + 4k - 3k$

(**e**) $w + 4w - 3w$

(**f**) $6y + 7y - 5y$

(**g**) $11g + 7g - 9g$

(**h**) $12q + 9q - 10q$

(**i**) $14x + 11x - 21x$

(**j**) $31p + 22p - 37p$

(**k**) $21h + 39h - 60h$

(**l**) $16t + 37t - 52t$

3 Simplify:

(**a**) $3f + 3v - 2f$

(**b**) $4d + 3r - 2d$

(**c**) $7e + 6g - 3e$

(**d**) $7k + 4s - 3k$

(**e**) $2w + 4y - w$

(**f**) $6y + 7p - 5y$

(**g**) $11g + 7w - 9g$

(**h**) $12q + 9b - 10q$

(**i**) $14x + 11y - 11x$

(**j**) $31p + 22k - 27p$

(**k**) $21h + 9z - 6h$

(**l**) $16t + 7e - 9t$

4 Simplify:
(a) $5a + 4b - 2a - 2b$ (b) $5f + 7g - 3f - 4g$ (c) $6y + 3h - 4y - 2h$
(d) $11d + 3e - 7d - e$ (e) $15m + 6t - 9m - 2t$ (f) $4s + 2t - 3s - t$
(g) $23y + 3z - 12y - 2z$ (h) $11c + 3g - 8c - 3g$ (i) $5y + 3z - 5y - 2z$
(j) $23g + 21t - 7t - 23g$ (k) $15t + 12q - 10t - 12q$ (l) $14r + 11s - 9r$
(m) $12w - 6w + 3a - 2a - 6w$ (n) $9f + 8y - 6f - 7y + 2y$ (o) $12h + 3b - 8h - 3b - 4h$

Review exercise 13

1 Solve each equation.
(a) $x + 5 = 8$ (b) $y + 1 = 21$ (c) $a + 9 = 15$ (d) $t + 10 = 50$
(e) $10 - p = 4$ (f) $2 - e = 1$ (g) $5 - u = 0$ (h) $12 - w = 3$
(i) $f - 6 = 1$ (j) $k - 7 = 5$ (k) $m - 9 = 10$ (l) $h - 7 = 16$
(m) $15 = a + 6$ (n) $12 = g - 4$ (o) $15 = c - 5$ (p) $0 = e - 11$

2 Solve the equations:
(a) $2x + 3 = 7$ (b) $2y + 5 = 11$ (c) $3a + 5 = 23$
(d) $5h + 1 = 21$ (e) $2x - 3 = 9$ (f) $4y - 3 = 17$
(g) $6p + 3 = 27$ (h) $7t - 4 = 24$ (i) $9k - 5 = 31$

3 Write an equation for each diagram. Solve each equation.
(a)

 gives

(b)

 gives

4 A bus leaving the station has an unknown number of passengers.
Six people get on at the first stop. The bus now has 14 passengers.
Write an equation and solve it to find the number of passengers on the bus at the station.

5 Copy and complete to simplify these expressions.
(a) $x + x + x =$ (b) $y + y + y + y =$ (c) $z + z + z + z + z + z + z =$
(d) $2x + 3x =$ (e) $5y + 4y =$ (f) $6a + 3a + 2a =$
(g) $5t + 3t + t =$ (h) $4e + e + 4e =$ (i) $7c + 3c + 2c + c =$

6 Simplify:
(a) $2a + 3b + 4a$ (b) $4x + 2y + 5x$ (c) $3t + 2w + 6t$
(d) $3y + 5t + 2y + 6t$ (e) $2w + 3z + w + z$ (f) $2c + 3k + 4c + 5k + c$

7 Simplify:
(a) $6a - 2a$ (b) $8t - 6t$ (c) $3t - 2t$
(d) $15z - 9z$ (e) $20s - 11s$ (f) $12b - 12b$

8 Simplify:
(a) $5a + 3b - 3a$ (b) $7x + 2y - 5x$ (c) $8t + 2w - 7t$
(d) $7y + 5t - 2y - 3t$ (e) $2w + 3z - w - z$ (f) $9c + 3k - 8c - 3k - c$

Summary

A letter may be used to represent an unknown number.

Solving equations

$x + 4 = 9$	$y - 3 = 7$	$8 - t = 1$	$2y + 3 = 11$	$3y - 10 = 2$
$x = 5$	$y = 10$	$t = 7$	$2y = 8$	$3y = 12$
			$y = 4$	$y = 4$

Forming equations

A bag contains an unknown number of marbles.

  gives

$$x + 3 = 10$$
$$x = 7$$

Simplifying expressions

$$y + y + y = 3y$$
$$4y + 2y = 6y$$
$$6g - 4g = 2g$$
$$4a + 3b + 2a = 6a + 3b$$
$$5t + 3u - t = 4t + 3u$$
$$7a + 5b - a - 4b = 6a + b$$

t is the same as $1t$

14 Tessellations

In this chapter you will learn about tiles and how they can be used to create patterns.

14.1 Drawing tessellations

When shapes or tiles are fitted together with no gaps or overlaps we call the pattern a **tessellation**.

Tessellations can be made using one shape repeatedly or a number of different tiles.

Shapes which are exactly the same shape and size are said to be **congruent**. You will look at tessellations using congruent shapes like the examples below.

> The word tessellation comes from the Greek word *tesserae* meaning tile

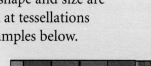
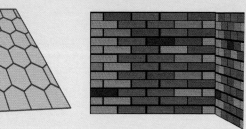

Exercise 14.1

1 Make a list of where you might see examples of tessellations.

You may use worksheets 14.1 to 14.6 for questions 2 to 5.

W

2 Using worksheet 14.1 or square dotted paper, copy and complete these tessellations using 12 congruent tiles.

(a)   (b)   (c)

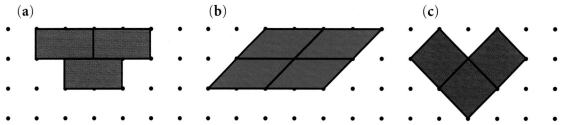

3 Using worksheets 14.2 and 14.3 or square dotted paper, copy and complete these tessellations using 12 congruent tiles.

(a)   (b)

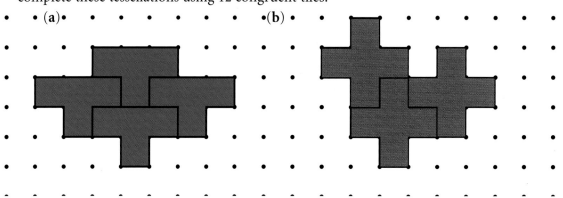

4 Using worksheets 14.4 and 14.5 or square dotted paper, copy
and complete these tessellations using 12 congruent tiles.

(a)   (b)   (c)

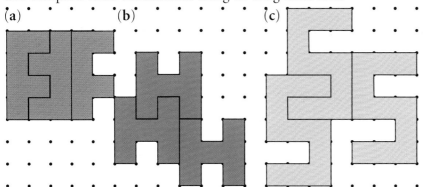

5 Using worksheet 14.6 or triangular dotted paper, copy and
complete these tessellations using 12 congruent tiles.

(a)   (b)   (c)

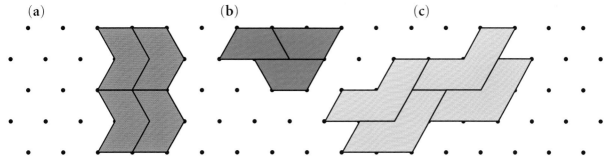

6 Here are two tessellations made using the same tile:

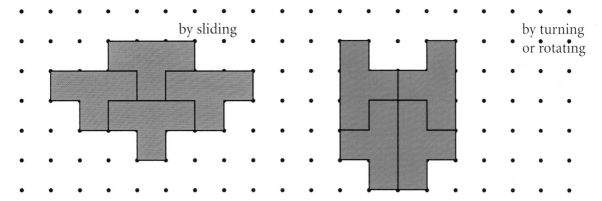

by sliding   by turning
                                              or rotating

Using square dotted paper, find two different tessellations which
can be made with each of these tiles. Use 12 congruent tiles in each.

(a)   (b)   (c)

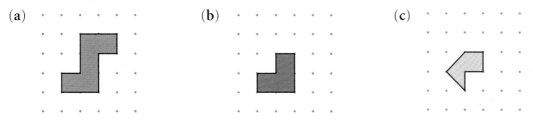

7 Bob is designing tiling for his patio using rectangular slabs.

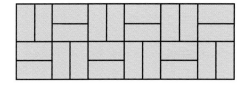

Find two other designs he could have for his patio.

8 A 4 cm by 6 cm rectangle can be filled with 8 'L shape' tiles like this:

Copy and complete the diagram to show how you could fit all the tiles into the rectangle.

9 (**a**) Which of these shapes tessellate?

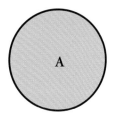 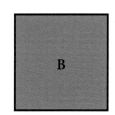 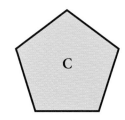 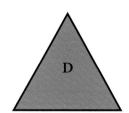

(**b**) For each shape that does, draw a tessellation using 12 congruent tiles.

10 Some traditional patchwork quilts were made from patches containing nine squares.

Using these tiles:

create patches which have:
(**a**) one line of symmetry
(**b**) two lines of symmetry
(**c**) four lines of symmetry.

14.2 Creating tessellations

M.C. Escher was a very famous 20th century Dutch artist. Most of his work contained mathematical ideas and he was well known for his tessellations. You can draw your own tessellation pictures.

Exercise 14.2

1 Step 1 – Create your starting tiles by drawing 12 congruent 3 cm by 3 cm squares on centimetre square dotted paper as shown.

Step 2 – *Start inside one tile.* To create the cat's ears draw diagonal lines through the bottom corner squares and move the highlighted triangles to the opposite side as shown in the diagram. Erase the extra lines and you have created a cat tile.

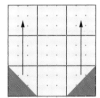 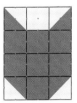

Step 3 – Repeat this for each of the other tiles to produce a tessellation of cats.

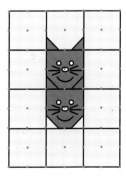

2 (**a**) Draw 12 congruent 2 cm by 4 cm rectangles on square dotted paper.

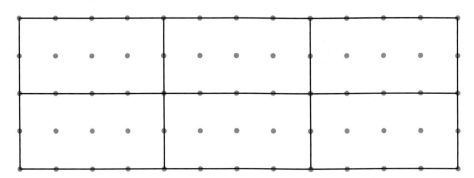

(**b**) To create a fish tile choose one rectangle and change its shape like this:

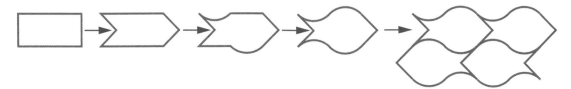

E **3** You will need a rectangular piece of card about 4 cm by 3 cm, scissors and sticky tape.

Step 1 Cut a piece out of one side.

Step 2 Stick it to the opposite side.

Step 3 Use your shape as a template.
Draw round it to create a tessellation of 12 tiles.

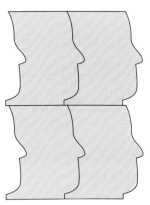

4 Create a tessellation pattern of your own.
You could use one of the ideas above to help you get started.

Review exercise 14

1 Which of the shapes below would tessellate?

A   B   C    D

2 Draw a tessellation using the tile shown.
Use 12 tiles in your drawing.

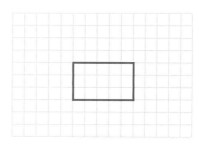

3 Copy and continue each tessellation.
Use 12 tiles in each diagram.

(a)

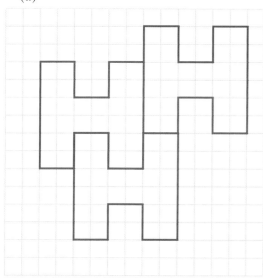

(b)

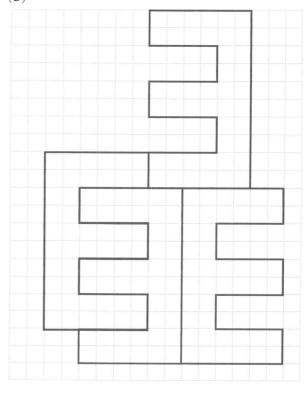

Summary

When shapes or tiles are fitted together with no gaps or overlaps the pattern is called a **tessellation**.

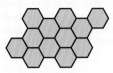

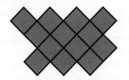

Identical shapes are called **congruent** shapes.

Not all shapes tessellate. Some shapes leave gaps.

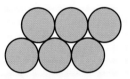

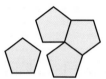

Some shapes tessellate by sliding: and by rotating:

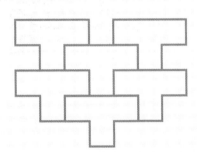

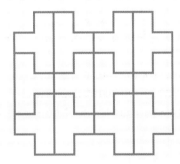

15 Ratio

In this chapter you will learn how to use ratios to calculate and share quantities.

15.1 Ratio

To make an orange squash drink you mix 1 part orange juice with 4 parts water.
The **ratio** of orange juice to water is 1 : 4. This is read as "1 to 4".

The ratio of water to orange juice is 4 : 1.

To make a shade of green, mix 2 tins of yellow with
3 tins of blue.
yellow : blue = 2 : 3
blue : yellow = 3 : 2

Exercise 15.1

1 Copy and complete each ratio statement to describe each situation.
   (**a**) To make a lemon squash drink you mix 1 part lemon juice
          with 5 parts water.
          The ratio of lemon juice to water is _____
          The ratio of water to lemon juice is _____
   (**b**) To make a shade of purple paint, mix 3 tins of red with
          5 tins of blue.
          The ratio of red paint to blue paint _____
          The ratio of blue paint to red paint _____
   (**c**) To make pastry, for every 1 gramme of fat you need
          2 grammes of flour.
          fat : flour = _____
          flour : fat = _____
   (**d**) To make concrete, mix 2 bags of cement with 7 bags of sand.
          cement : sand = _____
          sand : cement = _____

2 Give the ratio of red counters to blue counters for each of
   the following.
   (**a**)   (**b**)   (**c**)   (**d**)

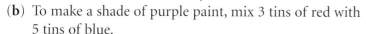

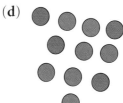

3 Find the ratio of:

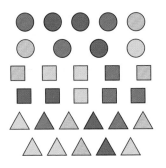

   (**a**) triangles to squares   (**b**) squares to circles
   (**c**) blue shapes to red shapes   (**d**) green shapes to yellow shapes
   (**e**) red squares to green triangles   (**f**) blue circles to yellow triangles
   (**g**) yellow squares to red squares   (**h**) green circles to red circles.

4 Give the ratio of purple to yellow parts for each diagram.

(**a**)   (**b**)   (**c**)   (**d**)

15.2 Simplifying ratios

4 tins of yellow can be mixed with 6 tins of blue.
This can be split to make two groups of 2 tins of yellow
with 3 tins of blue. Each group makes the same colour of
green as in the example on page 171.

The ratio of yellow paint to blue paint $= 4 : 6$
$$= 2 : 3$$

Example
Simplify each ratio.

(**a**) $4 : 8$ (**b**) $6 : 15$
       $4 : 8$ (divide each side by 4) $6 : 15$ (divide each side by 3)
   $= 1 : 2$ $= 2 : 5$

Exercise 15.2

1 Simplify each ratio.

   (**a**) $4 : 10$ (**b**) $6 : 15$ (**c**) $5 : 35$ (**d**) $12 : 28$ (**e**) $6 : 6$ (**f**) $18 : 4$
   (**g**) $9 : 6$ (**h**) $36 : 16$ (**i**) $28 : 12$ (**j**) $56 : 21$ (**k**) $14 : 35$ (**l**) $35 : 15$
   (**m**) $12 : 42$ (**n**) $40 : 50$ (**o**) $45 : 15$ (**p**) $36 : 54$ (**q**) $75 : 25$ (**r**) $60 : 12$

2 A shepherd uses 4 dogs to look after his 100 sheep.
   Write the ratio of dogs to sheep in simplest form.

3 Samir and Brian are business partners. Samir has shares in the business worth £300 000.
   Brian has the remaining shares worth £600 000.
   What is the ratio of the value of Samir's shares to Brian's in its simplest form?

4 Jehan has shares in business worth £450 000 000. Rachael has the remaining shares
   worth £150 000 000.
   What is the ratio of the value of Jehan's shares to Rachael's in its simplest form?

5 The green rectangle has length 24 metres and breadth 6 metres. The yellow rectangle measures 18 metres by 2 metres.
Find the ratios of their
   (**a**) lengths   (**b**) breadths.

24 m

18 m

6 m   2 m

6 The red square has sides of length 8 centimetres. The blue square has sides of 4 centimetres.
   (**a**) Find the ratio of the length of the red square to the length of the blue square.
   (**b**) (**i**) Calculate the area of each square.
          (**ii**) Find the ratio of the area of the red square to the area of the blue square.

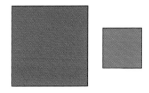

15.3 Ratio and proportion

The Citron Car Company makes cars in kit form.
Example 1
Liam paints the cars either yellow or green.
The ratio of yellow to green cars is 1 : 3.
This means that for every yellow car there will be 3 green cars.
If 4 cars were painted yellow, how many were painted green?

Yellow	Green
1	3
4	12

×4   ×4

There were **12** green cars.
Example 2
The Citron cars use either petrol or diesel.
The ratio of petrol to diesel is 5 : 2
How many petrol cars were made when the number of diesel cars was 16?

Petrol	Diesel
5	2

→

Petrol	Diesel
5	2
	16

→

Petrol	Diesel
5	2
40	16

×8   ×8

There were **40** petrol cars made.

Exercise 15.3

1 The ratio of yellow cars to green cars is 1 : 3.
   (**a**) How many green cars were there if the number of yellow cars was:
          (**i**) 5   (**ii**) 8   (**iii**) 9   (**iv**) 10   (**v**) 20   (**vi**) 100?
   (**b**) How many yellow cars were there if the number of green cars was:
          (**i**) 6   (**ii**) 15   (**iii**) 21   (**iv**) 33   (**v**) 66   (**vi**) 900?

2 The ratio of blue cars to red cars is 1 : 4.

 (**a**) How many red cars were there if the number of blue
 cars was:

 (**i**) 3   (**ii**) 5   (**iii**) 7   (**iv**) 10   (**v**) 40   (**vi**) 100?

 (**b**) How many blue cars were there if the number of red
 cars was:

 (**i**) 8   (**ii**) 12   (**iii**) 20   (**iv**) 32   (**v**) 60   (**vi**) 300?

3 The ratio of petrol cars to diesel cars is 5 : 2.

 (**a**) How many diesel cars were made when the number of petrol cars was:

 (**i**) 10   (**ii**) 25   (**iii**) 35   (**iv**) 50   (**v**) 75?

 (**b**) How many petrol cars were made, when the number of diesel cars was:

 (**i**) 6   (**ii**) 16   (**iii**) 18   (**iv**) 22   (**v**) 40?

4 The ratio of right hand drive cars to left hand drive cars is 3 : 8.

 (**a**) How many left hand drive cars were made when the number of right
 hand drive cars was:

 (**i**) 6   (**ii**) 15   (**iii**) 24   (**iv**) 30   (**v**) 300?

 (**b**) How many right hand drive cars were made when the number of left
 hand drive cars was:

 (**i**) 16   (**ii**) 24   (**iii**) 32   (**iv**) 56   (**v**) 72?

5 Rajiv and Bhavesh share the profit from their business in the ratio 1 : 2.
 What will Bhavesh receive if Rajiv's share is £2000?

6 George is Robert's grandfather. This year the ratio of their ages is 5 : 2.
 George is 85 years old. How old is Robert?

7 A shade of green paint is made by mixing yellow paint with blue paint in the ratio 2 : 3.
 How many tins of blue are needed to make this shade if 16 tins of yellow are used?

8 A large quantity of orange drink is needed
 for a sports day. The drink is made by mixing
 orange juice and water in the ratio 3 : 8.
 How much water is required if 6 litres of
 orange juice are used?

9 The ratio of the supporters of Inverness
 Caledonian Thistle to Ross County at the
 recent Highland derby was 4 : 3.
 There were 4400 Caledonian supporters.
 How many Ross County supporters were there?

10 A chocolate cake recipe states that sugar and
 flour should be mixed in the ratio of 3 : 4.
 If 120 grammes of flour are used, what weight
 of sugar is required?

11 The ratio of males to females who bought CDs for the rock group *Rubbish* was 8 : 7.
 How many males bought the CD if 3500 females bought it?

12 In a recent rugby international, the ratio of penalties awarded against Scotland to those
 awarded against England was 2 : 5. The Scottish team had 18 penalties awarded against it.
 How many penalties were awarded against the English team?

15.4 Sharing in a given quantity

Example 1
Rachael and Eilidh share the profit from their business in the ratio 2 : 3.
What will each receive if the total profit is £400 per week?

Step 1 Add up numbers in ratio to find the total number of parts.

No. of parts = 2 + 3 = 5

Step 2 Divide total by this number to find the value of 1 part.

Value of 1 part = £400 ÷ 5 = £80

Step 3 Multiply the value of 1 part by the each number in the ratio.

Rachael's share = 2 × £80 = £160
Eilidh's share = 3 × £80 = £240

Step 4 Check that the shares add to give the total.

£160 + £240 = £400 = correct total

Rachael receives **£160** and Eilidh receives **£240**.

This can be more conveniently set out in a proportion table:

Rachael	Eilidh	Total
2	3	5
		400

Rachael	Eilidh	Total
2	3	5
×80 160	240 ×80	400 ×80

Rachael receives **£160** and Eilidh receives **£240**.

Example 2 Share out 45 in the ratio of 1 : 2

1st share	2nd share	Total
1	2	3
×15 15	30 ×15	45 ×15

When 45 is shared in the ratio 1 : 2 the shares are **15** and **30** respectively.

Exercise 15.4

1 Share each amount in the given ratio:
(**a**) 21 in the ratio 2 : 1 (**b**) 16 in the ratio 3 : 1 (**c**) 21 in the ratio 4 : 3
(**d**) 35 in the ratio 3 : 2 (**e**) 36 in the ratio 2 : 7 (**f**) 54 in the ratio 4 : 5
(**g**) 60 in the ratio 7 : 3 (**h**) 66 in the ratio 8 : 3 (**i**) 72 in the ratio 5 : 3

2 Share these amounts in the ratios given:
(**a**) £20 in the ratio 3 : 2 (**b**) £25 in the ratio 4 : 1
(**c**) 48 centimetres in the ratio 1 : 5 (**d**) 24 kg in the ratio 3 : 5
(**e**) 60 minutes in the ratio 7 : 5 (**f**) 2000 metres in the ratio 3 : 7
(**g**) £60 in the ratio 1 : 1 (**h**) 24 hours in the ratio 5 : 3
(**i**) 100 litres in the ratio 12 : 13 (**j**) £80 in the ratio 7 : 3

3 Ruairidh and Calum invest in a new business. They agree to share the profit or losses in the ratio 2 : 3.

    (**a**) How much would each receive if the total profit gained is
        (**i**) £10 000   (**ii**) £50 000   (**iii**) £45 000   (**iv**) £1 000 000?

    (**b**) How much would it cost each person if the total losses were
        (**i**) £1000   (**ii**) £3500   (**iii**) £5500   (**iv**) £50 000?

4 The total volume of orange drink needed for a Beecraigs High School dance is 160 litres. Orange juice and water are mixed in the ratio 1 : 3. How much of each is needed?

5 A professional decorator requires 50 litres of green paint. This is made up by mixing blue and yellow paint in the ratio 7 : 3. Calculate the volume of each colour of paint which is needed to make the green paint.

6 The total profit of a business was £2500. This was shared between George and Mary in the ratio 2 : 3.
How much did each receive?

7 The total attendance at the Scotland versus England rugby match at Murrayfield was 60 000. The ratio of Scotland supporters to England supporters was 11 : 4.
How many Scotland supporters were there at the match?

8 During a complete football season Gairich High School football team scored a total of 54 goals. The ratio of goals scored in home matches to those scored in away matches was 7 : 2. How many goals were scored at home?

9 A sweet manufacturer makes mixed packets of fruit bon-bons.
He mixes lemon bon-bons and orange bon-bons in the ratio 2 : 5.
If the total number of bon-bons in a packet is 56, how many lemon bon-bons and how many orange bon-bons are there in each packet?

10 A gardener needs to mix red and white chips to lay around a patio.
The chips are mixed in the ratio 4 : 1.
A total of 560 kilograms are required.
Calculate the amount of each colour required.

11 The population of Scotland is 5 000 000.
If the ratio of Gaelic speakers to non Gaelic speakers is 3 : 197, how many Gaelic speakers are there?

Review exercise 15

1 Find, in simplest form, the ratio of:

(**a**) squares to triangles
(**b**) hexagons to circles
(**c**) red shapes to blue shapes
(**d**) yellow shapes to green shapes
(**e**) red circles to green hexagons
(**f**) yellow circles to yellow triangles
(**g**) green squares to blue squares
(**h**) blue hexagons to red circles.

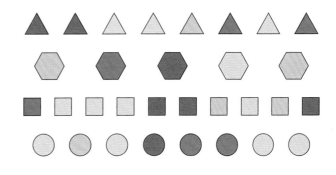

2 Simplify each ratio.

(**a**) 6 : 10   (**b**) 12 : 18   (**c**) 10 : 45   (**d**) 16 : 20
(**e**) 61 : 61   (**f**) 40 : 4   (**g**) 27 : 6   (**h**) 39 : 13

3 Auchenshoogle Juniors employ 20 stewards to look after a crowd of 600 supporters.
Write the ratio of stewards to supporters in simplest form.

4 The ratio of scores to misses for the penalty kick taker for the Scottish Borderers is 4 : 5.
If he misses 30 kicks, on how many
occasions does he score?

5 A market gardener plants seeds of
poppies and forget-me-nots in the
ratio 5 : 8. She buys 40 packets of
forget-me-nots. How many packets of
poppies should she buy?

6 A builder makes concrete by mixing
cement and sand in the ratio 3 : 7.
He has 21 bags of sand. How many bags
of cement does he need?

7 Share these amounts in the ratios given.

(**a**) £40 in the ratio 3 : 2   (**b**) £35 in the ratio 3 : 4
(**c**) 24 kilogrammes in the ratio 1 : 7   (**d**) 88 kg in the ratio 5 : 6
(**e**) 30 minutes in the ratio 7 : 3   (**f**) 2500 metres in the ratio 12 : 13

8 A motorist needs 2000 millilitres of screenwash for his car.
This is made up by mixing concentrate and water in the ratio 1 : 4.
Calculate the volume of concentrate and water which is needed to make the screenwash.

9 A brother and sister share the profit of their business in the ratio 4 : 3.
If the total profit in one month was £14 000, how much did each receive?

10 The total number of birds in a zoo's enclosure was 72. The ratio of native species
to tropical species was 7 : 5. How many native birds were in the enclosure?

11 The ratio of goals scored to goals conceded by Dundee in a season was 8 : 5.
The ratio of goals scored to goals conceded by Aberdeen in a season was 9 : 4.
Dundee scored 48 goals while Aberdeen scored 63 goals.
Which of the two teams conceded the most goals?

Summary

Ratio

The ratio of red counters to blue counters is 2 : 3.

Simplifying ratios

Simplify ratios by dividing each side by the same number.

6 : 15

= 2 : 5 (divide each side by 3)

The ratio of petrol to diesel is 5 : 2.

How many petrol cars were made when the number of diesel cars was 16?

Petrol	Diesel
5	2

→

Petrol	Diesel
5	2
	16

×8 →

Petrol	Diesel
5	2
40	16

×8

There were **40** petrol cars.

Use a proportion table to split a quantity into a given ratio.

Rachael and Eilidh share the £420 profit from their business in the ratio 3 : 4.

Rachael	Eilidh	Profit
3	4	7
		420

→

Rachael	Eilidh	Profit
×60 3	4 ×60	7 ×60
180	240	420

Rachael earns **£180** and Eilidh earns **£240**.

16 3D Shape

In this chapter you will learn more about solid shapes and look at ways of building them.

16.1 Dimensions

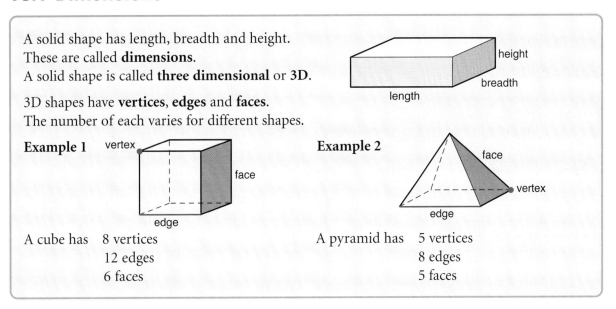

A solid shape has length, breadth and height.
These are called **dimensions**.
A solid shape is called **three dimensional** or **3D**.

3D shapes have **vertices**, **edges** and **faces**.
The number of each varies for different shapes.

Example 1

A cube has   8 vertices
              12 edges
              6 faces

Example 2

A pyramid has   5 vertices
                 8 edges
                 5 faces

Exercise 16.1

1 For each solid shape identify the red section as a vertex, edge or face.

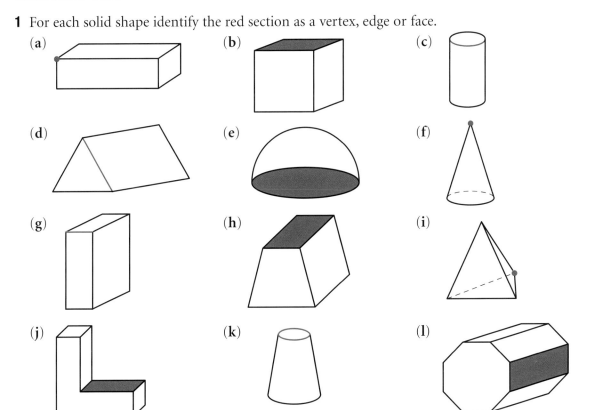

2 Name each shape in question 1, parts (**a**) to (**f**).

3 Copy and complete the table for each solid shape in question 1.

| | Number of | | |
Shape	Vertices	Edges	Faces
(a)			
(b)			
(c)			
(d)			
(e)			
(f)			

4 Copy and complete the table for each shape.

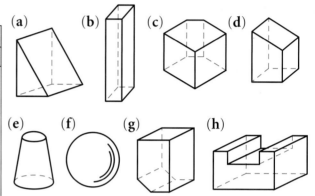

| | Number of | | |
Shape	Vertices	Edges	Faces
(a)			
(b)			
(c)			
(d)			
(e)			
(f)			
(g)			
(h)			

16.2 Naming faces

A face is identified by the letters at each vertex.
The letters are listed in order, starting at any vertex.

The red face on this cuboid may be named
  ABFE or BFEA or EFBA or …

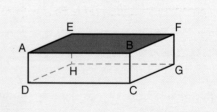

Exercise 16.2

1 There are eight ways of naming the red face in the example above.
Find the other five ways to name it.

2 On this cuboid find two names for
  (**a**) the blue face
  (**b**) the green face
  (**c**) the yellow face.

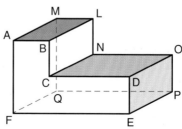

3 For each shape find two names for the red face.

(a)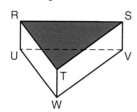

(b)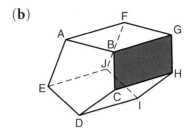

4 What colour is each face named below?
  (a) MLBA
  (b) BCNL
  (c) FEDCBA

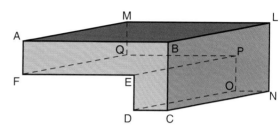

5 For this shape find two names for
  (a) the top
  (b) the back
  (c) the right hand face
  (d) the front

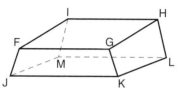

16.3 Diagonals

A line joining two vertices on the same face of a 2D shape is a **diagonal**.
The diagonal on the red face is AC or CA.

A line joining two vertices not on the same face
of a 3D shape is called a **space diagonal**.
The green space diagonal is BH or HB.

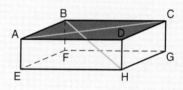

Exercise 16.3

 You may complete questions 1, 3 and 4 on worksheet 16.1

1 Copy the cube exactly as shown.
Draw in the diagonals on the top,
front and right hand side.

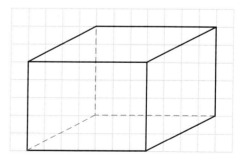

2 For this cuboid name the diagonals on
  (a) the front
  (b) the top
  (c) the left hand side
  (d) face DCGH.

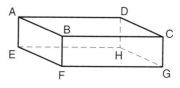

3 Copy the cube exactly as shown.
Draw in all four space diagonals.

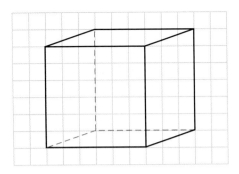

4 Copy the cuboid exactly as shown.
Draw in all the space diagonals.

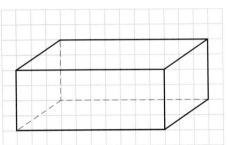

5 How many space diagonals
does this shape have?

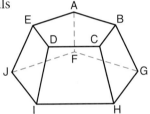

6 For each shape name both space diagonals drawn in red.

(**a**)
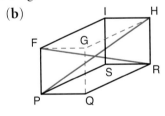

(**b**)
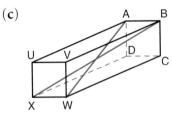

(**c**)

7 On the cube the space diagonal QW has been
drawn. Name the other three space diagonals.

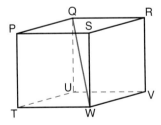

8 For each shape name all the space diagonals.

(**a**)
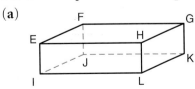

(**b**)
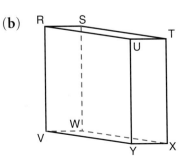

16.4 Angles

The angle shaded red is ∠PQW or ∠WQP.

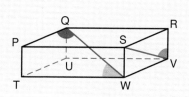

Exercise 16.4

1 On the cuboid above, name:
  (**a**) the blue angle   (**b**) the green angle

2 On the cuboid, name:
  (**a**) the green angle
  (**b**) the red angle
  (**c**) the blue angle

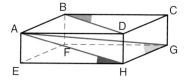

3 What colour is:
  (**a**) ∠SQO
  (**b**) ∠OQM
  (**c**) ∠MRN?

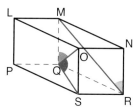

4 For each shape name the blue angle.
  (**a**) 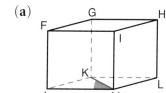 (**b**) 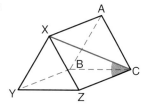 (**c**)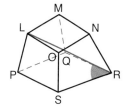

5 For each shape copy and complete the table.
  (**a** 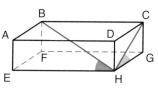 (**b**) 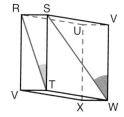 (**c**)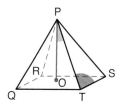

Angle	Colour
BHE	
	green

Angle	Colour
	blue
	green

Angle	Colour
	blue
	green

16.5 Drawing on isometric paper

Isometric dot paper is useful for drawing 3D shapes.

Exercise 16.5

You need isometric dot paper to complete this exercise.

1 Draw each 3D shape on isometric paper

(a)

(b)

(c)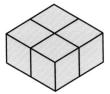

(d)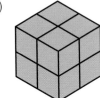

(e)

(f)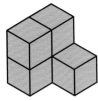

(g)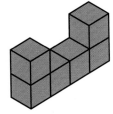

(h)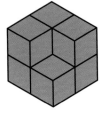

2 Draw these shapes with the red cubes removed.

(a)

(b)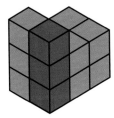

16.6 Calculating volume

The volume of a 3D shape is the space it occupies.

For a cuboid
volume = length × breadth × height

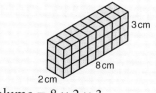

Volume = 8 × 2 × 3
= 48 cubic centimetres or cm^3

Example
Calculate the volume of each shape.

(a)

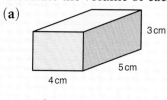

Volume = 4 × 5 × 3
= 60 cubic centimetres or cm^3

(b)

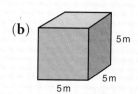

Volume = 5 × 5 × 5
= 125 cubic metres or m^3

Exercise 16.6

1 Calculate the volume of each 3D shape.

(a)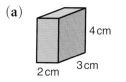

(b)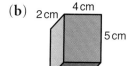

(c)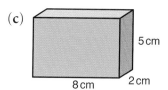

(d)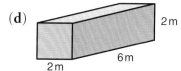

(e)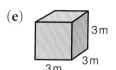

(f)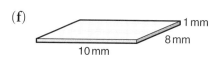

(g)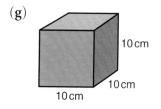

(h)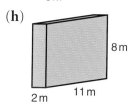

(i)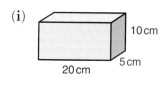

2 From the table find the volume of each cuboid.

Cuboid	Length	Breadth	Height
(a)	2 cm	3 cm	3 cm
(b)	5 m	2 m	5 m
(c)	6 mm	5 mm	7 mm
(d)	10 cm	10 cm	8 cm

3 Alan has built two storage boxes.
Which one is bigger and by how much?

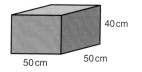

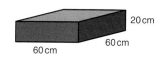

16.7 Building 3D shapes

This cuboid has:
   4 edges of 5 cm
   4 edges of 6 cm
   4 edges of 8 cm
   8 vertices

A **skeleton model**, using straws and pipe
cleaners, looks like this:

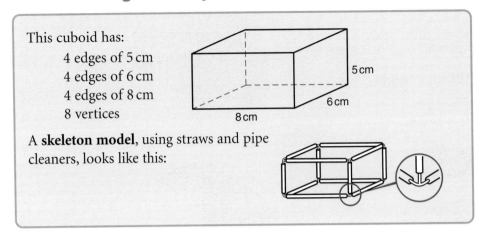

Exercise 16.7

W You may use worksheet 16.2 for this exercise.
To build the models you need straws, pipe cleaners, scissors and a ruler.
For each 3D shape (**a**)   list the number of each edge length required
                 (**b**)   write how many vertices are required
                 (**c**)   build a skeleton model if you have the materials.

1
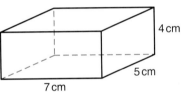

2
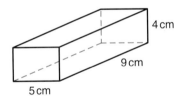

3
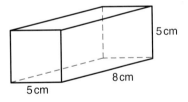

4
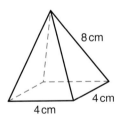

5
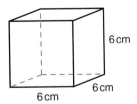

6
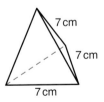

7
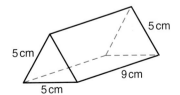

8
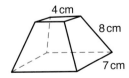

16.8 Nets

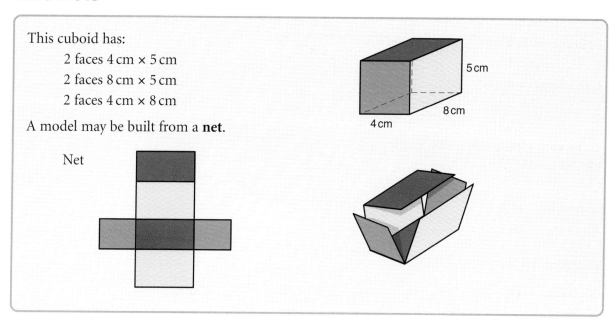

This cuboid has:

2 faces 4 cm × 5 cm
2 faces 8 cm × 5 cm
2 faces 4 cm × 8 cm

A model may be built from a **net**.

Net

Exercise 16.8

You may use worksheets 16.3 and 16.4 for questions 1 to 4.

To build the models you need 1cm squared paper, scissors and a ruler.

For each shape (**a**)   list the number of each size of face

             (**b**)   draw a net

             (**c**)   cut out the net and build the shape.

1   3 cm   6 cm   5 cm

2   5 cm   3 cm   2 cm

3   4 cm   4 cm   4 cm

4   3 cm   2 cm   4 cm

5   4 cm   7 cm   5 cm

6   6 cm   4 cm   4 cm

7   5 cm   5 cm   5 cm   7 cm

8   3 cm   3 cm   5 cm

16.9 Common 3D shapes

For some 3D shapes it is useful to know their properties.

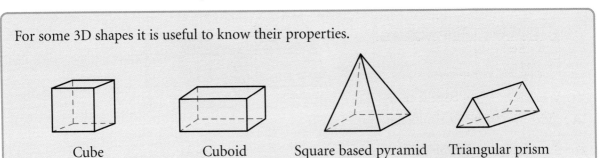

Cube   Cuboid   Square based pyramid   Triangular prism

Exercise 16.9

1 Copy and complete the table.

Shape	Number of			
	Vertices	Edges	Faces	Space diagonals
Cube				
Cuboid				
Square based pyramid				
Triangular prism				

2 For this cube:
   (**a**) What is the length of each edge?
   (**b**) What is the total edge length?
   (**c**) What is the area of each face?
   (**d**) What is the total area of all the faces?

Area = length × breadth

8 cm

3 For this cuboid:
   (**a**) Copy and complete the table.

Edge length	Number of edges
8 cm	
6 cm	
3 cm	

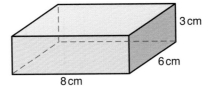

3 cm

6 cm

8 cm

   (**b**) What is the total edge length?
   (**c**) Calculate the area of the front face.
   (**d**) Copy and complete the table.
   (**e**) What is the total area of all six faces?

Face	Area
Front	
Top	
Left hand side	

4 For this pyramid:

(**a**) Copy and complete the table.

Edge length	Number of edges
5 cm	
11 cm	

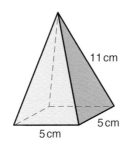

(**b**) What is the total edge length?

(**c**) What is the area of the base?

5 For this triangular prism:

(**a**) Copy and complete the table.

Edge length	Number of edges
4 cm	
12 cm	

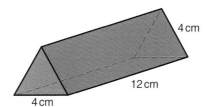

(**b**) What is the total edge length?

(**c**) What is the area of the base?

Review exercise 16

You need isometric dot paper for question 4.

1 For each shape identify the green section as a vertex, edge or face.

(**a**)   (**b**) 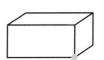   (**c**)

(**d**) 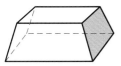   (**e**)   (**f**)

2 For the first three shapes shown in question 1, copy and complete the table.

Shape	Name	Number of			
		Vertices	Edges	Faces
(a)				
(b)				
(c)				

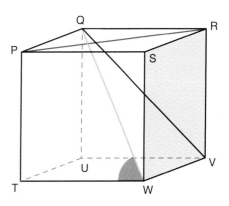

3 For this diagram, name the:

(**a**) red diagonal

(**b**) green space diagonal

(**c**) blue angle

(**d**) yellow face.

4 On isometric dot paper draw each 3D shape.

(a)

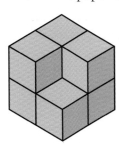

(b)

5 Calculate the volume of each 3D shape.

(a)

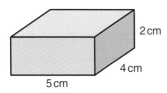

2 cm
4 cm
5 cm

(b)

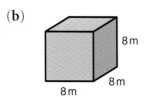

8 m
8 m
8 m

6 For each skeleton model below:
  (i) list the number of each edge length
  (ii) list the number of vertices.

(a)

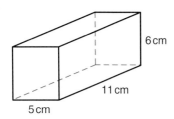

6 cm
11 cm
5 cm

(b)

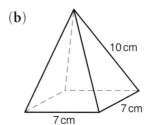

10 cm
7 cm
7 cm

7 Copy and complete the table to show which net would build each shape.

3D shape	Net
(a)	
(b)	
(c)	

(a)

(b)

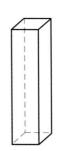

(c)

(i)

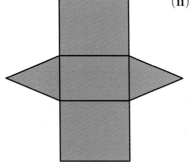

(ii)

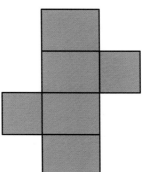

(iii)

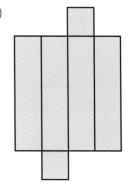

Summary

A solid shape has three dimensions: length, breadth and height.

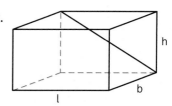

3D shapes have vertices, edges and faces.

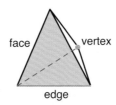

LMQP is a face.
SN is a diagonal.
MS is a space diagonal.

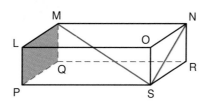

The green angle is ∠CEH or ∠HEC.

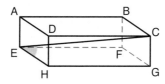

3D shapes may be drawn on isometric dot paper.

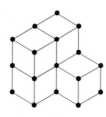

Volume = length × breadth × height
$= 6 \times 4 \times 3$
$= 72$ cubic cm or cm^3.

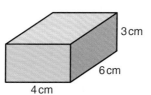

A 3D shape may be formed from a net.

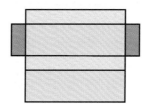

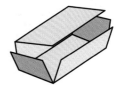

17 Formulae

In this chapter you will learn to construct and use formulae in both words and symbols.

17.1 Constructing formulae in words

Petals on flowers

1 flower

2 flowers

3 flowers

4 flowers

The next pattern in the sequence would be:

The number of flowers and petals can be shown in a table.

The number of petals increases 5 at a time.

Number of flowers	Number of petals
1	5
2	10
3	15
4	20

The number of petals is **5 times** the number of flowers.
You can use this **formula** to find the number of petals when you know the number of flowers.
For 6 flowers there would be 5 × 6 = 30 petals
For 20 flowers there would be 5 × 20 = 100 petals

Exercise 17.1

1 Leaves on stems

1 stem

2 stems

3 stems

(**a**) Draw the next pattern in the sequence.
(**b**) Copy and complete the table:
(**c**) Find the increase in the number of leaves each time.
(**d**) Copy and complete the formula:
The number of leaves is _____ times the number of stems.
(**e**) Use your formula to find how many leaves are on (**i**) 7 stems (**ii**) 12 stems.

Number of stems	Number of leaves
1	3
2	
3	
4	

2 Seedlings in pots

1 pot

2 pots

3 pots

(**a**) Draw the next pattern in the sequence.
(**b**) Copy and complete the table
(**c**) Find the increase in the number of seedlings each time.
(**d**) Copy and complete the formula:
The number of seedlings is _____ times the number of pots.
(**e**) Use your formula to find how many seedlings would be in
(**i**) 9 pots   (**ii**) 15 pots.

Number of pots	Number of seedlings
1	4
2	
3	
4	

3 Tomatoes on branches

1 branch

2 branches

3 branches

(**a**) Draw the next pattern in the sequence.
(**b**) Make a table using *Number of branches* and *Number of tomatoes*.
(**c**) Find the increase in the number of tomatoes each time.
(**d**) Write a formula for the number of tomatoes when you know the number of branches.
(**e**) Use your formula to find how many tomatoes are on
(**i**) 10 branches   (**ii**) 15 branches

Number of branches	Number of tomatoes
1	6

4 Carnations in a bunch

1 bunch

2 bunches

3 bunches

(**a**) Draw the next pattern in the sequence.
(**b**) Make a table using *Number of bunches* and *Number of carnations*.
(**c**) Find the increase in the number of carnations each time.
(**d**) Write a formula for the number of carnations when you know the number of bunches.
(**e**) Use your formula to find how many carnations are in
(**i**) 20 bunches   (**ii**) 25 bunches.

17.2 Word formulae from graphs

The graph shows the number of horns plotted against the number of cows

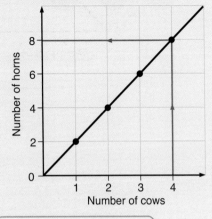

Notice that the graph is a straight line starting at zero.

From the graph you can make a table and then construct a formula as before.

Number of cows	Number of horns
1	2
2	4
3	6
4	8

The number of horns increases 2 at a time.

The number of horns is **2 times** the number of cows.

You can use this formula to find the number of horns when you know the number of cows. For 24 cows there would be 2 × 24 = 48 horns.

Exercise 17.2

1 (a) Using the graph, copy and complete the table.

Number of spiders	Number of legs
1	
2	
3	
4	

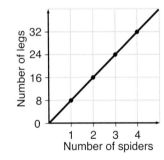

(b) Find the increase in the number of legs each time.
(c) Write a formula to find the number of legs when you know the number of spiders.
(d) Use your formula to find the number of legs on
    (i) 5 spiders   **(ii)** 12 spiders.

2 (a) Using the graph, make a table to show *Number of centipedes* and *Number of legs*.
(b) Write a formula to find the number of legs when you know the number of centipedes.
(c) How many legs are on
    (i) 10 centipedes   **(ii)** 15 centipedes?

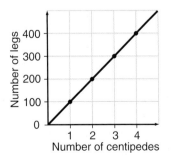

3 (**a**) Using the graph, make a table to show *Number of fish* and *Number of fins*.
   (**b**) Write a formula to find the number of fins when you know the number of fish.
   (**c**) How many fins are on
      (**i**) 8 fish　　　　　(**ii**) 20 fish?

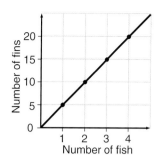

17.3 Formulae in symbols

A book costs £9.

The table shows the cost of books.

Number of books (*b*)	Cost in £s (*c*)
1	9
2	18
3	27
4	36

> *c* stands for the cost in pounds and *b* stands for the number of books.

The increase in the number of pounds each time is 9.

The formula is:　cost equals 9 times the number of books.

The formula in symbols is:　　$c = 9 \times b$
　　　　　　　　　　　　　　$c = 9b$

The cost of 8 books would be $9 \times 8 = £72$.

Exercise 17.3

1 A box holds 12 pencils.
   (**a**) Copy and complete the table.

Number of boxes (*b*)	Number of pencils (*p*)
1	12
2	
3	
4	

   (**b**) Find the increase in the number of pencils each time.
   (**c**) Write a formula in words to find the number of pencils when you know the number of boxes.
   (**d**) If *p* stands for the number of pencils and *b* stands for the number of boxes, write the formula in symbols.
   (**e**) Use your formula to find how many pencils are in
      (**i**) 6 boxes　　　　　(**ii**) 10 boxes.

2 A jotter has 48 pages.
   (**a**) Make a table to show the numbers of pages in up to 4 jotters.
   (**b**) Find the increase in the number of pages each time.
   (**c**) Using p to stand for the number of pages and j for the number of jotters, write a formula to find the number of pages when you know the number of jotters.
   (**d**) Use your formula to find how many pages are in a packet of
      (**i**) 10 jotters   (**ii**) 50 jotters.

3 A box contains 24 sharpeners
   (**a**) Make a table to show the number of sharpeners in up to 4 boxes.
   (**b**) Find the increase in the number of sharpeners each time.
   (**c**) Using s for the number of sharpeners and b for the number of boxes, write a formula for the number of sharpeners.
   (**d**) How many sharpeners are in 20 boxes?

4 A box contains 15 sets of compasses.
   (**a**) Make a table to show the number of compasses in up to 4 boxes.
   (**b**) Find the increase in the number of compasses each time.
   (**c**) Using c for the number of compasses and b for the number of boxes, write a formula for the number of compasses.
   (**d**) How many compasses are in 8 boxes?

5 A pad of graph paper has 50 sheets.
   (**a**) Make a table with s for the number of sheets and p for the number of pads. Use the table to show the number of sheets in up to 4 pads.
   (**b**) Use s and p to write a formula for the number of sheets.
   (**c**) How many sheets are in 12 pads?

6 The cost of a new computer is £900.
   (**a**) Make a table with c for the cost and n for the number of computers. Use the table to show the cost for up to 4 computers.
   (**b**) Write a formula for the cost of computers.
   (**c**) Find the cost of 9 computers.

7 Coaches hired for a school trip seat 57 passengers.
   (**a**) Using p for the number of passengers and c for the number of coaches, write a formula for the number of passengers on a trip when all the coaches are full.
   (**b**) How many passengers will travel on 7 full coaches?

17.4 More complex formulae in words

When escorting dangerous prisoners a guard is handcuffed to each side of the prisoner with another guard leading the way.

1 prisoner

2 prisoners

3 prisoners

4 prisoners

This can be shown in a table.

Number of prisoners	Number of guards
1	3
2	5
3	7
4	9

> The number of guards increases by 2 each time.

The number of guards is 2 times the number of prisoners **plus 1**.

You can use this formula to find the number of guards when you know the number of prisoners.

For 20 prisoners there would be 2 × 20 + 1 = 41 guards.

Exercise 17.4

1 Matchstick squares

Matchsticks have been arranged in a pattern of joined squares.

1 square

2 squares

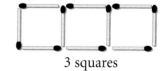

3 squares

(a) Draw the next pattern in the sequence.
(b) Copy and complete the table:

Number of squares	Number of matches
1	4
2	
3	
4	

(c) What is the increase in the number of matches each time?
(d) Copy and complete the formula.
     The number of matches is _____ times the number of squares plus _____ .
(e) How many matches are needed to make 9 squares?

2 Borders edging stones

Rectangular flower beds in a park have metre long edging stones.

1st bed   2nd bed   3rd bed

(a) Draw the next pattern in the sequence.

(b) Copy and complete the table:

(c) What is the increase in the number of edging stones each time?

Bed number	Number of stones
1	4
2	

(d) Copy and complete the formula.

The number of stones is _____ times the bed number plus _____

(e) How many stones are needed to go round the edge of bed number 15?

3 Garden slabs

In a large garden, paving slabs were laid around the edges of square flower beds.

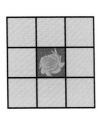 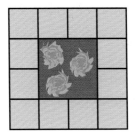 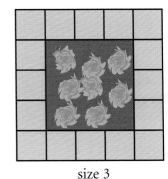

size 1   size 2   size 3

(a) Draw the next pattern in the sequence.

(b) Copy and complete the table:

Size of square	Number of slabs
1	8
2	

(c) What is the increase in the number of slabs each time?

(d) Write a formula for the number of slabs using the size of square.

(e) How many slabs are needed for a 9 metre square?

4 Seats round tables

 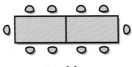 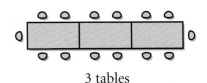

1 table   2 tables   3 tables

(a) Draw the next pattern in the sequence.

(b) Make a table to show *Number of tables* and *Numbers of seats*.

(c) Find the increase in the number of seats each time.

(d) Write a formula for the number of seats when you know the number of tables.

(e) How many seats should go round 8 tables?

5 Sheep pens

Sheep pens at the market are made by arranging portable barriers against a wall.

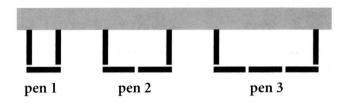

pen 1   **pen 2**   **pen 3**

(a) Draw the next pattern in the sequence.
(b) Make a table to show *Pen size* and *Number of barriers*.
(c) Write a formula to find the number of barriers when you know the pen size.
(d) How many barriers are needed for pen 9?

17.5 More complex formulae in symbols

Exercise 17.5

In this exercise, patterns of shapes have been made from matchsticks.
For each example in the exercise:

(i) Draw the next pattern in the sequence.
(ii) Make a table for the pattern of numbers.
(iii) Find the increase number.
(iv) Use the symbols s and n to write a formula.
(v) Use the formula to find the number of matchsticks in the 7th pattern.

Shape number (s)	Number of matchsticks (n)
1	
2	

1

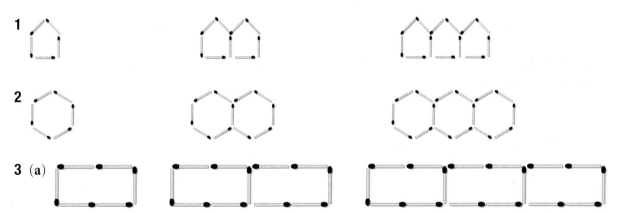

2

3 (a)

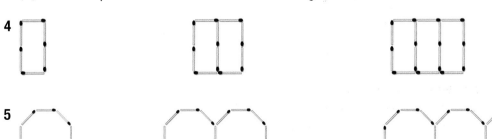

(b) What do you notice about the formulae for questions 2 and 3?

4

5

Review exercise 17

1 Bottles in a carrier

1 carrier   2 carriers   3 carriers

(**a**) How many bottles could be carried in 4 carriers?
(**b**) Make a table using *Number of carriers* and *Number of bottles*.
(**c**) Find the increase in the number of bottles each time.
(**d**) Write a formula in words for the number of bottles when you know the number of carriers.
(**e**) Use your formula to find how many bottles could be held in
    (**i**) 8 carriers   (**ii**) 12 carriers.

2 (**a**) Using the graph, make a table to show *Number of people* and *Number of toes*.
(**b**) Write a formula in words to find the number of toes when you know the number of people.
(**c**) How many toes are on
    (**i**) 9 people   (**ii**) 20 people?

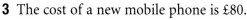

3 The cost of a new mobile phone is £80.
(**a**) Make a table with *Number of phones* (p) and *Cost in £s* (c).
    Use the table to show the cost for up to 4 phones.
(**b**) Using letters write a formula for the cost of this type of mobile phone.
(**c**) Find the cost of 11 phones.

4 This pattern has been made from matchsticks.

  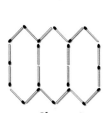

    Shape 1   Shape 2   Shape 3

(**a**) Draw the next pattern in the sequence.
(**b**) Copy and complete the table for 4 shapes.
(**c**) Find the increase number.
(**d**) Use symbols to write a formula for the number of matches.
(**e**) Use the formula to find the number of matches in the 7th pattern.

Shape number (s)	Number of matchsticks (n)
1	

Summary

To construct a formula

Identify the pattern by
– drawing the next picture
– studying the graph
– understanding the word
  explanation

Shrubs in plots

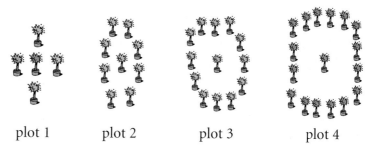

plot 1　　　plot 2　　　plot 3　　　plot 4

Draw a table to show the pattern of numbers.

Plot number (p)	Number of shrubs (n)
1	5
2	9
3	13
4	17

Find the increase number in the right-hand column of the table.

The number of shrubs increases by 4 each time.

Write the formula

– use the headings from the table or symbols for these headings.
– use the increase number to multiply
– check to see if a number must be added

The number of shrubs = 4 × the plot number + 1

$$s = 4p + 1$$

Use the formula

The number of shrubs in plot number 7 would be
$4 \times 7 + 1 = 29$

18 Problem solving

Exercise 18.1

1 • Colour this shape on squared paper and cut it out.
   • Cut the shape into 5 squares.
   • Fit the 5 squares together to make a rectangle.
   • Can you fit the 5 squares together to make a 10 by 3 rectangle? Explain.

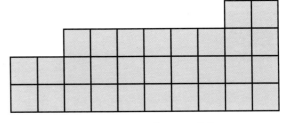

2 A family crosses a river on a raft.
   The maximum weight the raft can carry is 100 kg.

   Bud weighs 75 kg.   Jo-Anne weighs 57 kg.
   Ben weighs 46 kg.   Sue weighs 38 kg.

   (a) Jo-Anne, Sue and Ben want to cross the river using as few crossings as possible.
       In what order should they cross?
   (b) What is the least number of crossings needed for the whole family to cross?

3 A sprint team must have three members.
   One boy has to be chosen from **each** age group.
   List all the possible teams.

4 (a) You need a ruler for this question. Copy and complete.

Rectangle	P	Q	R	S
Length in cm				
Breadth in cm				
Area in cm^2				

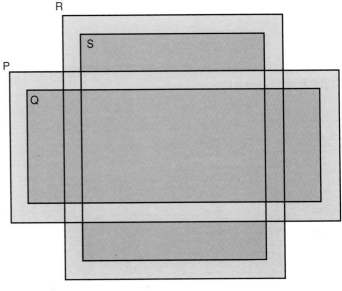

   (b) Find the area of this tile.

   (c) How many of these tiles cover each rectangle?
   (d) Show on centimetre squared paper how the tiles cover each rectangle.
   (e) Can you cover an 8 cm by 5 cm rectangle exactly with these tiles? Explain.

5 Chris makes rugs 5 feet by 3 feet from these carpet off-cuts.

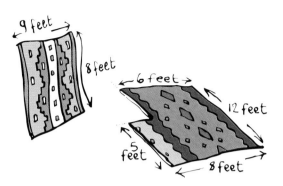

   (**a**) Sketch each carpet on squared paper.

   (**b**) Show how he could cut each carpet to make the greatest number of rugs.

6 Jean is using a scale drawing to plan the layout of the garden.
She has divided it into 16 equal squares, as shown below.
She wants to plant fruit (f), beans (b), carrots (c) and potatoes (p).

 The plots for each crop will have the **same shape and area**.
Here is the plot for fruit.
Copy the plan.

   (**a**) Design a layout for the garden.

   (**b**) Design a layout if each plot is T-shaped as shown.

7 Arundhati is an architect. She designs windows using identical panes of glass.
The panes are twice as long as they are broad.
The windows must be rectangles or squares.

Using 1 pane, 2 window designs are possible.

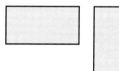

Using 2 panes, 4 window designs are possible.

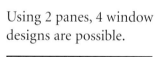

Here is one of Arundhati's designs for a 3-pane window.

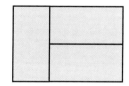

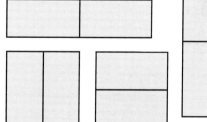

   (**a**) Draw all the possible window designs which use 3-panes.

   (**b**) Copy and complete:

Number of panes	1	2	3
Number of designs			

   (**c**) How many window designs do you think can be made using 4 panes?
Check your answer by drawing each design.

8

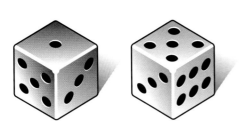

A game is played by throwing two dice, one red and the other blue.

List all the possible pairs of numbers in a table like this.

1, 1	1, 2	1, 3	1, 4	1, 5	1, 6
2, 1	2, 2	2, 3			
3, 1	3, 2				

(a) How many possible pairs are there?

(b) How many ways are there of scoring a **total** of
   (i) 12   (ii) 9   (iii) 7   (iv) 3?

9

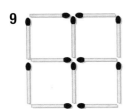

This pattern of 12 matches has five squares – four small squares and one large square.

Start with the same 12-match pattern each time.

(a) Draw the pattern left when you remove:
   (i) 2 matches to leave 3 squares   (ii) 4 matches to leave 1 square
   (iii) 5 matches to leave 2 squares   (iv) 4 matches to leave 2 squares.

(b) What is the least number of matches that have to be removed to leave
   (i) 2 squares   (ii) 3 squares?

10 You need scissors for part (b)

A flowchart lists instructions.
You have to follow them in order.

Every flowchart has:
- a title
- Start and Stop boxes
- Instruction boxes
- arrows between boxes

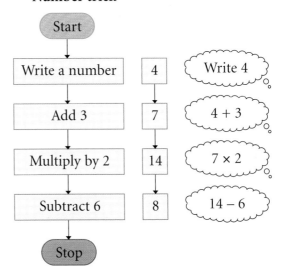

(a) Copy and complete this table:

Starting number	4	5	2	7
Answer	8			

(b) Copy the instructions and cut them out.
Design a flowchart which always gives the answer 6.

| Add 2 | | Multiply by 6 | | Think of a number | | Start |

| Subtract 12 | | Divide by the number you thought of | | Stop |

(c) Check your flowchart works using at least 3 starting numbers.

11 (a) Read this flowchart. Check that the correct path has been followed for each of the starting numbers 3 and 10.

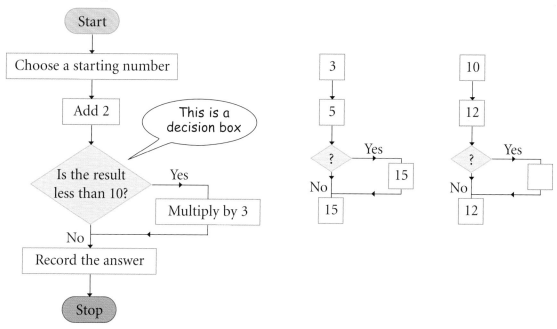

Number puzzle

(b) Copy and complete the table.

Starting number	3	10	7	4	12	21	8
Answer	15						

12 George Smith and Sarah Jones are buying cars at Mitchell's Motors.

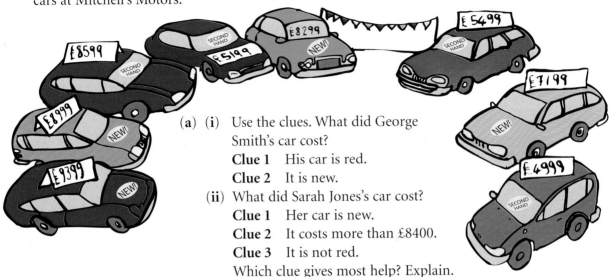

(a) (i) Use the clues. What did George Smith's car cost?

Clue 1   His car is red.

Clue 2   It is new.

(ii) What did Sarah Jones's car cost?

Clue 1   Her car is new.

Clue 2   It costs more than £8400.

Clue 3   It is not red.

Which clue gives most help? Explain.

(b) (i) Copy the number plates. To find George Smith's number plate, score out the number plates which are eliminated by each clue.

Clue 1   The number plate begins with G.

Clue 2   It contains a vowel.

(ii) Write George Smith's number plate.

G302 TYY	F614 YEP	D206 FYF	C426 GWN
F205 YCY	C299 AYW	G489 TYY	D167 EYN
E345 KJD	G183 UHM	E721 NWN	C400 HEP
F352 YEP	D516 EYN	C768 AYW	G253 FTH

(c) (i) Copy the number plates.

(ii) Which three of these number plates fit these clues?

Clue 1   They begin with F.

Clue 2   They contain a 2-digit number.

(iii) Write a third clue which will eliminate **two** of these number plates.

(iv) Write the number plate which remains.

F124 NYX	H91 VTH	F52 YEP	D22 NWN
E701 YEP	E503 KJD	H26 VCY	F986 NYW
D82 GWN	F49 YEP	F204 NYX	F430 YCY
H861 WYR	F560 NYW	E34 KJD	F50 YEP

(d) Mitchell's Motors had a prize draw. Some customers won free petrol.

The number of the ticket winning first prize was **even** and **between 1 and 41**.

(i) List the possible winning tickets.

(ii) Score out the numbers eliminated by these clues:

Clue 1   The number is a multiple of 4.

Clue 2   Its digits add up to 5.

(iii) Write the winning number.

(**e**) Mitchell's Motors had a raffle. Find the number of the ticket winning second prize. Read all the clues before you start.

Second prize

Clue 1   The number is greater than 50.   **Clue 4**   It is less than 140.
Clue 2   It is an odd number.   **Clue 5**   It is divisible by 9.
Clue 3   It is divisible by 5.

(**f**) Mitchell's Motors held a 'Win a Car' competition. Customers had to guess how far the car would travel on 5 litres of petrol. Who won the car?

Clue 1   The number of km is even.   **Clue 3**   The number of m is less than 300.
Clue 2   The number of km is greater than 50.   **Clue 4**   The number of m is odd.

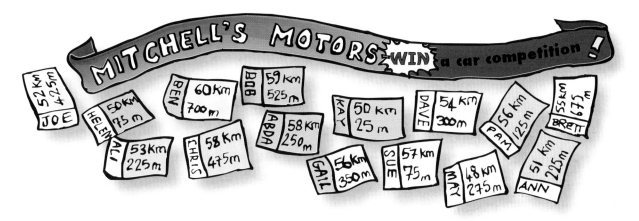

(**g**) Copy the table. Use the clues to help you complete the table showing the colour and model – saloon, estate, or hatchback – of each person's car.

Clue 1   George Smith's car is red.
Clue 2   Sarah Jones's car is the saloon.
Clue 3   Mark Wilson's car is not the white one.
Clue 4   The green car is not the estate.

Owner	Colour	Model
George Smith		

(**h**) Copy the table. Use the clues to help you complete the table showing the engine size and make – Ford, Rover or VW – of each person's car.

Clue 1   The 1600 cc engine is not in Ismael's car.
Clue 2   Dorothy's car is the VW.
Clue 3   The 1800 cc engine is in Ian's car.
Clue 4   The Rover has the 2000 cc engine.

Owner	Engine size	Make

(**i**) Four cars are each made in a different country – Britain, France, Italy and Japan. The four cars are different types and colours.

Clue 1   The French car is red.   **Clue 4**   The convertible is yellow.
Clue 2   The British car is a saloon.   **Clue 5**   The Japanese car is not white.
Clue 3   The white car is a hatchback.   **Clue 6**   The green car is not the estate.

Identify the colour, country and type for each car.

Truly impossible

The artist M C Escher was fascinated by impossible figures. Look carefully at the water flow in his drawing 'The Waterfall'.

You can find more impossible shapes and intriguing ideas on how to create your own in the book *Adventures with Impossible Figures* by Bruno Ernst.

13 You need 1 cm isometric paper.

This is an impossible triangle. You can draw it but it cannot be made.

Copy the shape.

Your impossible triangle has a side length of 6 cm.

Draw an impossible triangle with a side length of 8 cm.

This is an impossible rectangle.

Copy the shape.

Your impossible rectangle measures 8 cm by 4 cm.

Draw an impossible rectangle which measures 7 cm by 5 cm.

Copy and colour each of these impossible shapes.

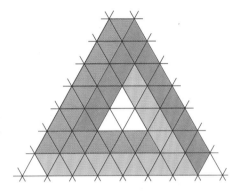

Answers

Chapter 1 Whole Numbers

Exercise 1.1

1 (a) 12 640 (b) 50 300 (c) 2 413 627 (d) 5 602 050
  (e) 14 220 000
2 (a) two thousand four hundred and six
  (b) fifteen thousand two hundred and twelve
  (c) five thousand and four
  (d) one hundred and twenty thousand three hundred
  (e) seven million three hundred and sixty four thousand
  (f) one million three hundred thousand and ten
  (g) four million two hundred and thirty thousand one hundred and forty six
  (h) three million thirty four thousand six hundred and fifty nine
4 (a) 10 840 (b) 99 400 (c) 1 455 200 (d) 61 520 (e) 17 100
  (f) 1 640 000
5 19 500   6 330 000   7 294 000
8 a = 670 b = 8200 c = 4230 d = 5620 e = 4200 f = 10 400
9 (a) 9090, 9099, 9800, 10 090, 10 110, 10 900
  (b) 312 000, 312 509, 312 540, 313 509, 314 217
10 293 702, 314 293, 314 442, 316 883, 360 642, 397 997, 407 844

Exercise 1.2

1 (a) 1130 m (b) 1150 m (c) 1340 m (d) 960 m
2 (a) (i) 7860 (ii) 70 (iii) 150 (iv) 290 (v) 700 (vi) 30
  (vii) 5110 (viii) 4000 (ix) 15 670 (x) 18 730
  (b) (i) 7900 (ii) 100 (iii) 100 (iv) 300 (v) 700 (vi) 0
  (vii) 5100 (viii) 4000 (ix) 15 700 (x) 18 700
3 2000 1500 2200
4 (a) 22 200 60 300 (b) 22 000 60 000
   13 700 10 700   14 000 11 000
   50 400 18 000   50 000 18 000
5 (a) (i) 1260 260 180 25 730 6320 6930 1440 260 360
   (ii) 1300 300 200 25 700 6300 6900 1400 300 400
  (b) (i) 120 900 451 700 611 400 208 600 227 400 146 800
      22 700 177 200 81 700
   (ii) 121 000 452 000 611 000 209 000 227 000 147 000
      23 000 177 000 82 000
   (iii) 120 000 450 000 610 000 210 000 230 000 150 000
      20 000 180 000 80 000
6 (a) 311 800 (b) 312 000
7 (a) 928 512 000 (b) 929 000 000
8 £51 100 000

Exercise 1.3

1 (a) 80 (b) 970 (c) 50 (d) 150 (e) 60 (f) 460
2 (a) 1100 (b) 100 (c) 8000 (d) 1500 (e) 800 (f) 700
3 (a) 11 000 (b) 10 000 (c) 18 000 (d) 1000 (e) 2000 (f) 10 000
4 700 °C
5 (a) 15 000 (b) 3000

Exercise 1.4

1 (a) 87 (b) 111 (c) 155 (d) 232 (e) 110
2 (a) 100 (b) 101 (c) 119 (d) 121 (e) 122
3 (a) 65 (b) 71 (c) 209 (d) 133 (e) 184
4 (a) 73 (b) 110 (c) 207 (d) 225 (e) 160 (f) 720
  (g) 305 (h) 284 (i) 151 (j) 1110 (k) 514 (l) 1998
5 93p 6 242 7 83 8 91m

Exercise 1.5

1 (a) 24 (b) 45 (c) 49 (d) 106 (e) 218
2 (a) 9 (b) 28 (c) 53 (d) 54 (e) 59
3 (a) 67 (b) 26 (c) 85 (d) 9 (e) 123

4 (a) 52 (b) 12 (c) 16 (d) 39 (e) 16 (f) 92
  (g) 88 (h) 69 (i) 1995 (j) 1014 (k) 146 (l) 255
5 44cm 6 265ml 7 375

Exercise 1.6

1 (a) 598 (b) 761 (c) 580 (d) 716 (e) 931 (f) 1218
  (g) 1217 (h) 1369 (i) 2900 (j) 5914 (k) 18 026 (l) 5144
2 (a) 234 (b) 234 (c) 737 (d) 619 (e) 544 (f) 374
  (g) 1167 (h) 77 (i) 763 (j) 2484 (k) 2465 (l) 3872
3 £472   4 (a) 17 162 (b) 2222
5 293   6 (a) 543 (b) 589
7 2139   8 £4584   9 Golden Gate 274m
10 £1874   11 £92 621
12 (a) 1089 (b) Always 1089

Exercise 1.7

1 (a) 30 (b) 32 (c) 54 (d) 35 (e) 56 (f) 30
  (g) 96 (h) 81 (i) 28 (j) 8 (k) 20 (l) 7
  (m) 6 (n) 7 (o) 6 (p) 8 (q) 8 (r) 8
  (s) 10 (t) 9
2 96p   3 8   4 £230
5 (a) 27 (b) 81   6 Yes 4m extra

Exercise 1.8

1 (a) 300 (b) 136 (c) 136 (d) 252 (e) 73 (f) 45
  (g) 310 (h) 306 (i) 176 (j) 1608
2 228   3 238   4 16   5 4736   6 154
7 (a) 184 (b) 91

Exercise 1.9

1 (a) 666 (b) 595 (c) 1026 (d) 1722 (e) 968 (f) 7662
  (g) 17 968 (h) 23 112
2 (a) 46 (b) 96 (c) 143 (d) 142 (e) 12 (f) 116
  (g) 370 (h) 267
3 £1029 4 24 5 2571 6 17 7 £920

Exercise 1.10

1 (a) 260, 2600 (b) 8230, 82 300 (c) 4500, 45 000
  (d) 3000, 30 000 (e) 56 200, 562 000 (f) 22 000, 220 000
  (g) 38 670, 386 700 (h) 30 300, 303 000 (i) 124 060, 1 240 600
  (j) 305 060, 3 050 600
2 (a) 420 (b) 810 (c) 1600 (d) 3000 (e) 3360
  (f) 6300 (g) 24 300 (h) 40 000 (i) 15 200 (j) 72 800
  (k) 61 800 (l) 144 000 (m) 51 270 (n) 70 200 (o) 630 000
3 £980   4 £8000   5 £1170   6 75 days

Exercise 1.11

1 (a) 30, 3 (b) 20, 2 (c) 800, 80 (d) 600, 60 (e) 340, 34
  (f) 620, 62 (g) 1780, 178 (h) 20 000, 2000 (i) 1550, 155
  (j) 28 950, 2895
2 (a) 44 (b) 32 (c) 8 (d) 17 (e) 13 (f) 90
  (g) 45 (h) 82 (i) 20 (j) 7 (k) 12 (l) 17
  (m) 32 (n) 8
3 5   4 (a) 6 (b) 20 (c) 48
5 (a) 10 (b) 50 (c) 300   6 11

Exercise 1.12

1 2100   2 (a) 600 (b) 2400
3 £200   4 40   5 7 days   6 1000

Exercise 1.13

1 735km   2 £936   3 £210   4 £912
5 (a) £442   (b) £1360   (c) £958
6 (a) £103 800 (b) £40 800 (c) £63 000
7 (a) 62 × 53 = 3286   (b) 2 × 356 = 712

Exercise 1.14

1 450 g flour, 225 g sugar, 150 g almonds, 375 g margarine
2 64   3 £1514   4 118 000   5 1600   6 212 520
7 (a) 1 172 800   (b) 311 500 (c) 784 300
8 1100 kg   9 22
10

Item 1	Item 2	Item 3	Cost
skirt	trousers	jumper	£68
skirt	trousers	blouse	£68
skirt	trousers	jacket	£76
skirt	blouse	jumper	£61
skirt	blouse	jacket	£76
skirt	jumper	jacket	£76
blouse	jumper	trousers	£57
blouse	jumper	jacket	£65
blouse	trousers	jacket	£72
jumper	trousers	jacket	£72

Review exercise 1

1 (a) four hundred and eighty two   (b) eight thousand and twenty
   (c) one hundred and twenty thousand three hundred and ten
   (d) two hundred and seventy one thousand and fifteen
   (e) two million six hundred and seventy two thousand
2 (a) 6082   (b) 24 500 (c) 64 587   (d) 150 020 (e) 9 672 300
3 16 809, 16 856, 16 865, 16 880, 16 980
4 (a) (i) 350   (ii) 490   (iii) 800   (iv) 5370   (v) 12 280
   (b) (i) 300   (ii) 500   (iii) 800   (iv) 5400   (v) 12 300
5 1 684 000   1 270 000   983 000   567 000
6 (a) 5000   (b) 4503
7 (a) £500   (b) £439
8 566   9 2413   10 £2273
11 (a) 11 923 (b) 5512   (c) 14 115   (d) 40 487   (e) 759
   (f) 11 990
12 (a) 86   (b) 90   (c) 282   (d) 632   (e) 179   (f) 57
   (g) 19   (h) 48   (i) 133   (j) 18   (k) 192   (l) 102
   (m) 749   (n) 1495   (o) 610   (p) 47   (q) 86   (r) 42
   (s) 63   (t) 24
13 £524 500
14 (a) 470, 4700   (b) 3600, 36 000   (c) 526, 400, 5 264 000
   (d) 134 560, 1 345 600 (e) 256 000, 2 560 000
15 (a) 280, 28   (b) 15 300, 1530 (c) 59 200, 5920 (d) 60 120, 6012
16 (a) 1080   (b) 4830   (c) 215 000   (d) 7200
   (e) 23 400   (f) 8400   (g) 84   (h) 21
   (i) 300   (j) 14   (k) 14   (l) 1550
17 6800   18 84   19 £1752

Chapter 2 Sequences, multiples and factors

Exercise 2.1

1 (i)   (a) 19, 23   (b) add 4
   (ii)   (a) 28, 33   (b) add 5
   (iii) (a) 88, 84   (b) subtract 4
   (iv)   (a) 80, 160   (b) multiply by 2
   (v)   (a) 30, 37   (b) add 7
   (vi)   (a) 3, 1   (b) divide by 3
   (vii) (a) 50, 0   (b) subtract 50
   (viii) (a) 24, 31   (b) add 1, then 2, then 3 etc
   (ix)   (a) 150, 75   (b) divide by 2
   (x)   (a) 107, 428   (b) multiply by 4, subtract 1 alternatively
2 (a) 98   (b) 87
3 £512   4 10, 40, 70, 100

5 (a) 21, 28, 36   (b) 42, 56, 72   (c) 36, 49, 64
6 (a) 21, 34   (b) 29, 47   (c) 112, 180   (d) 146, 237

7

5	7	12	19	31	50
18	15	33	48	81	129
23	22	45	67	112	179
41	37	78	115	193	308
64	59	123	182	305	487
105	96	201	297	498	795

8   1   5   10   10   5   1
     1   6   15   20   15   6   1

Exercise 2.2

2 (a) 16, 28, 52, 36   (b) 81, 36, 54   (c) 36
3 (a) 35   (b) 10, 20, 30…   (c) 52, 56…
   (d) 12, 24…   (e) 63, 126…   (f) 24
4 (a) 15   (b) 21   (c) 12   (d) 105
5 (a) 1, 3, 5, 15   (b) 1, 2, 3, 4, 6, 8, 12, 16, 24, 48
   (c) 1, 2, 4, 5, 10, 20, 25, 50, 100   (d) 1, 5
   (e) 1, 2, 3, 4, 6, 9, 12, 18, 36
6 (a) 1, 3, 15, 60   (b) 1, 3, 9, 15
7 1, 2 or 4
8 (a) (i) 1, 2, 4, 8   (ii) 1, 2, 3, 6   (b) 1, 2
   (c) (i) 1, 3   (ii) 1, 3, 5, 15   (iii) 1, 2, 3, 6, 9, 18   (d) 1, 3
9 (a) 2   (b) 4   (c) 15

Exercise 2.3

1 3, 4, 5   2 82
3 (a) 4056, 726, 111 111, 372, 1530, 27 132, 99, 273
   (b) 1250, 1530, 125
   (c) 1530
4 (a) ④ 28 ⑦   (b) 18   126   7   (c) 20   8000   400
        12   56   216   161   1200   3200
        ③ 24 ⑧   12   276   23   60   4800   80

5 (a)

9	4	5
2	6	10
7	8	3

   (b)

13	8	9
6	10	14
11	12	7

6

6	13	8
11	⑨	⑦
10	5	12

7

6	1	4	0
3	2	5	3
2	5	0	4

   5   0   7   1
8 (a)   16   (b)   134   (c)   29   (d)   3657
       +82   −85   ×5   +2438
       ___   ___   ___   ____
        98   49   145   6095
10 300

Review exercise 2

1 (i)   (a) 27, 30   (b) add 3
   (ii) (a) 76, 70   (b) subtract 6
   (iii) (a) 80, 40   (b) divide by 2
   (iv) (a) 243, 729   (b) multiply by 3
2 (a) (i) 7, 14, 56   (ii) 8, 20, 24, 32, 40, 56
   (b) (i) 2, 8, 20, 40   (ii) 2, 8, 32
   (c) 30
3 (a) 15   (b) 30   (c) 8   (d) 12
4 (a) 6   (b) 10   (c) 8   (d) 9

Chapter 3 Symmetry

Exercise 3.1

2 (a) (i)   (ii)
   (b) (iii)   (v)
   (c) 2   (d) 4
3 a, b, e, g

4 (a)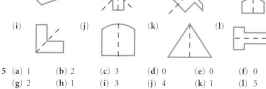

(b)　(c)　(d)

(e)　(f)　(g)　(h)

(i)　(j)　(k)　(l)

5 (a) 1　**(b)** 2　**(c)** 3　**(d)** 0　**(e)** 0　**(f)** 0
　(g) 2　**(h)** 1　**(i)** 3　**(j)** 4　**(k)** 1　**(l)** 5

6 (a)

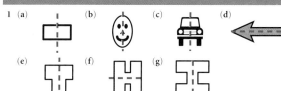

(b) 0

7 Worksheet 3.1

| 1 | 2 | 3 0 | 4 0 | 5 | 6 0 |
| 7 | 8 | 9 | 10 | 11 | 12 |

Exercise 3.2

1 (a)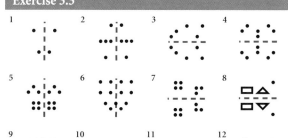

(b)　(c)　(d)

(e)　(f)　(g)

2 (a) HELLO, I LOVE MATHS　**(b)** MY NAME IS BOB
　(c) PASSWORD IS BADDY

3 (a)

4 (a) 3 + 10 = 13　**(b)** 33 ÷ 3 = 11
5 (a)　(b)　(c)　(d)

6 Worksheet 3.2

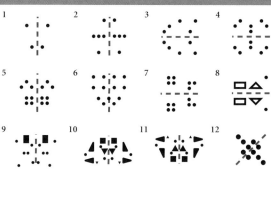

1	2	3	4
5	6	7	8
9	10	11	12

Exercise 3.3

1	2	3	4
5	6	7	8
9	10	11	12

13　**14**　**15**

Review exercise 3

1 a, b, c, d
2 (a) 2　**(b)** 0　**(c)** 2　**(d)** 1　**(e)** 3
3 (a)　(b)　(c)

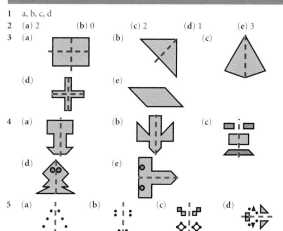

(d)　(e)

4 (a)　(b)　(c)

(d)　(e)

5 (a)　(b)　(c)　(d)

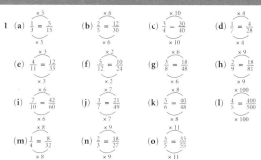

Chapter 4 Fractions

Exercise 4.1

1 (a) (i) $\frac{1}{3}$　**(ii)** $\frac{2}{3}$　**(b) (i)** $\frac{1}{5}$　**(ii)** $\frac{4}{5}$
　(c) (i) $\frac{3}{5}$　**(ii)** $\frac{2}{5}$　**(d) (i)** $\frac{1}{4}$　**(ii)** $\frac{3}{4}$
　(e) (i) $\frac{5}{11}$　**(ii)** $\frac{6}{11}$　**(f) (i)** $\frac{4}{9}$　**(ii)** $\frac{2}{9}$　**(iii)** $\frac{8}{9}$
　(g) (i) $\frac{3}{10}$　**(ii)** $\frac{7}{10}$　**(h) (i)** $\frac{3}{7}$　**(ii)** $\frac{4}{7}$
2 (a) (i) $\frac{1}{8}$　**(ii)** $\frac{3}{8}$　**(iii)** $\frac{7}{8}$
　(b) (i) 16　**(ii)** 4　**(iii)** 9

Exercise 4.2

1 (a) $\frac{1}{3} \overset{\times 5}{=} \frac{5}{15}$ (×5)　**(b)** $\frac{2}{5} \overset{\times 6}{=} \frac{12}{30}$ (×6)　**(c)** $\frac{3}{4} \overset{\times 10}{=} \frac{30}{40}$ (×10)　**(d)** $\frac{1}{7} \overset{\times 4}{=} \frac{4}{28}$ (×4)

(e) $\frac{4}{11} \overset{\times 3}{=} \frac{12}{33}$ (×3)　**(f)** $\frac{5}{12} \overset{\times 2}{=} \frac{10}{24}$ (×2)　**(g)** $\frac{3}{8} \overset{\times 6}{=} \frac{18}{48}$ (×6)　**(h)** $\frac{2}{9} \overset{\times 9}{=} \frac{18}{81}$ (×9)

(i) $\frac{7}{10} \overset{\times 6}{=} \frac{42}{60}$ (×6)　**(j)** $\frac{3}{7} \overset{\times 7}{=} \frac{21}{49}$ (×7)　**(k)** $\frac{5}{6} \overset{\times 8}{=} \frac{40}{48}$ (×8)　**(l)** $\frac{4}{5} \overset{\times 100}{=} \frac{400}{500}$ (×100)

(m) $\frac{1}{4} \overset{\times 8}{=} \frac{8}{32}$ (×8)　**(n)** $\frac{2}{3} \overset{\times 9}{=} \frac{18}{27}$ (×9)　**(o)** $\frac{3}{5} \overset{\times 11}{=} \frac{33}{55}$ (×11)

Exercise 4.3

1 (a) $\frac{3}{8} = \frac{6}{16}$　**(b)** $\frac{1}{5} = \frac{3}{15}$　**(c)** $\frac{7}{10} = \frac{21}{30}$　**(d)** $\frac{2}{3} = \frac{8}{12}$
　(e) $\frac{9}{10} = \frac{63}{70}$　**(f)** $\frac{3}{5} = \frac{21}{35}$　**(g)** $\frac{1}{4} = \frac{5}{20}$　**(h)** $\frac{2}{7} = \frac{6}{21}$
　(i) $\frac{5}{9} = \frac{40}{72}$　**(j)** $\frac{6}{11} = \frac{24}{44}$　**(k)** $\frac{7}{12} = \frac{14}{24}$　**(l)** $\frac{10}{11} = \frac{100}{110}$
2 (a) $\frac{1}{2} = \frac{2}{4} = \frac{4}{8}$　**(b)** $\frac{1}{3} = \frac{2}{6} = \frac{3}{9}$　**(c)** $\frac{2}{3} = \frac{4}{6} = \frac{10}{15}$　**(d)** $\frac{3}{4} = \frac{6}{8} = \frac{12}{16}$
　(e) $\frac{1}{5} = \frac{4}{20} = \frac{8}{40}$　**(f)** $\frac{4}{5} = \frac{20}{25} = \frac{40}{50}$　**(g)** $\frac{5}{6} = \frac{15}{18} = \frac{25}{30}$　**(h)** $\frac{4}{7} = \frac{24}{42} = \frac{36}{63}$
　(i) $\frac{3}{8} = \frac{9}{24} = \frac{18}{48}$　**(j)** $\frac{5}{9} = \frac{20}{36} = \frac{80}{144}$　**(k)** $\frac{7}{10} = \frac{14}{20} = \frac{42}{60}$　**(l)** $\frac{2}{11} = \frac{8}{44} = \frac{16}{88}$

Exercise 4.4

1 $\frac{1}{2}$	**2** $\frac{1}{2}$	**3** $\frac{1}{2}$	**4** $\frac{1}{2}$	**5** $\frac{1}{3}$	**6** $\frac{1}{3}$	**7** $\frac{1}{9}$	**8** $\frac{1}{3}$
9 $\frac{1}{3}$	**10** $\frac{1}{10}$	**11** $\frac{1}{5}$	**12** $\frac{1}{5}$	**13** $\frac{1}{5}$	**14** $\frac{1}{7}$	**15** $\frac{3}{4}$	**16** $\frac{2}{3}$
17 $\frac{3}{4}$	**18** $\frac{3}{5}$	**19** $\frac{3}{5}$	**20** $\frac{2}{7}$	**21** $\frac{1}{13}$	**22** $\frac{1}{15}$	**23** $\frac{1}{25}$	**24** $\frac{1}{2}$

Exercise 4.5

1 (a) $\frac{60}{80} = \frac{6}{8} = \frac{3}{4}$ (b) $\frac{30}{45} = \frac{6}{9} = \frac{2}{3}$ (c) $\frac{16}{40} = \frac{4}{10} = \frac{2}{5}$

(d) $\frac{36}{38} = \frac{9}{12} = \frac{3}{4}$ (e) $\frac{15}{45} = \frac{3}{9} = \frac{1}{3}$ (f) $\frac{28}{42} = \frac{4}{6} = \frac{2}{3}$

(g) $\frac{12}{36} = \frac{4}{12} = \frac{1}{3}$ (h) $\frac{12}{42} = \frac{6}{21} = \frac{2}{7}$ (i) $\frac{60}{75} = \frac{20}{25} = \frac{4}{5}$

(j) $\frac{45}{60} = \frac{9}{12} = \frac{3}{4}$ (k) $\frac{140}{700} = \frac{14}{70} = \frac{2}{10} = \frac{1}{5}$ (l) $\frac{90}{150} = \frac{18}{30} = \frac{6}{10} = \frac{3}{5}$

2 (a) $\frac{1}{6}$ (b) $\frac{2}{3}$ (c) $\frac{3}{4}$ (d) $\frac{1}{5}$ (e) $\frac{1}{2}$ (f) $\frac{6}{7}$

(g) $\frac{7}{8}$ (h) $\frac{4}{9}$ (i) $\frac{1}{7}$ (j) $\frac{7}{8}$ (k) $\frac{5}{8}$ (l) $\frac{1}{3}$

Exercise 4.6

1 (a) £15 (b) 21 g (c) 6 kg (d) 5 m (e) 8 tonnes (f) 9 cm
(g) 7 l (h) 8 p (i) £8 (j) 28 km (k) 9 l (l) 34
(m) 28 m (n) £13 (o) 12 cm (p) 31 m (q) £23 (r) 56 g
(s) £240 (t) 51°
2 (a) 480 (b) 320 (c) 240 (d) 192 (e) 120 (f) 96
3 (a) £1 400 (b) £1 120 (c) £800 (d) £700 (e) £560 (f) £1020

Exercise 4.7

1 (a) 250 (b) 10 (c) 10 (d) 27 (e) 8 (f) 24
2 (a) 12 tonnes (b) 63 mm (c) £44 (d) 84 cm
(e) £126 (f) 240 kg (g) 250 p (h) 630 g
(i) 6 km (j) 60 kg (k) 12 l (l) 80 km
3 (a) 640 (b) 720 (c) 800 (d) 384
(e) 576 (f) 600 (g) 840 (h) 864
4 (a) (i) 180 (ii) 80 (iii) 144 (b) 76
5 (a) 240° (b) 270° (c) 144° (d) 288° (e) 300° (f) 135°
(g) 80° (h) 280° (i) 108°

Exercise 4.8

1 (a) 2 (b) 4 (c) 6 (d) 10 (e) 3
2 (a) 3 (b) 6 (c) 9 (d) 15 (e) 5
3 (a) 4 (b) 8 (c) 16 (d) 5 (e) 14
4 (a) 5 (b) 15 (c) 7 (d) 14 (e) 28
5 (a) 6 (b) 15 (c) 40 (d) 5 (e) 23 (f) 17
6 (a) 2 (b) 9 (c) 35
7 (a) 6 (b) 9

Exercise 4.9

1 (a) 3 (b) 3 (c) $\frac{3}{4}$ (d) 2 (e) $\frac{5}{6}$ m (f) 1 km
(g) $\frac{5}{8} l$ (h) 1 m (i) $\frac{2}{5}$ g (j) 5 kg (k) $1\frac{1}{5}$ m (l) $2\frac{3}{4}$
2 (a) 5 kg (b) 3 kg (c) $2\frac{1}{3}$ kg (d) $2\frac{2}{5}$ kg (e) $2\frac{2}{9}$ kg (f) $1\frac{7}{10}$ kg
3 (a) $4\frac{2}{3} l$ (b) $3\frac{3}{5} l$ (c) $3\frac{1}{8} l$ (d) $3\frac{1}{3} l$

Exercise 4.10

1 (a) 2 (b) 6 (c) 3 (d) $\frac{9}{10}$
(e) $1\frac{1}{9} l$ (f) $2\frac{6}{7}$ m (g) $2\frac{5}{8}$ miles (h) $5\frac{5}{6}$ kg
(i) $3\frac{3}{5}$ km (j) $3\frac{3}{8}$ m (k) $6\frac{2}{3}$ cm (l) $1\frac{4}{5}$ kg
2 (a) $3\frac{1}{2} l$ (b) $4\frac{4}{5}$ kg (c) $1\frac{5}{7} l$ (d) $4\frac{3}{8}$ m (e) $5\frac{1}{4}$ h

Review exercise 4

1 $\frac{3}{7}$ **2** (a) $\frac{4}{11}$ (b) $\frac{3}{11}$ **3** (a) 10 (b) 25
4 (a) $\frac{5}{8} = \frac{10}{16}$ (b) $\frac{1}{5} = \frac{9}{45}$ (c) $\frac{7}{9} = \frac{35}{45}$ (d) $\frac{5}{12} = \frac{10}{24}$
5 (a) $\frac{1}{7} = \frac{3}{21} = \frac{6}{42}$ (b) $\frac{2}{9} = \frac{6}{27} = \frac{10}{45}$ (c) $\frac{3}{10} = \frac{12}{40} = \frac{15}{50}$
6 (a) $\frac{1}{2}$ (b) $\frac{3}{7}$ (c) $\frac{3}{4}$ (d) $\frac{2}{3}$ (e) $\frac{8}{9}$ (f) $\frac{3}{4}$
7 $\frac{5}{26}$ **8** (a) 4 (b) 12 (c) 10
9 (a) 9 pupils (b) 8 passengers **10** (a) 9 eggs (b) 30 people
11 12 **12** 2 kg **13** $1\frac{1}{3}$ miles
14 (a) $2\frac{1}{10}$ litre (b) $7\frac{1}{9}$ m

Chapter 5 Angles

Exercise 5.1

1 (a) ∠ABC, ∠CBA (b) ∠XYZ, ∠ZYX (c) ∠QOP, ∠POQ
(d) ∠HFG, ∠GFH (e) ∠RTS, ∠STR
2 (a) ∠SPQ (b) ∠QRS (c) ∠RSP (d) ∠PQR
3 (a) ∠ABC or ∠CBA (b) ∠BAC or ∠CAB (c) ∠BCA or ∠ACB
4 (a) (b) (c) (d)

5 (a) ∠SOR or ∠ROS (b) ∠TAG or ∠GAT (c) ∠HAR or ∠RAH
(d) ∠MON or ∠NOM

Exercise 5.2

(pupils own diagram)

Exercise 5.3

1 (a) 60° (b) 160° (c) 70° (d) 150°
2 ∠ABC = 43° ∠GEF = 20° ∠HIJ = 57° ∠KLM = 140°
3 (b) 2 triangles (c) *
(d) add to give 180°
(e) * (f) add to give 180°
4 (b) (i) ∠ABC = 120°, ∠BAC = 30°, ∠ACB = 30°
(ii) ∠ADC = 60°, ∠DAC = 30°, ∠ADC = 90°
(iii) ∠ADF = 30°, ∠DFA = 90°, ∠DAF = 60°
(iv) ∠DEF = 120°, ∠DFE = 30°, ∠FDE = 30°
(c) Always add to give 180°

Exercise 5.4

3 (a) 90° (b) 180° (c) 360°
4 (a) 3 o'clock, 9 o'clock
(b) No, hour hand is midway between 9 and 10
(c) 6 o'clock
(d) No, hour hand is midway between 12 and 1
5 (a) ∠ADL (b) ∠ABC, ∠BCD, ∠CDA, ∠DAB
(c) ∠QTS, ∠TSR, ∠SRQ, ∠RQT
(d) ∠KFG, ∠FGJ, ∠JGH, ∠GHI, ∠HIJ, ∠JIM, ∠INM, ∠NMJ, ∠JML,
∠MLK, ∠LKJ, ∠JKF, ∠GJK, ∠GJI, ∠IJM, ∠MJK
6 (a) 3 (b) ∠ABC, ∠CBD, ∠ABD
7 (a) ∠DCB, ∠ACE (b) ∠QOS, ∠TOR
(c) ∠ABD, ∠EBC (d) ∠ABC, ∠BCD, ∠EFG, ∠FGH, ∠GHI, ∠HIJ

Exercise 5.5

1 (a) 40° (b) 28° (c) 60° (d) 135° (e) 60° (f) 60°
(g) 70° (h) 130° (i) 50°
2 (a) 31° (b) 35° (c) 145° (d) 132° (e) 65°, 25° (f)
3 (a) (i) 55° (ii) 22° (iii) 73°
(b) decreases by 15° (c) increases by 20° (d) 0° (e) 90°
4 (a) (i) 40° (ii) 55° (iii) 65°
(b) decreases by 15° (c) increases by 20° (d) 0° (e) 180°

Exercise 5.6

1 (a) ∠CBD (b) ∠ABC (c) ∠ABD
2 (a) ∠LOM, ∠KON   (b) ∠LMN, ∠MNK, ∠NKL, ∠KLM
   (c) ∠LON, ∠KOM   (d) ∠LOK, ∠KLO, ∠OKL, ∠OLM, ∠LMO,
                        ∠OMN, ∠MON, ∠MNO, ∠ONK, ∠NKO
3 (a) ∠DBC acute, ∠DBA obtuse, ∠CBA obtuse
   (b) ∠ZXY acute, ∠XZY acute
   (c) ∠RST acute, ∠TSU obtuse
   (d) ∠JGI obtuse, ∠JGF acute, ∠FGH obtuse, ∠IGH acute
4 (a) ∠YXV, ∠WXZ, ∠QRU, ∠SRT
   (b) ∠YXZ, ∠VXW, ∠URT, ∠QRS, ∠PQR, ∠ESR, ∠OUR, ∠FTR,
      ∠NVX, ∠XWG, ∠MYX, ∠XZH, ∠XVU, ∠XWT, ∠WTR, ∠VUR,
      ∠RQB, ∠RSC, ∠XYK, ∠XZJ
   (c) ∠PAB, ∠CDE, ∠KLM, ∠HIJ
   (d) ∠ABQ, ∠BQP, ∠QPA, ∠PAB, ∠COE, ∠DES, ∠ESC, ∠SCD, ∠QBC,
      ∠BCS and others

Exercise 5.7

1 (a) 60°   (b) 50°   (c) 1°   (d) 19°   (e) 72°   (f) 87°
2 (a) ∠WXZ and ∠ZXY, ∠YZX and ∠WZX
   (b) ∠AED and ∠DEC, ∠EAD and ∠DAB
      ∠ABD and ∠CBD, ∠BCD and ∠DCE
   (c) ∠UQS and ∠RQS, ∠TQP and ∠RQP
3 (i) (a) ∠QPR and ∠RPS   (b) 35°
   (ii) (a) ∠NMO and ∠KMO   (b) 65°
   (iii)(a) ∠VUW and ∠WUX   (b) 47°
4 (90 − x)°

Exercise 5.8

1 (a) 60°   (b) 35°   (c) 1°   (d) 107°   (e) 168°   (f) 171°
2 (a) ∠BDC and ∠ADC
   (b) ∠LMO and ∠OMN, ∠MNO and ∠ONQ, ∠NOM and ∠MOP
   (c) ∠TSU and ∠USQ, ∠TQR and ∠RQP, ∠QPV, ∠OPV
3 (i) (a)   ∠EFH and ∠HFG   (b) 117°
   (ii) (a)   ∠LNM and ∠MNO   (b) 158°
                 ∠LNK and ∠KNO   67°
   (iii)(a) ∠SUX and ∠XUV   (b) 90°
                 ∠VUW and ∠WUS   137°
                 ∠VUT and ∠TUS   59°
4 (180 − x)°

Exercise 5.10

1 (a) 35°   (b) 128°   (c) 46°   2 85°, 95° 95°
3 (a) = 50   (b) = 120   (c) = 60   (d) = 125   (e) = 55   (f) = 125
   (g) = 110   (h) = 70   (i) = 70   (j) = 65   (k) = 35   (l) = 80
   (m) = 80   (n) = 60   (p) = 40   (q) = 60   (r) = 130   (s) = 50
   (t) = 65   (u) = 50
4 (a) ∠ACB = 37°, ∠BCD = 143°, ∠DCE = 37°
   (b) ∠XYW = 56°, ∠XYZ = 124°, ∠UYW = 124°
5 four angles formed giving 2 pairs

Exercise 5.12

1 (a) 80°   (b) 25°   (c) 96°
2 (a) = 60   (b) = 90   (c) = 110   (d) = 30   (e) = 70   (f) = 90
   (g) = 30   (h) = 75   (i) = 95   (j) = 64
3 (a) 55   (b) 36   (c) 61
4
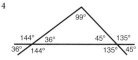
5 a = 19, b = 67

Exercise 5.13

1 (a) Thurso   (b) Oban   (c) Dunfermline (d) Portree
   (e) Stranraer   (f) Aberdeen   (g) Dunbar

2 (a) north   (b) southwest   (c) northeast   (d) south
   (e) east   (f) southeast
3 Portree
4 (a) 90°   (b) 45°   (c) 90°   (d) 180°   (e) 135°   (f) 135°
5 (a) east   (b) south   (c) northeast   (d) southeast
   (e) west   (f) northwest
6 (a) west   (b) north   (c) southwest   (d) northeast
   (e) east   (f) southeast

Exercise 5.14

1 (a) 180°   (b) 090°   (c) 135°   (d) 045°   (e) 315°
2 (a) 000°   (b) 045°   (c) 180°   (d) 270°   (e) 315°   (f) 225°
3 102°, 023°, 116°, 203°, 273°, 268°, 349°
4 (Pupil's diagram)

Review exercise 5

1 (a) ∠DEF, ∠FED   (b) ∠ZYW, ∠WYZ   (c) ∠KML, ∠LMK
2 (a) ∠CAB   (b) ∠XYW, ∠VWY   (c) ∠PRT, ∠SUT
3 (a) 55°   (b) 127°
4 (Pupil's diagram)
5 (a) ∠STU, ∠TUR, ∠URS, ∠RST   (b) ∠EFG
6 (a) ∠PQR, ∠TQS   (b) ∠ABE, ∠CBD, ∠EFG, ∠DFH, ∠HIJ, ∠GIK
7 (a) 64°   (b) 113°, 138°
8 (a) ∠DCB − obtuse   (b) ∠RPS − acute   (c) ∠GFE − obtuse
   (d) ∠SUN − reflex
9 (a) ACB and ∠BCD, 28°   (b) ∠STU and ∠UTV, 68°
                              ∠STW and ∠VTW, 112° and 68°
                              ∠MNL and ∠QNL, 145°
                              ∠MNP and ∠QNP, 90° and 90°
10 (a)   (b)
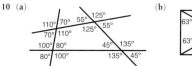

11 (a) 60   (b) 20   (c) 100   (d) 35   (e) 45   (f) 70
12 (a) 8   (b) 6   (c) 4   (d) 7   (e) 5   (f) 9   (g) 3
13 (a) west   (b) northwest   (c) north   (d) southeast
   (e) south   (f) southwest
14 P1 077° P108° P3 228°   P4 256° P5 288°

Chapter 6 Decimals

Exercise 6.1

1 (a) Eight thousand seven hundred and sixty-five four tenths and three
      hundredths
   (b) One thousand five tens two units seven tenths three hundredths
   (c) Seventy-two one tenth and six hundredths
   (d) Fifty and three tenths
2 (a) One hundred and twenty-three eight tenths and two hundredths
   (b) Thirty four and seven tenths and one hundredth
   (c) Twenty three and four hundredths
   (d) One hundred and fifty and two tenths
   (e) Two and one hundredth
   (f) Twenty and one tenth and three hundredths
   (g) One thousand and ten and one hundredth
   (h) One tenth

Exercise 6.2

1 (a) 0·5   (b) 0·8   (c) 1·6   (d) 2·4   (e) 3·4   (f) 4·9   (g) 0·2
   (h) 0·8   (i) 1·5   (j) 2·1   (k) 2·8   (l) 3·8   (m)4·9
2 (a) 1   (b) 1   (c) 2   (d) 2   (e) 3   (f) 5   (g) 0
   (h) 1   (i) 2   (j) 2   (k) 3   (l) 4   (m)5
3 (a) 18·5   (b) 18·9   (c) 19·4   (d) 20·3   (e) 21·1   (f) 21·7
   (g) 22·3   (h) 23   (i) 97·5   (j) 97·9   (k) 98·4   (l) 99·3
   (m)100   (n) 100·3   (o) 100·7   (p) 101·3

4 (a) 19 (b) 19 (c) 19 (d) 20 (e) 21 (f) 22
(g) 22 (h) 23 (i) 98 (j) 98 (k) 98 (l) 99
(m)100 (n) 100 (o) 101 (p) 101
5 (a) 4 (b) 6 (c) 7 (d) 1 (e) 11 (f) 16
(g) 1 (h) 93 (i) 0 (j) 100 (k) 32 (l) 23
(m)1 (n) 10 (o) 100
6 (a) 20 cm (b) 25 m (c) 13 km (d) 141 mm
7 34 km

Exercise 6.3

1 (a) 2·35 (b) 2·39 (c) 2·44 (d) 2·53 (e) 2·61 (f) 2·67
(g) 2·73 (h) 2·8 (i) 0·35 (j) 0·39 (k) 0·44 (l) 0·53
(m)0·61 (n) 0·67 (o) 0·73 (p) 0·8
2 (a) 2·4 (b) 2·4 (c) 2·4 (d) 2·5 (e) 2·6 (f) 2·7
(g) 2·7 (h) 2·8 (i) 0·4 (j) 0·4 (k) 0·4 (l) 0·5
(m)0·6 (n) 0·7 (o) 0·7 (p) 0·8
3 (a) 5·45 (b) 5·49 (c) 5·54 (d) 5·63 (e) 5·71 (f) 5·77
(g) 5·83 (h) 5·9 (i) 9·75 (j) 9·79 (k) 9·84 (l) 9·93
(m)10·01 (n) 10·07 (o) 10·13 (p) 10·2
4 (a) 5·5 (b) 5·5 (c) 5·5 (d) 5·6 (e) 5·7 (f) 5·8
(g) 5·8 (h) 5·9 (i) 9·8 (j) 9·8 (k) 9·8 (l) 9·9
(m)10·0 (n) 10·1 (o) 10·1 (p) 10·2
5 (a) 3·9 (b) 6·2 (c) 7·2 (d) 0·8 (e) 11·3 (f) 15·7
(g) 23·5 (h) 92·7 (i) 154·1 (j) 100·4 (k) 31·7 (l) 0·6
(m)0·7 (n) 1·0 (o) 10·0
6 (a) 0·5 (b) 1·1 (c) 1·9 (d) 2·7 (e) 3·4 (f) 4·9
(g) 0·2 (h) 1·4 (i) 2·1 (j) 3·1 (k) 4·5 (l) 18·8
(m)19·4 (n) 20·2 (o) 21 (p) 21·9 (q) 22·9 (r) 97·7
(s) 98·6 (t) 99·2 (u) 100·1 (v) 101·2
7 (a) 1 (b) 1 (c) 2 (d) 3 (e) 3 (f) 5
(g) 0 (h) 1 (i) 2 (j) 3 (k) 5 (l) 19
(m)19 (n) 20 (o) 21 (p) 22 (q) 123 (r) 98
(s) 99 (t) 99 (u) 100 (v) 101
8 (a) 0·05 (b) 0·11 (c) 0·19 (d) 0·27 (e) 0·34 (f) 0·49
(g) 0·03 (h) 0·12 (i) 0·19 (j) 0·27 (k) 0·39 (l) 0·49
(m)2·39 (n) 2·45 (o) 2·53 (p) 2·61 (q) 2·68 (r) 2·8
(s) 2·37 (t) 2·47 (u) 2·54 (v) 2·62 (w) 2·73
9 (a) 0·1 (b) 0·1 (c) 0·2 (d) 0·3 (e) 0·3 (f) 0·5
(g) 0·0 (h) 0·1 (i) 0·2 (j) 0·3 (k) 0·4 (l) 0·5
(m)2·4 (n) 2·5 (o) 2·5 (p) 2·6 (q) 2·7 (r) 2·8
(s) 2·4 (t) 2·5 (u) 2·5 (v) 2·6 (w) 2·7

Exercise 6.4

1 (a) 4·23 (b) 12·12 (c) 63·06 (d) 168·95 (e) 0·10
(f) 78·14 (g) 0·94 (h) 3·46 (i) 2·97 (j) 5·28
2 (a) 5·9 (b) 12·1 (c) 27·3 (d) 13·72 (e) 49·01
(f) 2·02 (g) 4·54 (h) 11·18 (i) 22·09 (j) 99·95
(k) 9·96 (l) 99·99 (m)24·66 (n) 2·09 (o) 8
(p) 0·44 (q) 100 (r) 98·99 (s) 22·61 (t) 34·44
(u) 176·21 (v) 111·1 (w) 8·89 (x) 0·1
3 (a) 23·6 (b) 11·8 (c) 40·64 (d) 6·5 (e) 108·79
(f) 27·38 (g) 110·1 (h) 12·87 (i) 0·93 (j) 30·8
(k) 5·59 (l) 90·11
4 (a) 6·3 (b) 14 (c) 25·65 (d) 6·8 (e) 12
(f) 21·5 (g) 3·6 (h) 4·4 (i) 10·18
5 (a) 23·4 m (b) 22·2 m
6 (a) 64·79 Bart 63·14 Pete 63·11 Mary (b) Mary (c) 0·03 s
7 0·85 l
8 (a) (i) 1·09 (ii) 2·82 (iii) 4·81
(b) 20·89 (c) 22·98
(d) 20·89 21·6 21·78 22·98 24·6 25·32 26·41
9 (a) Seonaid, Arlene, Katy, Meg, Stephanie, Ruth (b) 2·39 sec
(c) 27·59 sec (d) Arlene, Meg, Seonaid, Stephanie
(e) 26·22 sec, Seonaid

Exercise 6.5

1 (a) 6·8 (b) 12·2 (c) 12·63 (d) 12·72 (e) 73·6
(f) 4·2 (g) 6·3 (h) 4·3 (i) 12·14 (j) 4·21
(k) 29·24 (l) 94·04 (m)186·06 (n) 202·25 (o) 50·3
(p) 3·7 (q) 2·4 (r) 6·68 (s) 3·25 (t) 8·19

2 (a) 9·6 (b) 10·6 (c) 24·3 (d) 19·2 (e) 38
(f) 4·2 (g) 3·21 (h) 4·05 (i) 7·9 (j) 8·81
(k) 49·2 (l) 43·8 (m)85·56 (n) 133·36 (o) 59·94
(p) 1·4 (q) 1·05 (r) 3·97 (s) 4·88 (t) 33·34
3 (a) 4·86 m (b) 11·34 m 4 1·44 m
5 (a) 12 kg (b) 0·25 kg
6 0·25 litres 7 11·52 kg
8 (a) 134·21 g (b) 536·84 g (c) 1207·89 g
9 24·96 km 10 Mushrooms 0·06 kg cheese 0·2 kg onion 0·071 kg
11 10·68 litres
12 (a) 0·17 kg (b) 0·68 kg
13 (a) 2·1 litres (b) 0·3 litres
14 (a) £3.60 (b) 2·8 kg (c) 2·64 l

Exercise 6·6

1 (a) 721·6 (b) 513·3 (c) 123·7 (d) 803·4 (e) 21·6
(f) 503 (g) 20·1 (h) 527·8 (i) 9·8 (j) 1527·2
2 (a) 323·4 (b) 217·6 (c) 189·1 (d) 232 (e) 290·3
(f) 103·7 (g) 500·1 (h) 24·1 (i) 5 (j) 0·2
(k) 12321 (l) 3219·1 (m)1005·1 (n) 1432 (o) 1000·1
3 12·5 mins 4 53·2 secs 5 0·6 secs
6 180·8 secs 93·4 secs 106 secs

Exercise 6.7

1 (a) 3192·5 (b) 5272·8 (c) 1518·2 (d) 14 218·9 (e) 98·7
(f) 13 015·6 (g) 3001 (h) 13 420
2 (a) 3234·1 (b) 176·2 (c) 1890·1 (d) 2325 (e) 203
(f) 1037·5 (g) 5001 (h) 41·3 (i) 51 (j) 2
(k) 12321 (l) 32 190·1 (m)10 051·1 (n) 14 322 (o) 10 019
(p) 500·1 (q) 10 012 (r) 1001 (s) 430 (t) 210
3 641 secs or 10 mins 41 secs
4 6·3 secs 5 230 mm 6 561 cm 7 152 Euros

Exercise 6.8

1 (a) 3·192 (b) 5·27 (c) 1·5182 (d) 14·218 (e) 1·098
(f) 13·015 (g) 3·001 (h) 0·02
2 (a) 1·52 (b) 2·63 (c) 0·54 (d) 0·689 (e) 1·05
(f) 12·34 (g) 1·251 (h) 0·06 (i) 1·004 (j) 10·01
(k) 0·052 (l) 5·3 (m)20·4 (n) 0·002 (o) 11·11
3 (a) 0·152 (b) 1·263 (c) 0·254 (d) 0·768 (e) 0·105
(f) 11·234 (g) 0·1251 (h) 34·106 (i) 0·003 (j) 1·001
(k) 0·56 (l) 0·9 (m)0·0021 (n) 0·08 (o) 0·0002
4 0·985 m 5 53·2 ml
6 (a) 23·4 (b) 2·34
7 Potatoes 45·6 kg, carrots 8·25 kg, turnip 6·415 kg, peas 0·59 kg
8 (a) 0·06 secs (b) 0·006 secs

Exercise 6.9

1 (a) 104 (b) 246 (c) 642 (d) 1104 (e) 420
(f) 6170 (g) 625·5 (h) 849·6 (i) 21 (j) 6009
2 (a) 11 380 (b) 1818 (c) 21 (d) 236 (e) 516
(f) 1840 (g) 3690 (h) 8040 (i) 28 827 (j) 1200
3 (a) 1·17 (b) 0·316 (c) 0·213 (d) 0·03 (e) 2·003
(f) 0·71 (g) 0·001 (h) 0·151 (i) 0·011 (j) 0·011
4 (a) 0·69 (b) 1·32 (c) 0·061 (d) 0·087 (e) 0·0201
(f) 0·0193 (g) 0·0064 (h) 0·004

Exercise 6.10

1 (a) 36·43 (b) 58·51 (c) 225·11 (d) 3·38 (e) 8·56
(f) 63·28 (g) 187·2 (h) 729·92 (i) 393·07 (j) 12·75
(k) 153·38 (l) 90·09
2 (a) 7·6 (b) 0·8 (c) 0·5 (d) 0·9 (e) 1·8
(f) 10
3 £5·53 4 859·2 ml 5 3·2 l
6 (a) £37.25 (b) £31.29 (c) £8.94
7 (a) £89.06 (b) £135.05 (c) £117.53
8 (a) 266 (b) 1 l

Exercise 6.11

1 (a) £52·50 (b) £22·50 (c) £27·50 (d) £10·50 (e) £10·50
(f) £7·50 (g) £1·67 (h) £3·33 (i) £4·29 (j) £12·50
(k) £4·89 (l) £0·09 (m) £27·50 (n) £38·70 (o) £0·27
(p) £0·01

2 £1666·67   3 £0·45

4 (a) 3·2 p, 2·96 p, 2·99 p   (b) 250 ml

Exercise 6.12

1 (a) $\frac{9}{10}$ (b) $\frac{3}{10}$ (c) $\frac{5}{10} = \frac{1}{2}$ (d) $\frac{21}{100}$ (e) $\frac{99}{100}$
(f) $\frac{7}{10}$ (g) $\frac{2}{10} = \frac{1}{5}$ (h) $\frac{5}{100} = \frac{1}{20}$ (i) $\frac{25}{100} = \frac{1}{4}$ (j) $\frac{75}{100} = \frac{3}{4}$
(k) $\frac{17}{100}$ (l) $\frac{11}{100}$ (m) $\frac{1}{100}$ (n) $\frac{9}{10}$ (o) $\frac{1}{100}$
(p) $\frac{52}{100} = \frac{13}{25}$ (q) $\frac{97}{100}$ (r) $\frac{12}{100} = \frac{3}{25}$ (s) $\frac{45}{100} = \frac{9}{20}$ (t) $\frac{5}{1000} = \frac{1}{200}$

2 (a) $\frac{22}{100} = \frac{11}{50}$ (b) $\frac{3}{100}$ (c) $1\frac{3}{10}$ (d) $\frac{31}{100}$ (e) $6\frac{9}{100}$
(f) $7\frac{59}{100}$ (g) $\frac{3}{1000}$ (h) $\frac{1}{1000}$ (i) $\frac{27}{100}$ (j) $\frac{44}{100} = \frac{11}{25}$
(k) $\frac{3}{10}$ (l) $\frac{1}{100}$

Review exercise 6

1 (a) Five and six tenths
(b) Twenty three and five tenths and seven hundredths
(c) Eight tenths
(d) Five and two hundredths
(e) One hundred and three hundredths

2 (a) 8 (b) 13 (c) 2 (d) 56 (e) 100

3 (a) 5·6 (b) 18·9 (c) 29·5 (d) 99·2 (e) 200·0

4 (a) 7·6 (b) 10·4 (c) 19·32 (d) 34·18 (e) 182·01
(f) 1·4 (g) 1·4 (h) 9·3 (i) 18·54 (j) 88·69

5 (a) 6·3 (b) 8·32 (c) 22·14 (d) 35·01 (e) 1·1
(f) 2·68 (g) 4·94 (h) 4·49

6 (a) 8·6 (b) 18·3 (c) 13·23 (d) 25·44 (e) 92·15
(f) 3·2 (g) 4·2 (h) 3·18 (i) 4·03 (j) 4·02

7 (a) 15·4 (b) 136·4 (c) 640·4 (d) 9 (e) 1·8
(f) 231·2

8 (a) 162 (b) 937·5 (c) 5468 (d) 25 (e) 7
(f) 18

9 (a) 1·54 (b) 0·31 (c) 0·634 (d) 0·003 (e) 0·0005
(f) 0·0012

10 (a) 0·156 (b) 0·134 (c) 0·0034 (d) 0·0003 (e) 0·02
(f) 0·023

11 (a) 23·4 m (b) 26·46 m

12 (a) 7·21 (b) 1·41 (c) 8·71 (d) £2·91 (e) 1·21

13 (a) 29·2 m (b) 292 m

14 (a) 4·72 m (b) 47·2 m

15 (a) £2·50 (b) £0·63 (c) £13·50 (d) £27·50 (e) £0·06

16 (a) $\frac{9}{10}$ (b) $\frac{1}{5}$ (c) $\frac{57}{100}$ (d) $\frac{1}{4}$ (e) $\frac{3}{2}$

Chapter 7 Measurement

Exercise 7.1

2 50 miles/80 km

3 (a) 150 miles (b) 240 km

4 (a) cm (b) m (c) mm (d) cm (e) km
(f) km

6 (a) 3 cm (b) 8 cm (c) 12 cm (d) 4·5 cm

7 Ben Lomond 1000 m; Matterhorn 4000 m
Mt. McKinley 6000 m; Everest 9000 m

Exercise 7.2

2 (a) (i) 1 cm 5 mm (ii) 1·5 cm (iii) 15 mm
(b) (i) 2 cm 5 mm (ii) 2·5 cm (iii) 25 mm
(c) (i) 4 cm 2 mm (ii) 4·2 cm (iii) 42 mm
(d) (i) 4 cm 9 mm (ii) 4·9 cm (iii) 49 mm
(e) (i) 0 cm 5 mm (ii) 0·5 cm (iii) 5 mm
(f) (i) 1 cm 2 mm (ii) 1·2 cm (iii) 12 mm

3 (a) 2 cm 8 mm (b) 7 cm 9 mm (c) 12 cm 3 mm (d) 4 cm 4 mm

4 (a) 5·8 cm (b) 19·3 cm (c) 49·1 cm (d) 99·9 cm (e) 0·5 cm
(f) 2·5 cm (g) 0·2 cm (h) 45·5 cm (i) 62·5 cm

5 (a) 69 mm (b) 275 mm (c) 656 mm (d) 874 mm (e) 8 mm
(f) 58 mm (g) 150 mm (h) 256 mm (i) 1200 mm

7 (a) 5·25 m (b) 42·25 m (c) 67·83 m (d) 9·05 m (e) 12·345 m
(f) 18·023 m (g) 5·003 m (h) 4·259 m (i) 3·25 m (j) 4·85 cm
(k) 0·35 m (l) 0·09 m (m) 4 m (n) 0·7 m (o) 0·05 m

8 (a) 600 cm (b) 1260 cm (c) 1031 cm (d) 8754 cm (e) 850 cm
(f) 90 cm (g) 485 cm (h) 608 cm (i) 301 cm

9 (a) 3 km (b) 0·6 km (c) 0·02 km (d) 0·008 km (e) 4·567 km
(f) 65·89 km (g) 37·009 km (h) 200 km (i) 2400 km

10 (a) 8 cm (b) 3 cm (c) 2 m 2 cm (d) 5·02 m (e) 1 cm
(f) 9 cm (g) 1 cm (h) 34 cm (i) 167 cm

11 (a) 6 m (b) 46 m (c) 84 m (d) 10 m (e) 8 m
(f) 19 m (g) 7 m (h) 8 m (i) 5 m

Exercise 7.3

1 (b) 20 cm

2 (a) 46 mm × 32 mm, 15·6 cm (b) 62 mm × 28 mm, 18 cm
(c) 77 m × 46 mm, 24·6 cm (d) 34 mm × 32 mm, 13·2 cm

3 (b) 21·2 cm

4 (a) 14 cm (b) 17 cm

6 (a) 25·6 m (b) 26 m (c) £91

7 15·095 km

8 (a) 60 (b) 3 (c) 180 (d) £450

9 25 cm   10 1250

Exercise 7.4

2 Dinghy 100 kg, leaf 10 mg, CD 10 g, car 1 tonne, bottle 1 kg

3 (a) kg (b) mg (c) g (d) g (e) kg
(f) tonnes

4 (a) 100 g (b) 5 tonnes (c) 10 kg (d) 2 kg

Exercise 7.5

1 (a) 58·256 kg (b) 72·15 kg (c) 89·013 kg (d) 47·005 kg

3 (a) 6·5 g (b) 8·256 g (c) 4·028 g (d) 10·025 g (e) 25·75 g
(f) 0·268 g (g) 0·095 g (h) 0·005 g

4 (a) 3000 mg (b) 8953 mg (c) 4500 mg (d) 5980 mg (e) 8250 mg
(f) 2058 mg (g) 65 005 mg (h) 800 mg

5 (a) 5·5 kg (b) 12·045 kg (c) 58·25 kg (d) 8·005 kg (e) 0·8 kg
(f) 0·09 kg (g) 0·001 kg (h) 2·14 kg

6 (a) 8000 g (b) 5700 g (c) 12 007 g (d) 25 050 g (e) 1050 g
(f) 4009 g (g) 750 g (h) 3 g

7 (a) 5 tonnes (b) 0·3 tonne (c) 0·05 tonne (d) 0·002 tonne
(e) 5·982 tonnes (f) 6·87 tonnes (g) 10·002 tonnes (h) 67·09 tonnes

8 (a) 6 g (b) 5 g (c) 3 g (d) 0 g (e) 1 g
(f) 5 g (g) 45 g (h) 78 g

9 (a) 9 kg (b) 7 kg (c) 83 kg (d) 2 kg (e) 6 kg
(f) 46 kg (g) 26 kg (h) 8 kg

10 (a) 9 tonnes (b) 7 tonnes (c) 83 tonnes (d) 2 tonnes
(e) 9 tonnes (f) 24 tonnes (g) 25 tonnes (h) 125 tonnes

Exercise 7.6

1 (a) 8·633 kg (b) 14·03 kg (c) 7 kg (d) 19·217 kg

2 9·468 tonnes   3 437·34 kg   4 30·112 kg   6 7·5 tonnes

7 (a) 27 kg (b) £94·50   8 7·27 tonnes

9 (a) 40 (b) 24 (c) 960 (d) 14·4 tonnes

10 87·5 kg

11 No. Total weight 3·125 tonnes which is greater than 3 tonnes

12 40   13 2·5 kg

Exercise 7.7

1 (a) 400 ml, 0·4 *l* (b) 250 ml, 0·25 *l* (c) 1500 ml, 1·5 *l* (d) 1700 ml, 1·7 *l*
2 (a) 8·5 *l* (b) 9·375 *l* (c) 2·028 *l* (d) 120·025 *l* (e) 0·75 *l*
   (f) 2·275 *l* (g) 0·075 *l* (h) 0·005 *l*
3 (a) 4000 ml (b) 6275 ml (c) 8500 ml (d) 6520 ml (e) 2750 ml
   (f) 5675 ml (g) 8075 ml (h) 10 005 ml
4 (a) 6500 cm³ (b) 1325 cm³ (c) 275 cm³ (d) 5005 cm³ (e) 5750 cm³
   (f) 3075 cm³ (g) 2015 cm³ (h) 6002 cm³
5 (a) 5·75 m³ (b) 2·25 m³ (c) 1·625 m³ (d) 0·87 m³ (e) 5·2 m³
   (f) 6·245 m³ (g) 15·672 m³ (h) 1000 m³
6 (a) 2500 *l* (b) 6760 *l* (c) 10 545 *l* (d) 100 000 *l* (e) 4525 *l*
   (f) 2560 *l* (g) 8500 *l* (h) 5 *l*
7 (a) 7 *l* (b) 5 *l* (c) 8 *l* (d) 6 *l* (e) 5 *l*
   (f) 28 *l* (g) 42 *l* (h) 8 *l*

Exercise 7.8

1 (a) 2·1 *l* (b) 3·3 *l* (c) 4·4 *l* (d) 3·7 *l*
2 162·43 *l*   **3** 18 *l* 750 ml
4 (a) 4·5 *l* (b) 3 *l* (c) £5.25
5 No; the flask only holds 6 cups   **6** 1·5 *l*   **7** 8 glasses
8 5 × 500 cm³ only costs £1.95   **9** 272 *l*
10 (a) 125 *l* + 175 *l* + 60 *l* = 360 *l*   (b) £1186

Review exercise 7

1 (a) 24·8 cm (b) 16·016 m **2** 400 **3** 56 km **4** 1000
5 60 cm   **6** 20 tonnes 850 kg   **7** 11 kg 781 g
8 695·7 kg. Yes 24·3 kg spare   **9** 50
10 (a) 4000 kg = 4 tonnes (b) £1680 **11** 23 *l*
12 (a) 10·5 *l* (b) £8.75 **13** 58·44 m³

Chapter 8 Coordinates

Exercise 8.1

1 A(4,1) B(1,3) C(3,4)   **2** D(1,1) E(4,2) F(5,5)
3 G(4,0) H(3,3) I(5,3) J(0,1)   **4** K(3,1) L(1,2) M(4,5)
5 N(1,4) P(4,3) Q(0,3)
6 R(4,3) S(2,5) T(0,3) U(6,0) V(8,2) W(9,4) Z(10,1)

Exercise 8.2

1 (a) A(2,1) B(4,3) C(1,6) D(10,9) E(7,2) F(0,2) G(10,4)
      H(11,0) I(3,10) J(5,5)
   (b) (i) 10 (ii) 7 (iii) 0 (iv) 10 (v) 11 (vi) 5
   (c) (i) 5 (ii) 0 (iii) 4
   (d) G and D (e) E and F (f) J (g) K(7,9)
2 (a) (i) (2,2) (ii) (7,3) (iii) 10,0
   (b) swamp (c) (6,2) (d)(i) Hideout (ii) (6,10)
3 (a) A(1,4) B(1,1) C(5,1) (b) D(5,4) (c) E(3,1)
4 (a) E(1,1) F(5,1) (b) G(5,5) H(1,5)
Worksheet 8.1
5 Town (6,3) village (3,0) harbour (3,10) cave (6,6) hideout (9,8)
   lighthouse (11,1) rock (11,10) pirate port (0,7) mountain (3,7)
   cove (1,5) treasure (11,5) swamp (9,4) (9,5) (10,4) (10,5)
6 A(1,5) B(1,1) C(5,1) D(5,5) Diagonals meet (3,3)
   J(4,5) K(4,1) L(0,1) M(2,3)

Exercise 8.3

1 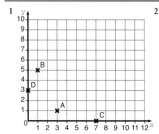   **2**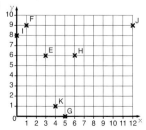

3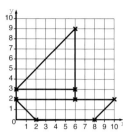

4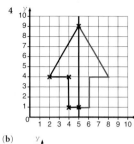

5 (a) 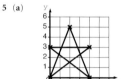   (b)

6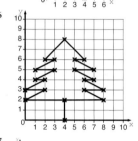

7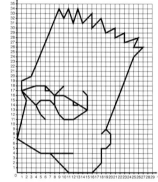

8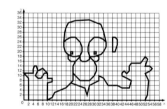

Exercise 8.4

1 (a)   (b) rectangle

2 (a) 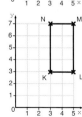   (b) rectangle

3 (a)   (c) E = (3,1)

4 (a)   (b) C = (5,4)   D = (2,4)
(c) E = $(3\frac{1}{2}, 2\frac{1}{2})$

5   Q = (6,5)   S = (1,3)

6 (e) 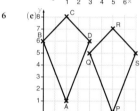   Q = (5,5)   R = (7,7)   S = (9,5)
(b) kite

Review exercise 8

1 (a) A(1,4)   B(5,4)   C(3,5)   D(5,0)   E(0,1)
(b) D and B   (c) (1,0)   (d) (3,2)

2 (a)   (b) (1,3)

3   S = (7,0)   T = (7,4)

Chapter 9 Percentages

Exercise 9.1

1 (a) $\frac{33}{100}$, 0·33   (b) $\frac{41}{100}$, 0·41   (c) $\frac{17}{100}$, 0·17   (d) $\frac{11}{100}$, 0·11   (e) $\frac{83}{100}$, 0·83
(f) $\frac{69}{100}$, 0·69   (g) $\frac{9}{100}$, 0·09

2 (a) 21%, 0·21   (b) 19%, 0·19   (c) 61%, 0·61   (d) 93%, 0·93   (e) 43%, 0·43
(f) 31%, 0·31   (g) 7%, 0·07

3 (a) 37%, $\frac{37}{100}$ (b) 57%, $\frac{57}{100}$ (c) 67%, $\frac{67}{100}$ (d) 77%, $\frac{77}{100}$ (e) 81%, $\frac{81}{100}$
(f) 29%, $\frac{29}{100}$ (g) 3%, $\frac{3}{100}$

4

Percentage	Fraction	Decimal	Percentage	Fraction	Decimal
51%	$\frac{51}{100}$	0·51	47%	$\frac{47}{100}$	0·47
49%	$\frac{49}{100}$	0·49	59%	$\frac{59}{100}$	0·59
53%	$\frac{53}{100}$	0·53	63%	$\frac{63}{100}$	0·63
19%	$\frac{19}{100}$	0·19	73%	$\frac{73}{100}$	0·73
23%	$\frac{23}{100}$	0·23	89%	$\frac{89}{100}$	0·89
99%	$\frac{99}{100}$	0·99	39%	$\frac{39}{100}$	0·39
79%	$\frac{79}{100}$	0·79	1%	$\frac{1}{100}$	0·01
27%	$\frac{27}{100}$	0·27			

Exercise 9.2

1 (a) $\frac{2}{5}$ (b) $\frac{1}{5}$ (c) $\frac{1}{2}$ (d) $\frac{3}{5}$ (e) $\frac{3}{4}$
(f) $\frac{1}{25}$ (g) $\frac{3}{25}$ (h) $\frac{13}{25}$ (i) $\frac{4}{25}$ (j) $\frac{4}{5}$
(k) $\frac{7}{20}$ (l) $\frac{19}{20}$ (m) $\frac{11}{20}$ (n) $\frac{16}{25}$

2 Water $\frac{3}{10}$, tomato $\frac{27}{50}$, oil $\frac{1}{10}$, spices $\frac{3}{50}$

3 Total fat $\frac{6}{25}$, saturated fat $\frac{3}{20}$, cholesterol $\frac{1}{50}$, sodium $\frac{2}{25}$

4 Sunbathing $\frac{11}{50}$, swimming $\frac{7}{50}$
shopping $\frac{13}{50}$, scuba diving $\frac{3}{20}$
sport $\frac{1}{4}$, sightseeing $\frac{9}{25}$

5 May $\frac{13}{20}$, June $\frac{29}{50}$, July $\frac{14}{25}$

6 Savings account $\frac{3}{50}$, current account $\frac{1}{25}$, credit card $\frac{9}{50}$

Exercise 9.3

1

Percentage	Fraction	Decimal
50%	$\frac{1}{2}$	0·5
25%	$\frac{1}{4}$	0·25
75%	$\frac{3}{4}$	0·75
1%	$\frac{1}{100}$	0·01
10%	$\frac{1}{10}$	0.1
20%	$\frac{1}{5}$	0·2
$33\frac{1}{3}$%	$\frac{1}{3}$	0·333
$66\frac{2}{3}$%	$\frac{2}{3}$	0·667

2 (a) 50%   (b) 25%   (c) 75%   (d) $33\frac{1}{3}$%   (e) 20%
(f) 10%   (g) 10%   (h) $66\frac{2}{3}$%   (i) $33\frac{1}{3}$%   (j) 75%
(k) 20%   (l) 1%

Exercise 9.4

1 (a) £42   (b) £250   (c) £1·60   (d) 4 g   (e) 64 kg
(f) £3   (g) 22·5 km   (h) £9   (i) 5·2 ml   (j) 31 kg
(k) £48   (l) £16

Exercise 9.5

1 (a) 30 g   (b) 48 km   (c) 24 m   (d) £42   (e) 49·2 cm
(f) 26·4 kg
2 (a) 22 ml   (b) £33.60   (c) 48 g   (d) 25·2 mm   (e) 168 km
(f) £29·16
3 (a) £18·40   (b) £14·40   (c) £25·60   (d) £38.40
4 (a) 7·2 g   (b) 6·3 g   (c) 10·8 g   (d) 19·8 g

Exercise 9.6

1 (a) £344   (b) 220 cm   (c) 960 m   (d) £337·20   (e) £2616
(f) 258 ml
2 (a) £204   (b) 504 g   (c) 28·2 m   (d) £31·50   (e) 400 g
(f) 268 ml
3 40% of £600

Exercise 9.7

1 (a) £50·40   (b) £55·80   (c) £31·50   (d) £26·10
2 (a) £3800   (b) £5600   (c) £6380
3 (a) £336   (b) £552   (c) £708
4 (a) 25 g   (b) 50 g   (c) 100 g   (d) 187·5 g   (e) 375 g
5 (a) £3780   (b) £46 000   (c) £1140   (d) £600   (e) £468
6 (a) 6 g   (b) 8 g   (c) 10 g   (d) 2·7 g

Exercise 9.8

1 (a) 76·8 ml   (b) £50·60   (c) 18·9 ml   (d) £81·92   (e) 49·5 m
   (f) £80·75   (g) £646   (h) 2·94 kg
2 Starch 70 g, sugar 17·5 g, fat 40 g, fibre 27·5 g
3 Water 1080 ml, orange juice 120 ml, grape juice 165 ml, apple juice 135 ml

Exercise 9.9

1 (a) £80·60   (b) £62·40   (c) £42·25   (d) £37·70
2 (a) £35·84   (b) £27·44   (c) £72·80   (d) £96·32   (e) £138·88
3 (a) £9·36   (b) £113·88   (c) £183·30
4 (a) £81·70   (b) £198·12   (c) £320·40

Exercise 9.10

1 (a) 35%   (b) 30%   (c) 22%   (d) 28%   (e) 30%
   (f) 30%   (g) 90%   (h) 55%   (i) 40%   (j) 80%
   (k) 90%   (l) 84%   (m) 40%   (n) 62%
2 (a) Maths 90%, French 80%, English 72%, Science 75%   (b) Maths

Exercise 9.11

1 Sol e Mar 18%, Mirabar 30%, Guadelupe 8%, Costa Azur 40%,
   Grande 4%
2 Magaluf 20%, Palma 40%, Cala D'Or 25%, Santa Ponsa 15%
3 (a) 60   (b) Boat 45%, Market 15%, Beach 30%, Castle 10%
4 History 37·5%, Geography 40%, Modern Studies 22·5%

Review exercise 9

1
Percentage	Fraction	Decimal
50%	$\frac{1}{2}$	0·5
10%	$\frac{1}{10}$	0·10
25%	$\frac{1}{4}$	0·25
75%	$\frac{3}{4}$	0·75
20%	$\frac{1}{5}$	0·2
1%	$\frac{1}{100}$	0·01

2 (a) $\frac{41}{50}$ (b) $\frac{9}{20}$ (c) $\frac{12}{25}$ (d) $\frac{3}{25}$
3 (a) 0·13   (b) 0·77   (c) 0·08   (d) 0·333
4 (a) £24   (b) 20 kg   (c) 32 ml
5 (a) £20·40   (b) 93·5 g   (c) 3·06 kg   6 £98
7 (a) £363·80   (b) £497·55   8 72%
9 (a) 70%   (b) 20%   (c) 95%

Chapter 10 2D Shape

Exercise 10.1

1 (a) one of three children   (b) 4 sided shape
   (c) a competition with 5 events   (d) 6 sided shape
   (e) 3-wheeled cycle   (f) one of four children
   (g) 5 sided shape   (h) 2-wheeled cycle
   (i) 10 years   (j) a competition with 10 events
   (k) sea creature with 8 tentacles   (l) a competition with 7 events
2 (a) 4   (b) 6   (c) 3   (d) 5   (e) 8
3 See worksheet answer

Shape	Name	Regular or not regular	Number of sides	Number of angles
(a)	triangle	regular	3	3
(b)	quadrilateral	not regular	4	4
(c)	pentagon	regular	5	5
(d)	hexagon	regular	6	6
(e)	triangle	not regular	3	3
(f)	square	regular	4	4
(g)	pentagon	not regular	5	5
(h)	hexagon	not regular	6	6
(i)	rectangle	not regular	4	4

Exercise 10.2

1 (a)   (b) A square has 4 equal sides
                                  A square has 4 right angles

2 (a)   (b) The opposite sides of a rectangle
                                  are equal
                                  A rectangle has 4 right angles

3 (a)   (b) A square has 4 axes of
             symmetry
             A rectangle has 2 axes of
             symmetry

Exercise 10.3

1 (a) Pupils' drawings   (b) For each shape diagonals are equal
   (c) E marked on diagrams   (d) For each shape diagonals bisect each other
2 (a) Pupils' drawings   (b) T marked on diagrams
   (c) for square all angles 90°, for rectangle vertically opposite angles equal
3 (a) False   (b) True   (c) True   (d) False   (e) True
   (f) True   (g) False   (h) True   (i) True   (j) True

Exercise 10.4

1 (i) d, e, h   (ii) a, c, g   (iii) b, f
2 (a) 3   (b) 1   (c) 0
3 (a) 8   (b) 6
4 (a) (i) 3 cm   (b) (i) 4 cm   (c) (i) 4 cm
      (ii) 60°   (ii) 70°   (ii) 76°
   (d) (i) 2·5 cm   (e) (i) 6 cm   (f) (i) 3·7 cm
      (ii) 60°   (ii) 70·5°   (ii) 60°

Exercise 10.5

1 (a) A, D, J   (b) B, E, F, I   (c) C, G, H

Exercise 10.6

1 (a) K, L, N, P, O   (b) L, M, P, Q   (c) L, P
2 (a) T, U, V, W, X   (b) R, S, T, U   (c) T, U
3 (a) Isosceles and right angled   (b) Scalene and right angled
   (c) Isosceles and obtuse angled   (d) Scalene and obtuse angled
   (e) Scalene and obtuse angled   (f) Scalene and obtuse angled
   (g) Isosceles and acute angled

4 (a)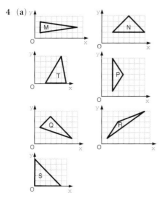

(b)

	Acute	Right	Obtuse
Isosceles	M	N, S	P
Scalene	T	Q	L, R

Exercise 10.7

1 (a) 40 cm, 96 cm²   (b) 36 cm, 81 cm²
  (c) 44 mm, 105 mm²   (d) 100mm, 625 mm²
2 (a) 10 cm, 6 cm²   (b) 12 cm, 9 cm²
  (c) 14 cm, 10 cm²   (d) 16 cm, 16 cm²
  (e) 14 cm, 6 cm²

Exercise 10.8

1 (a) 6 cm²   (b) 24 mm²   (c) 54 cm²   (d) 45·5 cm²   (e) 40·5 m²
  (f) 56 mm²
2 (a) 40 mm, 60 mm²   (b) 48 m, 96 m²   (c) 56 cm, 84 cm²
  (d) 60 mm, 120 mm²   (e) 70 cm, 210 cm²   (f) 80 m, 240 m²

Exercise 10.9

1 (a) 24 cm²   (b) 17 cm²   (c) 10 cm²
2 (c) P = 40 cm²   Q = 56 cm²   R = 58 cm²   S = 127 cm²   T = 60 cm²

Exercise 10.10

1 (a) A 16 cm²   B 16 cm²   C 16 cm²   D 16 cm²
  (b) All the same area.
2 (a)(i) 36 cm²   (ii) 36 cm²   (iii) 36 cm²   (iv) 36 cm²
  (b) All the same area.
3

4 (a) 64 cm²   (b) 8 cm by 8 cm
5 (a) 36 cm²   (b) 12 cm
6 (a) 10 mm   (b) 4 mm

Review exercise 10

1 (a) Pentagon reg., 5, 5, 5   (b) Quadrilateral, not reg., 4, 4, 2
  (c) Hexagon, reg., 6, 6, 9
2 (a) (ii), (iv), (v)
  (b) (i), (ii), (iii), (iv), (v), (vi)
3 (a) Isosceles and right angled   (b) Equilateral and acute angled
  (c) Scalene and obtuse angled   (d) Isosceles and obtuse angled
4 (a) 22 cm, 28 cm²   (b) 36 m, 81 m²   (c) 12 cm, 6 cm²
  (d) 30 mm, 30 mm²   (e) 16 cm, 14 cm²

Chapter 11 Time

Exercise 11.1

1 (a) 36   (b) 104   (c) 66
  (d) 240   (e) 120   (f) 35

2 (a) 10 080   (b) 8760   (c) 86 400
  (d) 4320   (e) 43 800   (f) 30 240
3 (a) Tuesday   (b) Monday   (c) Thursday
4 (a) Wednesday   (b) Wednesday   (c) Monday
5 8th September
6 (a) 16   (b) 13   (c) 20   (d) 36   (e) 42   (f) 132
7 25   8 88   9 4th

Exercise 11.2

1 (a) 1·15pm   (b) 8·45am   (c) 11·25pm
  (d) 6·50pm   (e) 11·55pm   (f) 12·20pm
2 (a) 3·45am, quarter to four (morning)
  (b) 8·20pm, twenty past eight (evening)
  (c) 4·25pm, twenty five past four (afternoon)
  (d) 11am, eleven o'clock (morning)
  (e) 1·30pm, half past one (afternoon)
  (f) 9·20am, twenty past nine (morning)
  (g) 11pm, eleven o'clock (evening)
  (h) 1·15am, quarter past one (morning)
  (i) 12·30am, half past midnight
3 (a) 0600 hours   (b) 1400 hours   (c) 2000 hours
  (d) 2245 hours   (e) 1115 hours   (f) 0317 hours
  (g) 1545 hours   (h) 1205 hours
4 (a) 10·50pm, 2250 hours   (b) 2pm, 1400 hours
  (c) 3·15pm, 1515 hours   (d) 11·55am, 1155 hours
  (e) 5·30pm, 1730 hours   (f) 10·55am, 1055 hours

Exercise 11.3

1 (a) 7 hrs   (b) 12 hrs   (c) 6 hrs   (d) 7 hrs
  (e) 6 hrs   (f) 11 hrs   (g) 3 hrs 18 mins   (h) 4 hrs 40 mins
  (i) 1 hr 10 mins   (j) 57 mins   (k) 3 hrs 10 mins   (l) 5 hrs 55 mins
  (m) 3 hrs 20 mins   (n) 7 hrs 51 mins   (o) 5 hrs 47 mins   (p) 16 hrs 27 mins
2 2·25 pm   3 2028 hours
4 (a) 2115 hours   (b) 2345 hours   (c) 1915 hours
5 (a) 1·15 pm   (b) 3 hrs 34 mins
6 (a) 2 hrs 45 mins   (b) 7·15 pm   (c) 9·51 pm   (d) 9 mins
7 (a) 1 hr 12 mins   (b) 11 45   (c) 2·25 pm   (d) 1 hr 32 mins
  (e) 20 mins
8 (a) 0505 on Tuesday 24th July   (b) 0110 hours
9 (a) Animal Kingdom   1 hr
       Colour of Money   1 hr 5 mins
       Number Magic   55 mins
       Science of Cinema   1 hr 50 mins
  (b) 4 hrs 50 mins

Exercise 11.4

1 (a) 1 min 10 secs   (b) 1 min 45 secs   (c) 2 mins 50 secs
  (d) 3 mins 20 secs   (e) 4 mins   (f) 5 mins 50 secs
2 (a) 5 mins 8 secs   (b) 7 mins 42 secs   (c) 12 mins 50 secs
  (d) 25 mins 40 secs
3 (a) Joan   (b) 6 mins 43 secs
4 (a) 2·41 secs   (b) 2 mins 53·3 secs   (c) Ben by 0·26 secs
5 (a) 1·4 secs   (b) 0·88 secs   (c) 1·45 secs   (d) 0·93 secs
6 1·83 secs

Exercise 11.5

1 and 2 Pupils' own answers
3 60mph
4 (a) 50 miles   (b) No   5 4 km per hour   6 53 mph
7 8 mph   8 (a) 10   (b) 1hr 24mins   (c) 25

Review exercise 11

1 (a) 5760   (b) 30 240
2 No, due on 15th May   3 50 days
4 (a) 0730   (b) 2115   (c) 1745   (d) 0020   (e) 1245   (f) 1045
5 (a) 3·35 pm   (b) 11·55 am   (c) 10·05 pm
  (d) 12·15 am   (e) 6·43 am   (f) 12·19 pm

6 2 hrs 35 mins **7** 2310 **8** 8 hrs 30 mins
9 Tina by 0·72 secs **10** 45 km/hr **11** 60 miles per hour

Chapter 12 Information Handling

Exercise 12.1

1 (**a**) 12 (**b**) IWI (**c**) 7
2 (**a**) £9 (**b**) Circle (**c**) £18 (**d**) £5·50
3 (**a**) 8·7 (**b**) 4·4 (**c**) Elbow to wrist (**d**) 1 inch
(**e**) 2·5 inches
4 (**a**) £249 (**b**) £215 (**c**) £324
(**d**) (**i**) 3 nights in August (**ii**) £12
5 (**a**) UA0401, 5 hrs (**b**) 4 hrs 55 mins (**c**) RE 1371 (**d**) $360
6 (**a**) 4% (**b**) 1% (**c**) 1% (**d**) 5%

Exercise 12.2

1

Size	Low	Medium	High
12	3	2	3
14	1	4	2
15	1	1	3

2 (**a**)

	8	10	12	14
Short	2	3	1	2
Medium	1	2	4	4
Long	1	2	2	5

(**b**) 10
(**c**) Long

3 (**a**)

Width	38	39	40	41	42
D	1	2	5	1	1
E	3	2	0	1	1
F	1	2	2	0	1

(**b**) 7

4

Sleeve length	38	40	42	44
S	1	3	2	1
M	2	2	4	2
L	0	1	3	1

Exercise 12.3

1 (**a**) 55% (**b**) 2001 and 2002 (**c**) 15%
(**d**) 2000 and 2001
2 (**a**) 12 (**b**) 12 (**c**) 24 (**d**) 2B2 (**e**) 2B2
3 (**a**) 80 (**b**) Baked potato (**c**) 10
(**d**) Yes. Healthy choices are popular.
4 (**a**) 15 (**b**) 45 (**c**) 45
5 (**a**)

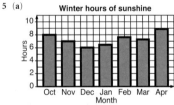

(**b**) April
(**c**) March and April

6 (**a**)

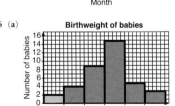

(**b**) 6
(**c**) 8

7 (**a**)

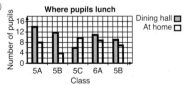

(**b**) 5C
(**c**) 5A

Exercise 12.4

1 (**a**) 5 °C (**b**) 17·5 °C (**c**) 2·5 °C
2 (**a**) May (**b**) 25 mm (**c**) 350 mm
3 (**a**) 65 (**b**) 70 (**c**) 10 years (**d**) World War II
4 (**a**)

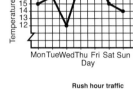

(**b**) Wednesday
(**c**) Monday and Saturday
(**d**) 7°

5 (**a**)

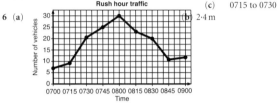

(**b**) 0800
(**c**) 0715 to 0730

6 (**a**) (**b**) 2·4 m

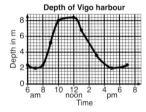

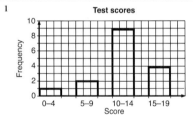

(**c**) 8·30 a.m. and 3·15 p.m.
(**d**) 9 a.m. and 2 p.m.

Exercise 12.5

1

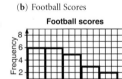

2 (**a**)

Goals Scored	Tally marks	Frequency
0	﹋I	6
1	﹋I	6
2	IIII	5
3	III	3
4	II	2

(**c**) 3

(**b**) Football Scores

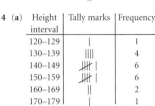

3 (**a**)

Weight interval	Tally marks	Frequency
25–29	III	3
30–34	IIII	4
35–39	﹋II	7
40–44	﹋III	8
45–49	II	2

(**b**) 10

4 (**a**)

Height interval	Tally marks	Frequency
120–129	I	1
130–139	IIII	4
140–149	﹋I	6
150–159	﹋I	6
160–169	II	2
170–179	I	1

(**c**) 17

(**b**)

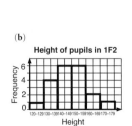

5 (a)

Golf	Tally marks	Frequency
66–68	|||	3
69–71	||||	4
72–74	|||||	5
75–77	||	2
78–80	||||||	7
81–83			1

(b)

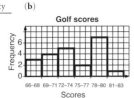

Golf scores

(c) 12

6 (a)

Temp	Tally	Frequency
12–16	||||	4
17–21	||||	4
22–26	||||| ||	7
27–31	||||| |||	8
32–36	|||	3

(b)

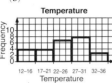

Temperature

(c) 11 times

Exercise 12.6

1 (a)(i) 25   **(ii)** 20   **(b)** 20

2 (a)

Activity	TV	Sport	IT	Help at home	Other
Number of pupils	35	10	30	15	10

(b) 5

3 (a) 5   **(b)** 15   **(c)** 30

4 (a) Red   **(b)** 10   **(c)** 40

5 (a) Income tax   **(b)** Income tax
     VAT
     N.I.
     Other
     Oil

Review exercise 12

1 (a) 7   **(b)** 10   **(c)** January   **(d)** 62

2

	Size in ml		
	200	300	400
Dry	2	3	1
Normal	0	2	2
Greasy	1	1	3

3 (a) February   **(b)** January and May *or* March and June
(c) 125ml   **(d)** February and March   **(e)** 25ml

4

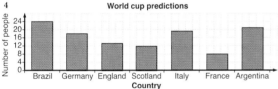

World cup predictions

5 (a) 80°   **(b) (i)** 60°C   **(c)** 20 mins   **(d)** 48 mins
          (ii) 36°C
          (iii)28°C

6 (a)

Test Score	Tally marks	Frequency
0–4	||	2
5–9	||||| |||	8
10–14	||||| ||||| |||	13
15–19	|||||	5

(b) 10

Chapter 13 Simple Algebra

Exercise 13.1

1 (a) $x = 3$ **(b)** $y = 5$ **(c)** $b = 1$ **(d)** $p = 6$ **(e)** $x = 6$
   (f) $y = 1$ **(g)** $c = 11$ **(h)** $q = 16$ **(i)** $h = 38$ **(j)** $z = 15$
   (k) $e = 1$ **(l)** $p = 16$ **(m)**$x = 30$ **(n)** $k = 5$ **(o)** $y = 10$
   (p) $d = 9$ **(q)** $x = 30$ **(r)** $y = 50$ **(s)** $b = 9$ **(t)** $p = 0$
2 (a) $x = 1$ **(b)** $y = 3$ **(c)** $b = 5$ **(d)** $p = 10$ **(e)** $y = 8$
   (f) $p = 5$ **(g)** $g = 4$ **(h)** $j = 12$ **(i)** $k = 8$ **(j)** $h = 15$
   (k) $v = 17$ **(l)** $d = 0$ **(m)**$d = 33$ **(n)** $m = 28$ **(o)** $k = 104$
   (p) $b = 99$ **(q)** $b = 24$ **(r)** $f = 7$ **(s)** $q = 46$ **(t)** $t = 115$

3 (a) $k = 1$ **(b)** $k = 2$ **(c)** $k = 5$ **(d)** $k = 8$ **(e)** $c = 7$
   (f) $h = 6$ **(g)** $p = 8$ **(h)** $s = 10$ **(i)** $h = 10$ **(j)** $f = 7$
   (k) $q = 12$ **(l)** $w = 0$ **(m)**$c = 8$ **(n)** $g = 16$ **(o)** $r = 19$
   (p) $v = 18$ **(q)** $c = 10$ **(r)** $a = 20$ **(s)** $t = 60$ **(t)** $c = 25$
4 (a) $a = 3$ **(b)** $a = 7$ **(c)** $a = 11$ **(d)** $a = 9$ **(e)** $b = 7$
   (f) $z = 11$ **(g)** $w = 11$ **(h)** $u = 15$ **(i)** $k = 15$ **(j)** $d = 18$
   (k) $s = 20$ **(l)** $h = 24$ **(m)**$m = 56$ **(n)** $z = 28$ **(o)** $k = 27$
   (p) $p = 26$
5 (a) $b = 7$ **(b)** $z = 7$ **(c)** $e = 4$ **(d)** $u = 15$ **(e)** $w = 5$
   (f) $y = 23$ **(g)** $w = 16$ **(h)** $p = 54$ **(i)** $c = 35$ **(j)** $v = 7$
   (k) $m = 43$ **(l)** $k = 67$ **(m)**$s = 4$ **(n)** $w = 60$ **(o)** $t = 12$
   (p) $u = 118$
6 (a) $w = 2$ **(b)** $t = 11$ **(c)** $p = 10$ **(d)** $g = 9$ **(e)** $c = 16$
   (f) $k = 3$ **(g)** $p = 29$ **(h)** $k = 1$ **(i)** $x = 9$ **(j)** $s = 0$
   (k) $f = 30$ **(l)** $z = 25$ **(m)**$h = 40$ **(n)** $x = 4$ **(o)** $w = 64$
   (p) $c = 8$

Exercise 13.2

1 (a) $x = 5$ **(b)** $a = 6$ **(c)** $m = 4$ **(d)** $p = 10$
2 (a) $y = 3$ **(b)** $z = 5$ **(c)** $b = 3$ **(d)** $y = 3$ **(e)** $t = 5$
   (f) $q = 7$ **(g)** $s = 9$ **(h)** $x = 22$
3 (a) $y = 10$ **(b)** $x = 9$ **(c)** $r = 12$ **(d)** $s = 8$ **(e)** $t = 5$
   (f) $y = 7$ **(g)** $a = 7$ **(h)** $q = 7$ **(i)** $x = 5$ **(j)** $m = 5$
   (k) $x = 6$ **(l)** $t = 5$

Exercise 13.3

1 (a) $y = 3$ **(b)** $y = 4$ **(c)** $y = 1$ **(d)** $y = 8$ **(e)** $y = 4$
   (f) $y = 7$ **(g)** $y = 5$ **(h)** $y = 2$ **(i)** $y = 1$ **(j)** $y = 8$
   (k) $y = 4$ **(l)** $y = 8$ **(m)**$y = 4$ **(n)** $y = 5$ **(0)** $y = 4$
   (p) $y = 11$
2 (a) $y = 2$ **(b)** $y = 2$ **(c)** $y = 1$ **(d)** $y = 10$ **(e)** $y = 6$
   (f) $y = 3$ **(g)** $y = 3$ **(h)** $y = 2$ **(i)** $y = 7$ **(j)** $y = 11$
   (k) $y = 7$ **(l)** $y = 0$
3 (a) $y = 5$ **(b)** $y = 7$ **(c)** $y = 13$ **(d)** $y = 2$ **(e)** $y = 3$
   (f) $y = 5$ **(g)** $y = 5$ **(h)** $y = 6$
4 (a) $x = 3$ **(b)** $a = 6$ **(c)** $a = 3$ **(d)** $b = 7$ **(e)** $p = 4$
   (f) $q = 3$ **(g)** $t = 8$ **(h)** $f = 6$ **(i)** $s = 8$ **(j)** $x = 1$
   (k) $k = 2$ **(l)** $w = 0$

Exercise 13.4

1 (a) $x + 3 = 5$ **(b)** $x + 1 = 8$
     $x = 2$ $x = 7$
2 (a) $2x + 3 = 5$ **(b)** $2x + 4 = 10$ **(c)** $x + 2 = 3$
     $x = 1$ $x = 3$ $x = 1$
   (d) $3x + 1 = 10$ **(e)** $x + 4 = 6$ **(f)** $4x + 1 = 9$
     $x = 3$ $x = 2$ $x = 2$
3 (a) $x + 12 = 15$ **(b)** 3

Exercise 13.5

1 (a) $2a$ **(b)** $3b$ **(c)** $3c$ **(d)** $4k$ **(e)** $6m$
   (f) $7f$ **(g)** $5v$ **(h)** $8z$ **(i)** $6a$ **(j)** $5c$
   (k) $9j$ **(l)** $8q$ **(m)**$4m$ **(n)** $3e$ **(o)** $5d$
   (p) $8i$ **(q)** $2u$ **(r)** $11f$ **(s)** $10g$ **(t)** $12s$
   (u) $9h$ **(v)** $14l$
2 (a) $4a$ **(b)** $6b$ **(c)** $9c$ **(d)** $5k$ **(e)** $12m$
   (f) $24f$ **(g)** $12v$ **(h)** $20z$ **(i)** $8a$ **(j)** $5a$
   (k) $7b$ **(l)** $8g$ **(m)**$7p$ **(n)** $9y$ **(o)** $6x$
   (p) $15y$ **(q)** $19k$ **(r)** $45t$ **(s)** $15y$ **(t)** $18k$
   (u) $40t$ **(v)** $15e$

Exercise 13.6

1 (a) $4a + b$ **(b)** $4b + 2c$ **(c)** $5c + 3d$ **(d)** $4k + 5f$ **(e)** $6m + 6p$
   (f) $10a + 5f$ **(g)** $8v + 4z$ **(h)** $15z + 4a$ **(i)** $4a + 5b$ **(j)** $5a + 7b$
   (k) $5b + 7g$ **(l)** $9g + 5w$ **(m)**$8p + 10b$ **(n)** $8y + 5w$ **(o)** $6x + 6y$
   (p) $12y + 10h$ **(q)** $17k + 4s$ **(r)** $35t + 20u$ **(s)** $11e + 15u$ **(t)** $25t + 6w$
   (u) $12h + 20g$ **(v)** $7m + 4p$

2 (a) $5a + 4b + 6c$ **(b)** $9t + 5s + 6u$ **(c)** $9p + 5q + 7r$
   (d) $8e + 9i + 2a$ **(e)** $7g + 4h + 5k$ **(f)** $11j + 2s + 10y$
   (g) $4f + 3t + 4w$ **(h)** $3d + 6k + 3w$ **(i)** $5r + 4t + 5y$
   (j) $3a + 2b + 3c + 3d + 2e$ **(k)** $9d + 7e + 6u$ **(l)** $4a + m + 8v$
3 (a) $6e + 4w$ **(b)** $4s + 5t + 6u$ **(c)** $5a + 8b + 11c$
   (d) $10m + 3p + 11y$ **(e)** $9k + 11t + 10y$ **(f)** $12g + 11i + 13p$
   (g) $17a + 14b + 8v$ **(h)** $40k + 47t + 6u + z$

Exercise 13.7

1 (a) $2a$ **(b)** $4b$ **(c)** $2c$ **(d)** d **(e)** $2y$
   (f) w **(g)** u **(h)** $2t$ **(i)** $10h$ **(j)** $5m$
   (k) q **(l)** $8p$ **(m)** 0 **(n)** $23s$ **(o)** $15x$
   (p) $36k$ **(q)** $3z$ **(r)** 0 **(s)** $100w$ **(t)** $12y$
2 (a) $6c$ **(b)** $2d$ **(c)** $6e$ **(d)** $8k$ **(e)** $2w$
   (f) $8y$ **(g)** $9g$ **(h)** $11q$ **(i)** $4x$ **(j)** $16p$
   (k) 0 **(l)** t
3 (a) $f + 3v$ **(b)** $2d + 3r$ **(c)** $4e + 6g$ **(d)** $4k + 4s$ **(e)** $w + 4y$
   (f) $y + 7p$ **(g)** $2g + 7w$ **(h)** $2q + 9b$ **(i)** $3x + 11y$ **(j)** $4p + 22k$
   (k) $15h + 9z$ **(l)** $7t + 7e$
4 (a) $3a + 2b$ **(b)** $2f + 3g$ **(c)** $2y + h$ **(d)** $4d + 2e$ **(e)** $6m + 4t$
   (f) $s + t$ **(g)** $11y + z$ **(h)** $3c$ **(i)** z **(j)** $14t$
   (k) $5t$ **(l)** $5r + 11s$ **(m)** a **(n)** $3f + 3y$ **(o)** 0

Review exercise 13

1 (a) $x = 3$ **(b)** $y = 20$ **(c)** $a = 6$ **(d)** $t = 40$ **(e)** $p = 6$
   (f) $e = 1$ **(g)** $u = 5$ **(h)** $w = 9$ **(i)** $f = 7$ **(j)** $k = 12$
   (k) $m = 19$ **(l)** $h = 23$ **(m)** $a = 9$ **(n)** $g = 16$ **(o)** $c = 20$
   (p) $e = 11$
2 (a) $x = 2$ **(b)** $y = 3$ **(c)** $a = 6$ **(d)** $h = 4$ **(e)** $x = 6$
   (f) $y = 5$ **(g)** $p = 4$ **(h)** $t = 4$ **(i)** $k = 4$
3 (a) $2x + 1 = 9$ **(b)** $3x + 2 = 8$
      $x = 4$ $x = 2$
4 $x + 6 = 14$
   $x = 8$
5 (a) $3x$ **(b)** $4y$ **(c)** $7z$ **(d)** $5x$ **(e)** $9y$
   (f) $11a$ **(g)** $9t$ **(h)** $9e$ **(i)** $13c$
6 (a) $6a + 3b$ **(b)** $9x + 2y$ **(c)** $9t + 2w$ **(d)** $5y + 11t$ **(e)** $3w + 4z$
   (f) $7c + 8k$
7 (a) $4a$ **(b)** $2t$ **(c)** t **(d)** $6z$ **(e)** $9s$ **(f)** 0
8 (a) $2a + 3b$ **(b)** $2x + 2y$ **(c)** $t + 2w$ **(d)** $5y + 2t$ **(e)** $w + 2z$
   (f) 0

Chapter 14 Tessellations

Exercise 14.1

1 Pupils' own list
2 to 7 Pupils' complete tessellations
8

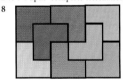

9 (a) B D   **(b)** Pupils' tessellations
10 Pupils' tessellations

Exercise 14.2

Pupils' own tessellations.

Review Exercise 14

1 A C
2 and 3 Pupils' own tessellations.

Chapter 15 Ratio

Exercise 15.1

1 (a) The ratio of lemon juice to water is $1:5$
      The ratio of water to lemon juice is $5:1$
   (b) The ratio of red paint to blue paint is $3:5$
      The ratio of blue paint to red paint is $5:3$
   (c) fat : flour = $1:2$ flour : fat = $2:1$
   (d) cement : sand = $2:7$ sand : cement = $7:2$
2 (a) $2:3$ **(b)** $3:5$ **(c)** $4:3$ **(d)** $4:7$
3 (a) $11:10$ **(b)** $10:9$ **(c)** $8:7$ **(d)** $7:8$ **(e)** $2:3$
   (f) $3:4$ **(g)** $3:2$ **(h)** $2:3$
4 (a) $3:1$ **(b)** $1:3$ **(c)** $2:3$ **(d)** $3:3$

Exercise 15.2

1 (a) $2:5$ **(b)** $2:5$ **(c)** $1:7$ **(d)** $3:7$ **(e)** $1:1$
   (f) $9:2$ **(g)** $3:2$ **(h)** $9:4$ **(i)** $7:3$ **(j)** $8:3$
   (k) $2:5$ **(l)** $7:3$ **(m)** $2:7$ **(n)** $4:5$ **(o)** $3:1$
   (p) $2:3$ **(q)** $3:1$ **(r)** $5:1$
2 $1:25$ **3** $1:2$ **4** $3:1$
5 (a) $4:3$ **(b)** $3:1$
6 (a) $2:1$ **(b)(i)** red $64\,\text{cm}^2$, blue $16\,\text{cm}^2$ **(ii)** $4:1$

Exercise 15.3

1 (a) (i) 15   **(ii)** 24   **(iii)** 27   **(iv)** 30   **(v)** 60   **(vi)** 300
   (b) (i) 2   **(ii)** 5   **(iii)** 7   **(iv)** 11   **(v)** 22   **(vi)** 300
2 (a) (i) 12   **(ii)** 20   **(iii)** 28   **(iv)** 40   **(v)** 160   **(vi)** 400
   (b) (i) 2   **(ii)** 3   **(iii)** 5   **(iv)** 8   **(v)** 15   **(vi)** 75
3 (a) (i) 4   **(ii)** 10   **(iii)** 14   **(iv)** 20   **(v)** 30
   (b) (i) 15   **(ii)** 40   **(iii)** 45   **(iv)** 55   **(v)** 100
4 (a) (i) 16   **(ii)** 40   **(iii)** 64   **(iv)** 80   **(v)** 800
   (b) (i) 6   **(ii)** 9   **(iii)** 12   **(iv)** 21   **(v)** 27
5 £4000   **6** 34   **7** 24   **8** 16 litres   **9** 3300
10 90 g   **11** 4000   **12** 45

Exercise 15.4

1 (a) 14, 7   **(b)** 12, 4   **(c)** 12, 9   **(d)** 21, 14   **(e)** 8, 28
   (f) 24, 30   **(g)** 42, 18   **(h)** 48, 18   **(i)** 45, 27
2 (a) £12, £8   **(b)** £20, £5   **(c)** 8 cm, 40 cm
   (d) 9 kg, 15 kg   **(e)** 35, 25 minutes   **(f)** 600, 1400 m
   (g) £30, £30   **(h)** 15 h, 9 h   **(i)** 48 l, 52 l
   (j) £56, £24
3 (a) (i) £4000, £6000   **(ii)** £20 000, £30 000
     (iii) £18 000, £27 000   **(iv)** £400 000, £600 000
   (b) (i) £400, £600   **(ii)** £1400, £2100
     (iii) £2200, £3300   **(iv)** £20 000, £30 000
4 Orange juice 40 l, water 120 l   **5** 35 l blue, 15 l yellow
6 George £1000, Mary £1500   **7** 44 000
8 42   **9** 16 lemon, 40 orange
10 448 kg red, 112 kg white   **11** 75 000

Review exercise 15

1 (a) $5:4$ **(b)** $5:8$ **(c)** $7:6$ **(d)** $2:1$ **(e)** $1:2$
   (f) $4:3$ **(g)** $2:1$ **(h)** $1:1$
2 (a) $3:5$ **(b)** $2:3$ **(c)** $2:9$ **(d)** $4:5$ **(e)** $1:1$
   (f) $10:1$ **(g)** $9:2$ **(h)** $3:1$
3 $1:30$ **4** 24 scores   **5** 25 packets   **6** 9 bags
7 (a) £24, £16   **(b)** £15, £20   **(c)** 3 kg, 21 kg
   (d) 40 kg, 48 kg   **(e)** 21 mins, 9 mins   **(f)** 1200 m, 1300 m
8 400 ml concentrate, 1600 ml water   **9** £8000, £6000
10 42 birds   **11** Dundee (30 goals)

Chapter 16 3D Shape

Exercise 16.1

1 (a) vertex (b) face (c) edge (d) edge (e) face
  (f) vertex (g) edge (h) face (i) vertex (j) face
  (k) edge (l) face
2 (a) cuboid (b) cube (c) cylinder (d) triangular prism
  (e) hemisphere (f) cone
3

		Number of		
Shape	Name	Vertices	Edges	Faces
(a)	cuboid	8	12	6
(b)	cube	8	12	6
(c)	cylinder	0	2	3
(d)	triangular prism	6	9	5
(e)	hemisphere	0	1	2
(f)	cone	1	1	2

4

	Number of		
Shape	Vertices	Edges	Faces
A	6	9	5
B	8	12	6
C	10	15	7
D	8	12	6
E	0	2	3
F	0	0	1
G	10	15	7
H	16	24	10

Exercise 16.2

1 FBAE, BAEF, AEFB, FEAB, EABF
2 (a) ABLM, AMLB, BAML, BLMA, LBAM, LMAB, MABL, MLBA
  (b) CDON, CNOD, DCNO, DONC, ONCD, ODCN, NCDO, NODC
  (c) DOPE, DEPO, EDOP, EPOD, PODE, PEDO, ODEP, OPED
3 (a) RST or TRS or STR or SRT or RTS or TSR
  (b) BCHG or CHGB or HGBC or GBCH or BGHC or GHCB or HCBG
     or CBGH
4 (a) red (b) blue (c) green
5 (a) IHGF or HGFI or GFIH or FIHG or IFGH or FGHI or GHIF or HIFG
  (b) IMLH or MLHI or LHIM or HIML or MIHL or IHLM or HLMI
     or LMIH
  (c) GHLK or HLKG or KGHL or LKGH or KLHG or GKLH or LHGK
     or HGKL
  (d) FGKJ or GKJF or KJFG or JFGK or JKGF or FJKG or GFJK or KGFJ

Exercise 16.3

1 Pupils copy shape
2 (a) BG, CF (b) AC, BD (c) AF, BE (d) DG, CH
3   4

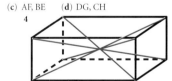

5 10
6 (a) PV, RT (b) FR, HP (c) AW, BX
7 PV, RT, SU 8 (a) EK, HJ, GI, FL (b) SY, TV, UW, RX

Exercise 16.4

1 (a) ∠SVR or ∠RVS (b) ∠TWQ or QWT
2 (a) ∠AGH or ∠HGA (b) ∠AHE or EHA (c) ∠DBC or ∠CBD
3 (a) red (b) blue (c) green
4 (a) ∠KMJ or ∠JMK (b) ∠XCZ or ∠ZCX (c) ∠LRS or ∠SRL
5 (a) | Angle | Colour | (b) | Angle | Colour | (c) | Angle | Colour |

Angle	Colour
BHE	blue
CHG	yellow

Angle	Colour
SWV	blue
RTS	yellow

Angle	Colour
PTS	blue
OPT	yellow

Exercise 16.5

Pupils copy shapes.

Exercise 16.6

1 (a) 24 cm³ (b) 40 cm³ (c) 80 cm³ (d) 24 m³ (e) 27 m³
  (f) 80 mm³ (g) 1000 cm³ (h) 176 m³ (i) 1000 cm³
2 A 180 cm³, B 50 m³, C 210 mm³, D 800 cm³
3 Blue by 28 000 cm³

Exercise 16.7

1 (a) 4 of 7 cm (b) 8   2 (a) 4 of 5 cm (b) 8
     4 of 5 cm   4 of 9 cm
     4 of 4 cm   4 of 4 cm
3 (a) 4 of 8 cm (b) 8   4 (a) 4 of 4 cm (b) 5
     8 of 5 cm   4 of 8 cm
5 (a) 12 of 6 cm (b) 8   6 (a) 6 of 7 cm (b) 4
7 (a) 6 of 5 cm (b) 6   8 (a) 4 of 4 cm (b) 8
     3 of 9 cm   4 of 8 cm
                           4 of 7 cm

Exercise 16.8

1 (a) 2 of 5 cm × 3 cm   2 (a) 2 of 2 cm × 3 cm
     2 of 5 cm × 6 cm   2 of 3 cm × 5 cm
     2 of 3 cm × 6 cm   2 of 2 cm × 5 cm
3 (a) 6 of 4 cm × 4 cm
4 (a) 2 of 4 cm × 2 cm   5 (a) 2 of 7 cm × 5 cm
     2 of 2 cm × 3 cm   2 of 5 cm × 4 cm
     2 of 4 cm × 3 cm   2 of 7 cm × 4 cm
6 (a) 1 of 4 cm × 4 cm   7 (a) 2 of 5 cm triangles
     4 of 4 cm × 6 cm triangles   3 of 7 cm × 5 cm
8 (a) 2 of 3 cm triangles
     2 of 5 cm × 3 cm
     1 of 5 cm × 4·25 cm

Exercise 16.9

1

	Number of			
Shape	Vertices	Edges	Faces	Space diagonals
Cube	8	12	6	4
Cuboid	8	12	6	4
Square based pyramid	5	8	5	0
Triangular prism	6	9	5	0

2 (a) 8 cm (b) 96 cm (c) 64 cm² (d) 384 cm²
3 (a)

Edge length	Number of edges
8 cm	4
6 cm	4
3 cm	4

  (b) 68 cm
  (c) 24 cm²

  (d)

Face	Area
Front	24 cm²
Top	48 cm²
L.H. Side	18 cm²

  (e) 180 cm²

4 (a)

Edge length	Number of edges
5 cm	4
11 cm	4

  (b) 64 cm
  (c) 25 cm²

5 (a)

Edge length	Number of edges
4 cm	6
12 cm	3

  (b) 60 cm
  (c) 48 cm²

Review exercise 16

1 (a) edge (b) vertex (c) edge (d) face
  (e) face (f) edge
2

		Number of		
Shape	Name	Vertices	Edges	Faces
(a)	tetrahedron	4	6	4
(b)	cuboid	8	12	6
(c)	cone	1	1	2

3 (a) PR (b) QW (c) QWT (d) SRVW

4 Pupils copied shapes
5 (a) $40\,\text{cm}^3$ (b) $512\,\text{m}^3$
6 (a) (i) 4 of 5 cm   (ii) 8   (b) (i) 4 of 7 cm   (ii) 5
         4 of 11 cm   4 of 10 cm
         4 of 6 cm
7

3D Shape	Net
A	(ii)
B	(iii)
C	(i)

Chapter 17 Formulae

Exercise 17.1

1 (a) 4 stems each with 3 leaves

(b)
Number of stems	Number of leaves
1	3
2	6
3	9
4	12

(c) 3   (d) The number of leaves is 3 times the number of stems.
(e) (i) 21   (ii) 36

2 (a) 4 pots each with 4 seedlings

(b)
Number of pots	Number of seedlings
1	4
2	8
3	12
4	16

(c) 4   (d) The number of seedlings is 4 times the number of pots.
(e) (i) 36   (ii) 60

3 (a) 4 branches each with 6 tomatoes

(b)
Number of branches	Number of tomatoes
1	6
2	12
3	18
4	24

(c) 6
(d) The number of tomatoes is 6 times the number of branches.
(e) (i) 60   (ii) 90

4 (a) 4 bunches each with 8 carnations

(b)
Number of bunches	Number of carnations
1	8
2	16
3	24
4	32

(c) 8
(d) The number of carnations is 8 times the number of bunches.
(e) (i) 160   (ii) 200

5 (a) 4 bracelets each with 4 charms

(b)
Number of bracelets	Number of charms
1	4
2	8
3	12
4	16

(c) 4
(d) The number of charms is 4 times the number of bracelets.
(e) (i) $4 \times 7 = 28$
(ii) $4 \times 10 = 40$

6 (a) 4 necklaces each with 6 beads

(b)
Number of necklaces	Number of beads
1	6
2	12
3	18
4	24

(c) 6
(d) The number of beads is 6 times the number of necklaces.
(e) (i) $6 \times 8 = 48$
(ii) $6 \times 11 = 66$

Exercise 17.2

1 (a)
Number of spiders	Number of legs
1	8
2	16
3	24
4	32

(b) 8
(c) The number of legs is 8 times the number of spiders.
(d) (i) 40
(ii) 96

2 (a)
Number of centipedes	Number of legs
1	100
2	200
3	300
4	400

(b) The number of legs is 100 times the number of centipedes.
(c) (i) 1000
(ii) 1500

3 (a)
Number of fish	Number of fins
1	5
2	10
3	15
4	20

(b) The number of fins is 5 times the number of fish.
(c) (i) 40
(ii) 100

Exercise 17.3

1 (a)
Number of boxes (b)	Number of pencils (p)
1	12
2	24
3	36
4	48

(b) 12
(c) The number of pencils is 12 times the number of boxes.
(d) $p = 12b$
(e) (i) 72
(ii) 120

2 (a)
Number of jotters (j)	Number of pages (p)
1	48
2	96
3	144
4	192

(b) 48
(c) $p = 48j$
(d) (i) 480
(ii) 2400

3 (a)
Number of boxes (b)	Number of sharpeners (s)
1	24
2	48
3	72
4	96

(b) 24
(c) $s = 24b$
(d) 480

4 (a)
Number of boxes (b)	Number of compasses (c)
1	15
2	30
3	45
4	60

(b) 15
(c) $c = 15b$
(d) 120

5 (a)
Number of pads (p)	Number sheets (s)
1	50
2	100
3	150
4	200

(b) $s = 50p$
(c) 600

6 (a)
Number of computers (n)	Cost in £'s (c)
1	900
2	1800
3	2700
4	3600

(b) $c = 900n$
(c) £8100

7 (a) $p = 57c$ (b) 399

Exercise 17.4

1 (a)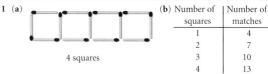

4 squares

(b)
Number of squares	Number of matches
1	4
2	7
3	10
4	13

(c) 3
(d) The number of matches is 3 times the number of squares plus 1.
(e) 28

2 (a)

4th bed

(b)
Bed number	Number of stones
1	4
2	6
3	8
4	10

(c) 2   (d) The number of stones is 2 times the bed number plus 2.
(e) 32

3 (a)

size 4

(b)
Size of square	Number of slabs
1	8
2	12
3	16
4	20

(c) 4   (d) The number of slabs is 4 times the size plus 4.
(e) 40

4 (a)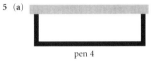

4 tables

(b)
Number of tables	Number of seats
1	6
2	10
3	14
4	18

(c) 4
(d) The number of seats is 4 times the number of tables plus 2.
(e) 34

5 (a)

pen 4

(b)
Pen size	Number of barriers
1	3
2	4
3	5
4	6

(c) The number of barriers is 1 times the pen size plus 2.
(d) 11

Exercise 17.5

1 (i)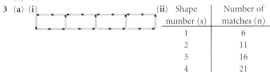

(ii)
Shape number (s)	Number of match sticks (n)
1	5
2	9
3	13
4	17

(iii) Increase 4
(iv) $n = 4s + 1$
(v) 29

2 (i)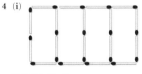

(ii)
Shape number (s)	Number of matches (n)
1	6
2	11
3	16
4	21

(iii) Increase 5
(iv) $n = 5s + 1$
(v) 36

3 (a) (i)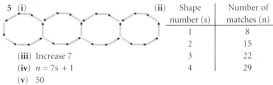

(ii)
Shape number (s)	Number of matches (n)
1	6
2	11
3	16
4	21

(b) The same

4 (i)

(ii)
Shape number (s)	Number of matches (n)
1	6
2	10
3	14
4	18

(iii) Increase 4
(iv) $n = 4s + 2$
(v) 30

5 (i)

(ii)
Shape number (s)	Number of matches (n)
1	8
2	15
3	22
4	29

(iii) Increase 7
(iv) $n = 7s + 1$
(v) 50

Review exercise 17

1 (a) 24

(b)
Number of carriers	Number of bottles
1	6
2	12
3	18
4	24

(c) 6   (d) 6 times   (e) (i) 48   (ii) 72

2 (a)
Number of people	Number of toes
1	10
2	20
3	30
4	40

(b) The number of toes is 10 times the number of people.
(c) (i) 90   (ii) 200

3 (a)
Number of phones (n)	Cost in £'s (c)
1	80
2	160
3	240
4	320

(b) c = 80p   (c) £880

4 (a)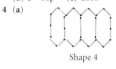

Shape 4

(b)
Shape number (s)	Number of matches (n)
1	8
2	14
3	20
4	26

(c) 6   (d) $n = 6s + 2$ (e) 44

Chapter 18 Problem solving

Exercise 18.1

1 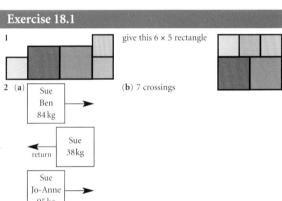   give this 6 × 5 rectangle

2 (a)    (b) 7 crossings

```
Sue
Ben
84 kg      →

       ←  Sue
return    38 kg

Sue
Jo-Anne    →
95 kg
```

3
JBC	JAC	JKC	JEC
JBG	JAG	JKG	JEG
JBD	JAD	JKD	JED
TBC	TAC	TKC	TEC
TBG	TAG	TKG	TEG
TBD	TAD	TKD	TED

4 (a)
Rectangle	P	Q	R	S
Length in cm	9	8	7	6
Breadth in cm	4	3	6	5
Area in cm²	36	24	42	30

(b) 6 cm²
(c) P6, Q4
R7, S5

(d) P   Q   R   S

(e) No. Rectangle area 40 cm².
Tile area 6 cm². 40 does not divide exactly by 6.

5

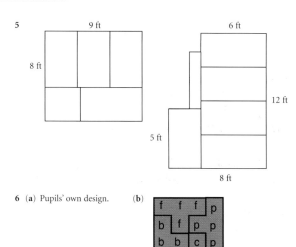

6 (a) Pupils' own design. (b)

7 (a)

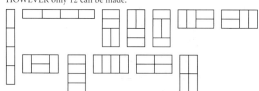

(b) (i)

Number of panes	1	2	3
Number of designs	2	4	8

(c) 16 designs if we continue the pattern in the table.
HOWEVER only 12 can be made.

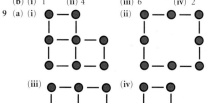

8 (a) 36
(b) (i) 1   (ii) 4   (iii) 6   (iv) 2
9 (a) (i)   (ii)   (iii)   (iv)

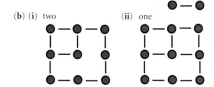

(b) (i) two   (ii) one

10 (a)

Starting number	4	5	2	7
Answer	8	10	4	14

(b)

Start → Think of a number → Add 2 → Multiply by 6 → Subtract 12 → Divide by the number you thought of → Stop

11 (b)

Starting number	3	10	7	4	12	21	8
Answer	15	12	27	18	14	23	10

12 (a) (i) £9399
(ii) £8999 Clue 2 because only 3 cars cost more than £8400
(b) (ii) G 183 UHM
(c) (ii) F 52 YEP F 49 YEP F 50 YEP
(iii) It contains an odd number
(iv) F 49 YEP
(d) (iii) 32   (e) 135   (f) Pam
(g)

Owner	Colour	Model
George Smith	red	estate
Sarah Jones	white	saloon
Mark Wilson	green	hatchback

(h)

Owner	Engine Size	Make
Ishmael	2000cc	Rover
Dorothy	1600cc	VW
Ian	1800cc	Ford

(i)

Colour	Country	Type
Red	France	Estate
Green	Britain	Saloon
White	Italy	Hatchback
Yellow	Japan	Convertible

Index